£11·95
(2)

CORA KAPLAN was born in New York City in 1940, and has lived in England since 1966. A Lecturer in the School of English and American Studies at the University of Sussex, where she teaches courses in feminism, history and literature, she has edited and introduced a critical anthology of women's poetry, *Salt and Bitter and Good: Three Centuries of English and American Women Poets* (1975) and a new edition of Elizabeth Barrett Browning's *Aurora Leigh* (1978). She has lectured on feminism and literature in both America and Australia, and her essays have appeared in various journals and collections. She is on the editorial collective of the journals *Feminist Review* and of *New Formations*.

Cora Kaplan

Sea Changes
Essays on Culture and Feminism

VERSO
London · New York

British Library
Cataloguing in Publication Data

Kaplan, Cora
    Sea changes: culture and feminism. —
    (Questions for feminism)
    1. English literature — Women authors —
    History and criticism
    I. Title   II. Series
    820.9′9287   PR111

    ISBN 0-86091-151-9
    ISBN 0-86091-864-5 Pbk

First published 1986
Second impression 1990
© Cora Kaplan 1986

Verso
6 Meard Street, London W1

Typeset in Parliament by
Leaper & Gard Ltd, Bristol, England

Printed in Great Britain by Bookcraft (Bath) Ltd, Midsomer Norton, Avon

Contents

For Emma and Sid

Acknowledgements

'Language and Gender' appeared originally in a pamphlet, *Papers on Patriarchy Conference London 76*, Lewes, Sussex 1976. 'Radical Feminism and Literature: Rethinking Millett's *Sexual Politics*' appeared originally in *Red Letters*, no. 9, 1979. 'The Indefinite Disclosed: Christina Rossetti and Emily Dickinson' appeared originally in *Women Writing and Writing about Women*, edited by Mary Jacobus, London 1979 and is published by kind permission of Croom Helm. 'Wicked Fathers: A Family Romance' appeared originally in *Fathers: Reflections by Daughters* edited by Ursula Owen, London 1983 and is published by kind permission of Virago Press. 'Speaking/Writing/Feminism' appeared originally in *On Gender and Writing* edited by Micheline Wandor, London 1983 and is published by kind permission of Pandora Press, a subsidiary of Routledge and Kegan Paul. 'Wild Nights: Pleasure/ Sexuality/Feminism' appeared originally in *Formations of Pleasure*, London 1983 and is published by kind permission of Routledge and Kegan Paul. 'Pandora's Box: Subjectivity, Class and Sexuality in Socialist Feminist Criticism' appeared originally in *Making a Difference* edited by Gayle Greene and Coppelia Kahn, London 1985 and is published by kind permission of Methuen and Co. 'The Feminist Politics of Theory' appeared originally in *Ideas from France*, ICA Publications, London 1985. 'Keeping the Color in *The Color Purple*' appeared originally in *Papers* from Literature/ Teaching/Politics Conference, Bristol, 1985. 'Red Christmases' appeared originally in *New Statesman*, vol. 108, No. 2805/2806, 21/28 December 1984.

Thanks to the editors of the publications in which these essays first appeared for all their help at the time.

For proposing this collection my grateful thanks to all the series editors of *Questions for Feminism*. My especial thanks to Michèle Barrett, whose idea the book was, and whose editorial advice, criticism, warm support and patience at every stage of its preparation has been exemplary. I would also like to thank Neil Belton of Verso for making the final editorial processes almost pleasant.

Discussions with friends, colleagues and students over a long period have helped to shape and focus the questions addressed in these essays. I have both benefited from and enjoyed many demanding and enlightening conversations over the years with Jacqueline Rose about the use of psychoanalysis in cultural and historical analysis. For acute comments and criticism on the matter and texts of individual essays I would like especially to thank Michèle Barrett, Rosalind Delmar, Paul Gilroy, Ann Rosalind Jones, Jill Lewis, Alison Light, Keith McClelland, Ursula Owen, Mark Pegram, Denise Riley and Helen Taylor.

For their unstinting intellectual and emotional generosity, my deepest gratitude to Barbara Taylor and Annie Whitehead whose work and friendship have been a stimulus and support for many years.

My son Jacob has provided me with loving companionship over the decade in which these pieces were written. For that pleasure, and his patience with me, heartfelt thanks.

Introduction

Full fathom five thy father lies;
  Of his bones are coral made
Those are pearls that were his eyes,
  Nothing of him that doth fade
But doth suffer a sea-change
Into something rich and strange
                    Ariel's Song, *The Tempest* Act 1, scene 2

Sea-changes. I want to use Ariel's song not to announce, prematurely, the death of patriarchal authority at the hands of contemporary feminism, but rather to suggest, in a cheerless political moment, that positive transformations have been enabled by its many sided assault on the meanings and practices attached to such authority. It is fashionable in some sections of the British and American left at the moment to identify the 'utopianism' of the social movements of the sixties and seventies and the theoretical deviations of their projects and programmes as largely responsible for the fragmented state of progressive politics in the west. Contemporary feminism has been one of the major targets of this attack; even socialist feminism today stands accused of too much attention to the personal, psychological and cultural and not enough to economic issues and 'traditional' social hierarchies.

This collection of essays, written over the last ten years grew out of, and in an important sense still draws upon, the productive optimism of that earlier political moment which sought to 'marry' socialism and feminism and, at the very least, to consider a temporary alliance between Marx and Freud. Running through them is the premise that an historical and materialist analysis of fiction, poetry, autobiography and feminist polemic must centre questions about the representation of sexual difference, sexuality and subjectivity, together with questions about the representation of social hierarchy. Several of these essays look at subjectivity, and sexuality as they were articulated

1

in feminist and literary discourse in the late eighteenth and nine-teenth century. Almost every piece argues for an historically appropriate use of psychoanalysis as a way of integrating the analysis of both class and gender and social and psychic mean-ing.

An emphasis on ideological forms of oppression has been the main strength of radical feminist theories of women's subordina-tion, but also their main weakness, in the sense that cultural forms are too often seen as directly expressing universal patri-archal values, unmediated by history, economics or politics. In its approach to questions of ideology socialist feminism has developed an historically specific analysis that has tried with some success to theorize the relationship between class and gender. A very substantial body of work on visual, written and oral representation — everything from ads to Rembrandt and Brontë to Billie Holliday — has defined itself as socialist feminist and has used Marxism, semiotics and psychoanalysis as one of its theoretical orientations. But artistic practices have always had a somewhat marginal place in the wider political agendas of the tendency; socialist feminism has never been as enthusiastically committed to cultural intervention as other sections of the women's movement. On the contrary it has often been critical of an overemphasis on culture at the expense of more direct kinds of activism. Moreover too much attention to high art — canon-ized literature, painting or music as it is taught in universities — produces a familiar socialist queasiness that is caused by a set of old and still unsettled questions in Marxist aesthetics about art and value. Is the literature and visual art of past generations only useful to socialism as examples of the power of bourgeois ideol-ogy to narrate and depict the myth of individual freedom and autonomy within capitalism? If we enjoy it too much (while, of course, solemnly exploring its organization of ideology) have we too been seduced by its fantasies? Do we end up unconsciously mimicking its social values and orientation, by paying too much attention to the lives and consciousness of the ruling groups represented in text and image? How do we link our analyses of these dominant representations with the history of subordinated groups whose oppressed labour made artistic production possi-ble for the leisured classes?

These are real, recurring questions for socialism and they

come up in a particularly acute form for socialist feminism since imaginative writing is one of the few public discourses in which women, albeit privileged women only, were able to speak from the seventeenth century onwards. How then can we read their work for something more than a representation of the social and psychic values of their class? First of all we must read them together with other contemporary discourses that construct class, race and gender, so that we may hear more accurately how their writing appropriates and changes dominant ideas of sexual difference. Moreover because of the subordinated place of women within the ruling classes, and because sexual difference is constructed through the hierarchies of class and race — and vice versa — women's writing both articulates and challenges the dominant ideology from a decentered position within it. Women's texts often move through the rhetoric of radical individualism towards a critique of both patriarchal and capitalist relations. Yet this same writing will be painfully class-bound and often implicitly or explicitly racist, displacing on to women in subordinate groups the 'bad' elements of female subjectivity so that a reformed and rational feminine may survive. *Jane Eyre* is the emblematic example of this process in mid-nineteenth-century writing, a proto-feminist text that both moves within and pushes beyond 'bourgeois ideology'. Women's fiction and poetry is a site where women actively structured the meaning of sexual difference in their society, especially and powerfully as it applied to difference between women. Nevertheless these writings properly considered undermine the programmatic way in which bourgeois ideology is used as shorthand by male marxist critics for a unified, genderless, hegemonic system of ideas. And while socialist feminist critics are prevented by their consciousness of the class and race bias in much women's writing from taking a purely celebratory stance towards it, they do not use it either as a stick to beat liberal humanism. The kind of political, critical pugilism actively at work in male Marxist cultural analysis — a verbal roughing up of the reactionary text — seems less appropriate when socialist feminist critics are looking at women's own representations, which, as social narrative and as fantasy, remain within the history of the development of feminist discourse, a history in itself full of disturbance and division.

As one dives deeper into socialist feminism's relationship to cultural practice and cultural criticism the waters grow more rather than less troubled. Because the issue of the value of high culture, in the past, present and in some post-revolutionary future remains unresolved, various common-sense reservations flood in to fill the gap between the political and economic concerns of socialist feminism and its work on culture. Cultural criticism is seen as simultaneously elitist and frivolous, both in what it looks at — bourgeois literature, film, visual art — and how it writes about it — in difficult theoretical language. Cultural critics have accepted both these reservations in part, broadening the range of texts and making analysis more access-ible. But behind this compound negative characterization of the project as 'elitist' and 'lightweight' there stands another type of disapproval equally directed at the content of imaginative repre-sentation — its concern with subjectivity and sexuality — and at psychoanalysis, the particular theoretical tool that has proved so useful in tackling literature, visual art and film. Apart from a critique of the supposed ahistoricity of psychoanalysis and its phallocentric bias, psychoanalysis clearly lends a valorizing legitimacy to cultural criticism's interest in sexuality, fantasy and femininity. This is not particularly surprising, for while the perils and dangers of sexuality are a familiar theme in all forms of femin-ism sexuality as potentially productive and pleasurable has only quite recently become a major question for socialist feminism as a whole. Socialist feminism inherits a general left wing asceticism, with its deep commitment to the rational and its mistrust of emotion, and adds to it the understanding that women are most vulnerable, materially and symbolically, when their sexuality is at stake.

It seems to me that this puritanism turns us away from what we most need to understand about the intimate relationship between the specific forms of women's subordination and other kinds of oppression. Throughout the book I have argued for a politics that includes and debates concepts of subjectivity and issues of sexuality. In particular I have tried to demonstrate that a psychoanalytic understanding of the construction of sexual difference does not turn feminism or socialism away from a political analysis of subordination or a political practice of resist-ance but consistently informs and enriches theory and practice. For if social life is ordered through psychic structures that to some extent organize its meanings, that psychic life in turn is only ever lived through specific social histories and political and economic possibilities. Ignore that shifting reciprocal relationship, which constructs the particular subjectivities lived by women and men of different historical periods, classes, races and cultures and it becomes especially problematic to discuss how both individual and collective resistance to oppression is shaped and enabled. We need a perspective on history and subjectivity to understand why social movements develop and fail, what sustains the collective morale of a strike, the popularity of a peace movement, the anger of an ethnic community, the defiance of a young civil servant. Without an analysis of the structure of feeling, it is hard to get below the surface of sexual differentiation and subordination, and to understand in what circumstances and in what terms women will rebel or submit. Femininity is never lived in the abstract however, but always, insistently, through a particular set of histories. Several essays in the book — 'Wicked Fathers', 'Speaking/Writing/Feminism', 'Red Christmases' take up and explore this question.

We must go on insisting therefore that cultural expression, subjectivity and 'utopian' questions about the quality of social and psychic life in general stay on the agendas of socialism and feminism. For a narrowing of the political vision of the left to traditional issues of economics and politics in the face of a massive shift to the right in western societies speaks not of a new materialist realism but is, in itself part of a conservative retrenchment. Class conflict and struggle needs to remain high on the political agenda but the strategies of such struggle and the alliances that can be made between oppressed groups have changed and must change further; and ought to include, not exclude, the questions raised about sexuality and subjectivity. We do not need a left version of Victorian values, or our own self-punishing vision of a personally commiserating restructuring of the economic and social framework of our lives. Such a response misunderstands the political needs of the present moment by seriously underestimating the ways in which feminist and anti-racist initiatives have altered the terms of political debate for the dominant culture and for the left. To a great extent sexist and racist language in the public domain, however aggressive in tone, is strategically on the defensive. A normative, subliminal, natural consensus around the subordinate status of women and Blacks has been successfully challenged, and the right has now to argue for a new repression, not an old 'gentleman's agreement'. This breaking up of the natural language of subordination has worked to reform practices too, though it produces in its wake a formidable reaction. Although the political climate has profoundly changed for the worse, the need to develop an historically informed understanding of the intertwined social and psychic effects of productive relations is more urgent than ever. While it is true that the social and political movements out of which the socialist feminist cultural project grew are dispersed and fragmented and that with their dispersal has gone any easy conviction that cultural intervention is part of a grand orchestration of resistance and change, it is also obvious that those interventions have produced dynamic effects that move beyond the original constituencies which they addressed.

Dominant and alternative discourses now move uneasily between old languages of natural, transhistorical sexuality and new languages in which masculinity and femininity are contingent terms whose meanings can be changed. Within a whole range of institutions from the Labour Party to the medical establishment patriarchal modes of authority, politics and science are being challenged. At points of collective struggle, in the miners' strike of 1984–85, within the growing forms of Black consciousness in Britain the raising of sexual politics in the community has been productive of political energy rather than of draining internal conflict.

How precisely has feminism contributed to these changes? It has sometimes seemed that feminism's own profound internal disagreements about the nature of sexual difference have blurred and impeded its challenge to dominant definitions. Looking back on the debates within feminism over the last twenty years I would argue that these conflicts, if often politically painful and divisive at the time have in other ways been necessary — even productive, contributing to a general opening up of questions about sexuality and gender. As I have noted earlier, feminism has developed, through its own internal dialectic, a political language about gender that refuses the fixed and transhistorical definitions of masculinity and femininity in the dominant culture. Some feminists might argue that the inability to resolve the questions posed by that critique of gender has been a weakness. Yet I would argue instead that it is a positive aspect of the difference between feminisms that it has not easily produced a set of alternative definitions, but instead, secured a public hearing in government, civil service, courts, schools, workplace, theatre, unions and media for challenges to those meanings and the practices that flow from them. Socialist feminism has insistently linked those issues with a critique of capitalism. Where an offensive is launched against feminist initiatives the outcome is by no means predictably on the side of reaction. Not only has the incidence of such struggles become more rather than less numerous in the last six or seven years, but the range of public issues inflected by feminist ideas has broadened. There is now in Britain a differentiated vocabulary of sexual power relations that can be appropriated and mobilized by men and women from almost every place in the social system. Such a widely contested arena is an important stage in any transformation of social and political relations. (We do not yet even remotely have such a nuanced debate about race in this country). A kind of premature despair that relegates, for example, issues of subjectivity and sexuality to a time when progressive forces are in ascendance will inevitably produce a progressive agenda that excludes them and is the other, darker side of a naive optimism that sees all aspects of change flowing naturally from a shift in political leadership or productive relations. All of these advances are tentative and none are irreversible; most have contradictory aspects. But in a time when broad social movements do not stand behind specific interventions, when the left itself can come to no agreement about where to pitch its appeal, these uneven but undeniable destabilizations of the terms through which patriarchal power and masculine identity are secured are not politically negligible. If Ariel's song — appropriated through a feminist reading — still exaggerates reports of the death of the father as a figure of symbolic and real authority, there is little doubt that his iconic hegemony has been shaken.

I begin with this political broadside as a point of entry to these essays, and as a way of suggesting that an 'optimism of the intellect' as well as the will is still an appropriate mode for socialist feminism in the eighties. I have been sitting here with a pile of pamphlets, books, and periodicals from the early through late seventies trying to reconstruct for myself the mood and moment in which the political and intellectual project behind these essays was conceived. Thinking back from now to then it is hard to avoid letting a self-indulgent nostalgia colour my recollections; for me those years were as close as I have ever come to an unalienated experience of political life, as I think they were for many other women who came to feminism with a history of left political activism. Nostalgia produces a particular kind of fictional idealization of the past that is unhelpful as a present analysis, but equally the brutal rejection of the 'liberationist' political modes and 'false' euphoria of the sixties and seventies sets up another mythology in which these decades appear as a naive political childhood assessed from a realistic adult perspective. What seems important to emphasize here, is the way in which that period altered the conditions under which many of us produced intellectual work, and what that change in turn effected in the objects of our study, our strategies of analysis and our general sense of the possibility of political transformation.

Much of the writing I did in those years was either collective, ephemeral or both: writing for conferences, as agit–prop, for group meetings — position papers and hand-outs. Behind each reading group or event as support and reference lay the women's movement itself — in some ways a heuristic concept as a coherent political tendency — but very real as a form of ongoing political practice. While the first course on gender at my university was taught in 1973, I myself did not teach such a course until about seventy-six. My 'feminist' teaching was therefore a semi-subversive restructuring of courses already in the syllabus and non-degree teaching in further education or alternative day schools. The sense in which feminism as an intellectual orientation was extra-institutional and, indeed, deeply illegitimate from the point of view of my own work-place was profound, and did not really shift until seventy-eight or seventy-nine.

Like many people on the left in the seventies I was a member of a variety of study groups. For two years from seventy-six through seventy-eight most of my developing ideas and projects emerged from my involvement in a London-based working group. The Marxist-Feminist Literature Collective, whose genesis and activities I discuss in 'The Feminist Politics of Literary Theory.'

Throughout the seventies I taught men and women (but mostly women) of all ages in adult education classes in East Sussex. All those experiences, of learning, writing and teaching outside the structures of formal, degree-granting, career-advancing education and in relation to a political movement to which in some sense (though not a party political sense) one was responsible offered a model of intellectual work radically at odds with that of competitive scholarship and isolated authorship, of teaching as a purely didactic hierarchical practice. I was never so unhappy in my work and life, and so intellectually insecure as when a postgraduate; the experience seemed the formal essence of ideologies of cultural individualism. Conversely I was never so content and productive as when I felt my ideas fed into collective practice and were sure of a critical response that had an immediate political inflection. This period redefined for me the meaning of freedom and autonomy in relationship to intellectual work, highlighting the marketplace model of the profession with its notion of isolated, original labour and competition. Instead freedom and autonomy were achieved through the sense that politics and scholarship were connected; new ideas emerged from ongoing dialogues and the energy generated constant argument and critique in which the implications of one's own work could be drawn out into many different areas, and used to address current social and political questions. As long ago as 1792, Thomas Paine observed that revolutions released 'a mass of sense' and 'talent' in society. That sustained excitement, and a belief in the possibility of collective change is hard to evoke today as a general mood. As a political legacy and practical precedent it is still alive and at work in many places, informing educational and other kinds of political work, resisting the pressures that urge us back to the marketplace of ideas.

So far I have chosen to use this introductory space to offer an historical and political context for the essays that follow. In most cases they argue internally for the theoretical perspectives they use, but perhaps it is worth saying a few words about how and why I came to focus so closely in so many of these pieces on the late eighteenth and mid-nineteenth centuries. Before I began to write about feminism and cultural production I was working on the development of the radical press in Britain and America in the 1790s as an historical instance of the transformation of political language in a decade of revolution. That project came directly out of the political upheavals from the late fifties onwards in which I had been involved: Civil Rights, anti-Vietnam agitation, the beginnings of the student movement.

When, in the early seventies, I rewrote my intellectual agenda in feminist terms I incorporated many of the questions from that early project into my new set of concerns. I kept my interest in the 1790s as a decade in which journalists like Tom Paine and Mary Wollstonecraft argued for a politics of language along with a new language of politics. As I began to look more closely at poetry and fiction, especially women's writing, I became fascinated with the 1840s and 1850s as decades in which debates about sexual difference and the role of women were spoken through and against Chartism and European revolution. Feminism, in the period 1750–1850 does not have a collective voice; even the title is an anachronism. But there is, from the 1790s a public terrain and a growing agenda around 'the rights of woman' or 'emancipation' where a medley of voices, male and female, may be heard. Imaginative literature was the traditional secular space where issues of gender relations and sexuality could be discussed, a form too where the social and psychic meanings of sexual difference were simultaneously represented. In contrast to the male political pamphlets and didactic texts I had been reading in the 1790s in which an already existing rational common man could, through collective struggle, banish the corrupt politics of an international *ancien régime* woman seemed always in struggle with her own subjectivity, whose reform must precede any public campaign for female emancipation. Early emancipatory texts like Wollstonecraft's *A Vindication of the Rights of Woman* centre the troubled question of woman's psychic being, as do most fictions by women and men.

The supposed natural psychic and sexual frailty of woman as compared to men dominates debates on gender in the period on which I have concentrated. Its ideological development is related implicitly to the simultaneous elaboration of theories about the psychic inadequacy of subordinated races and classes. The emphasis in these essays on questions of subjectivity in the autobiographical, didactic and imaginative writing of women is therefore twofold. First of all I have tried to show how psychological categories constructed dominant definitions of sexual difference, and how these naturalized distinctions around gender were already inflected with class and racial ideologies. From what set of assumptions did eighteenth and nineteenth-century women argue against dominant sexual ideologies?

We can see, for example, how women's writing develops a

'discourse of the self' in the nineteenth century whose relationship to those dominant ideologies of race, class and gender is always unsettled, neither wholly collusive with them nor wholly defiant. The emphasis on female subjectivity in the nineteenth century women's novel is not only or primarily an example of the genre's preoccupation with norms of bourgeois individualism, although a socially reductive reading of these texts inexorably leads to an analysis of them as conduct books for women. Read less literally, for psychic as well as social meaning, they point towards the contradictions in those humanist ideas of the unified self that femininity, as ideal, fallible or degraded always called up. If we understand femininity and masculinity in a psychoanalytic sense as descriptive terms that no individual psychic or social subject can actually embody, we make better sense of the symbolic narratives about gender which past fictions, poems and autobiography offer us. In using psychoanalysis to explore sexual difference in the past I have emphasized the persistence of psychic structure in relation to the shifting social elements of psychic content. In nineteenth century Britain for example, class meaning organizes and orders the split representation of women as good and bad, for women as much as for men. The languages of class, in turn, are steeped in naturalized concepts of sexual difference. In order to understand the boundaries of gendered consciousness in a particular historical moment, we need to examine both the social and psychic elements of difference.

A change in the political weather in the middle of a project leads to shifts in emphasis and perspective. In the mid-seventies I took it for granted that political transformation was possible. Submission rather than resistance needed to be explained, and submission seemed to me then to be, in a kind of unexamined way, still shamefully attached to the feminine. Now it seems rather the reverse. We are only too familiar these days with the modes through which reaction is rationalized and accepted. Feminism has so far weathered the political winter better than one might have expected, riding its rough seas with comparative skill and stamina. It isn't at all clear why this should be so. There has been an ironic tendency lately among male cultural analysts to pose feminist cultural intervention born of the seventies as a model for what socialism ought to be doing in the eighties. It is true that feminism continues to be highly productive and imaginative both in its theory and practices — its influence has survived the break up of a broad 'movement' and been appropriated by groups of women who were not affected by the earlier wave at all. It is also true that cultural expression is not 'in sync' historically with the political developments that inspire it. Without a range of political practices to relate to, however, no amount of receptive publishers or eager producers will keep feminist cultural production from becoming, once again, isolated and individual. Indeed the invention of 'post-feminism', a position without a practice of any kind, which argues that sexual subordination no longer needs to be struggled against, is symptomatic of a desire to make cultural expression stand in for actual social and political transformation, to mistake the texts that argue for change for the instance of change itself. Among the many literary manifestos that the feminisms of the last twenty years have inspired, some have called for a new 'women's language', for 'women's writing' in place of rationalist, patriarchal discourse. Like post-feminism, this demand imagines a place where sexual difference is uncontested, either secured as feminine essence or dissolved entirely. I imagine no such place and desire no such language.

Somewhere in his cultural writings Antonio Gramsci has argued that it is not important to decide the form that a radical art practice should take but very important to specify and work towards the conditions of production that will bring it into being. A future that continues to keep open and fluid the forms of contestation and struggle around sexual difference has a chance of reinventing masculinity and femininity as things both 'rich and strange'.

I

Feminism and Cultural Politics

1.

Radical Feminism and Literature: Rethinking Millett's *Sexual Politics*

With the publication of Kate Millett's *Sexual Politics* (1970) radical feminist theory can be said to have 'come out', costumed, not surprisingly, in something old — refurbished bits and pieces of sixties New Left radicalism — as well as something new — 'a systematic overview of patriarchy as a political institution'.[1] Millett's reworking of 'patriarchy' is conceptually co-ordinated with the left-libertarian policies that underwrote the civil rights, anti-imperialist and counter-culture movements. From this tendency *Sexual Politics* retained a violent hostility to the 'functionalist' bias of the academy coupled with a mildly receptive if somewhat duff ear for Marx and Engels, the latter modified by a firm rejection of Stalinist old-left politics. Patriarchy was defined as 'a political institution' rather than an economic or social relation, and political institutions were in their turn conceived as hierarchical power relations. Institutions were conceptualized as expressing oppression in homologous or analogous ways, so that the State, the Family, the University, the Mental Hospital or the Army, instead of having differentiated structures and a complex articulation, were, instead, metaphors for each other, emphasising through their similarities the dominance relations of the society as a whole, which were characterized by racism, sexism and capitalism. This type of analysis, which owed a great deal to

---

1. Kate Millett, *Sexual Politics*, London 1977, p. xi.

the functionalism it refused, provided a theoretical justification for struggle on all possible sites in the sixties. The campus thus became as valid a place to fight as Mississippi. While it is unfair to ridicule or denigrate the resistance of the decade, it is crucial for us now to understand where this analysis, so simple, and often so simply wrong, was instrumental in the creation of radical feminist theory.

Millett's influential book is especially useful if one asks why so disproportionate a number of declared feminists have chosen literature as the particular object of their analysis of female subordination. For even given the relatively large numbers of academic women who read arts subjects rather than economics, politics or labour relations, and taking into account the primacy that 'ideology' holds in feminist theories of all political complexions, the attention given to literature as a source of patriarchal ideology or feminist liberation is peculiar, and surely requires some explanation and political justification. *Sexual Politics*, one of the most readable and innovative texts of the modern women's movement, helps to make sense of this tendency. Almost half the book is devoted to the theoretical and historical development of patriarchy; the third section examines *The Literary Reflection* as revealed in the work of four male authors, D.H. Lawrence, Henry Miller, Norman Mailer and Jean Genet. In this final section Millett has made a lasting intervention in literary criticism. Since *Sexual Politics* it has been difficult for critics to ignore the wider social and political implications of the representation of sexual practice in fiction. In taking issue with Millett's interpretations, critics, myself included, have been forced on to her ground, made to admit that the depiction of sex in literature is an ideological issue for author, reader and critic. Once you have read Millett, an 'innocent' enjoyment of the sexual in literature is almost sure to be lost. This breaking-up of an unthinking 'broadminded', liberal consensus about sexual representation has been a major achievement. *Sexual Politics* sets another excellent precedent, not generally acknowledged. Unlike most recent feminist books on literature, even including Ellen Moers' brilliant, eclectic study of *Literary Women*,[2] *Sexual Politics* sets literary analysis against a specific theory of women's subordination, in relation to ideologies of gender difference inscribed in other contemporary

2. Ellen Moers, *Literary Women*, London 1978.

discourses and practices. The book provides the material for its own critique.

Rereading the first half of *Sexual Politics* is still rewarding. Millett had researched very widely; she touched most of the issues that feminists had developed in the seventies. The historical section marks off the period 1830–1930 as a time of 'Sexual Revolution' and the period of 1930–60 as 'The Counter-revolution'. Even this periodization, indicating radical putsch and inevitable backlash, harks back to a very sixties left description of the ebb and flow of radical movements. In the course of her historical exposition there are valuable discussions of Mill and Engels, and a more central if wildly uneven account of the sinister patriarchal implications in the development of psychoanalytic and social theory.

Millett's prose is often richer than her arguments, but even so the first half of the book is so full of matter that it is sometimes difficult to keep track of the logic of her analysis. She is centrally concerned to show how patriarchal ideology has kept pace with profound changes in attitudes towards sexuality, which in Millett's broad definition generally means social, economic and political relations between men and women, but occasionally means sexuality alone. It would require a much longer piece to deal fully with Millett's concept of the workings of patriarchy; for the purposes of this essay I want to concentrate on two theoretical issues which have far-reaching implications for Millett's literary analysis: the first is her understanding of 'ideology' within her larger definition of patriarchy, and the second, related to the first but narrower in scope, is her critique of Freud. Once Millett's position on these subjects has been located it becomes much easier to see why she has tackled literature through male writers almost exclusively, and why Lawrence, Miller, Mailer and Genet have been chosen instead of an alternative group composed say, of James, Fitzgerald, Updike and Baldwin, novelists equally obsessed with the social and political implications of sexuality. We can see why literature, such an important area of concern for radical feminism, remains, even in the hands of a skilful and academically trained critic like Millett, virtually untheorized.

Radical Feminism and Ideology

Under the sixties' slogan 'the personal is political' a space was made for feminists to include the psychological effects of female socialization as one of the principal oppressions suffered by women in male-dominated societies. Franz Fanon and Kenneth Clark (the Black sociologist) had offered prior analyses of the internalized effects of racism in colonial countries and in the United States. It was easy to see that if racial stereotyping could induce feelings of inferiority and difference, gender distinctions, even more widely held by human societies, could be instilled at a deep level. Successful struggle by Africans and American Blacks against racism showed that its effects were damaging but not permanent. At the same time as Fanon, Clark and others were exploring the psychological implications of racist and imperialist ideologies, the radical right were heralding the end of ideology — by which they meant the political and social theories held by the left. In choosing a working definition of ideology, feminists did not hesitate to choose a loosely Marxist conception in which ideology was a world seen upside-down, alienated, mystified — a false representation that reflected the alienating conditions in which people lived. This definition is largely drawn from early Marxist texts that liberal academics in the sixties were pulling out of the dying fires to which they had been consigned by zealous book-burning McCarthyites a few years earlier. However, both the early and late Marx held that ideologies are formed by material conditions of existence related to historically specific modes of production. One may go quite far in insisting on the relative autonomy of ideology, and still call oneself a Marxist, but one can never see ideology escaping a necessary dialectical relation with a given mode of production. However much the American New Left in the sixties concentrated on the political at the expense of the economic, however much it confused consciousness with struggle, it never quite forgot about capitalism, nor did it generally abandon the Marxist concept of determination by the base, the economy, in the last instance, even if the last instance seemed as far off as the last trump. However, a sea change occurs with the development of radical feminist theory, which insists on the primacy of gender difference over all other determinations. In Marxist theory ideologies of the bourgeoisie and the proletariat were seen as class specific ideologies dictated by class divisions created by capitalism, with bourgeois ideology dominant. 'Ideology' in Marxist shorthand means bourgeois ideology. In radical feminist theory the notion of a dominant ideology of a ruling group as distinct, say, from a 'national' ideology is retained, as is the concept of ideology as a false representation. However now *only* patriarchal ideology ruled, an ideology that ignored and/or transcended class division. Radical feminism is by no means a theoretical unity, any more than Marxism, or Marxist–feminism. Within radical feminism the origin of women's subordination is variously described, yet it is always at pains to point out that the transhistorical, transcultural, transclass character of women's oppression proves that patriarchy is much more fundamental in the determination of women's condition of existence than the effects of any given mode of production. The original conditions under which men seized power over women, or maintained it at subsequent historical moments, hardly matters. What does matter is that power is maintained by men through ideologies of gender inequality. Just as Marx characterises capital as having as its raison d'etre the extraction of surplus value (unpaid labour) from the worker, so patriarchy's reason-for-being in this un-mediated definition is to ensure the domination of men over women. It is easy to see how patriarchy becomes, given this emphasis, primarily a power relation, and patriarchal ideology its energy source.

Millett on Freud has become so familiar a part of anti-patriar-chal rhetoric that there is some danger when looking again at Millett's anti-Freud passages[3] of watching mesmerized as the knife blade makes a telling stroke here and there at Viennese phallocentrism, and assuming the rest of the argument, as it has been taken up by Shulamith Firestone and others.[4] A more dutiful rereading is interesting. Millett's technique is to isolate elements of Freudian theory drawn from different periods and kinds of writing in order to emphasise the gross chauvinism of certain passages on women — as well as to ridicule the method-ology together with the conclusions. She sees Freud's work on women as giving a pseudo-scientific imprimatur to biological determinism, and, further, to be motivated centrally by Freud's

3. Millett, pp. 176-203.
4. Shulamith Firestone, *The Dialectic of Sex*, London 1979.

distaste for 'feminist insurgence'. Penis envy, Millett's particular bête, noir or blanc, was 'in fact a superbly timed accusation, enabling masculine sentiment to take the offensive again as it had not since the disappearance of overt misogyny when the pose of chivalry became fashionable'.[5] As Millett herself points out later, in a rather more acute and milder discussion of Erik Erikson on women, chivalry is simply a polite form of misogyny. In any case her dating of the disappearance of overt misogyny is fuzzy. Did it ever disappear? Or does it simply recede in Millett's account so that she can place Freud in the foreground as the arch-enemy of feminism? Here is an unhappily typical example of Millett's polemic, which itself commits the errors which she lays at Freud's door:

> Freud's circular method in formulating penis envy begins by report-ing children's distorted impressions, gradually comes to accept them as the correct reaction, goes on to present its own irresponsible version of the socio-sexual context, and then, through a nearly imperceptible series of transitions, slides from description to a form of prescription which ensures the continuance of the patriarchal status quo, under the guise of health and normality. Apart from ridicule, the counter-revolutionary period never employed a more withering or destructive weapon against feminist insurgence than the Freudian accusation of penis envy.[6]

Note the ambiguous use of 'children's distorted impressions' and the substitution of 'irresponsible' for incorrect. Millett concen-trates on Freud's ascription of penis envy, narcissism and masochism to women. She does not concern herself very much *here* with oedipalization and its consequences, or the concept of the unconscious, nor nearly enough with Freud's general point that our social identity is constructed through our taking on the position of one sex or another at an early age. Millett even feels that Freud's promisingly liberated theory that all humans are basically bisexual is vitiated because he still wishes to see healthy adults as normal at widely differentiated points in the spectrum of socialized gender difference. She insists that Freud's theories on women are an example of biological determinism, with women locked into their natural role of mothers. But even

---

5. Millett, p. 189.
6. Ibid.

here she is convinced that Freud manages to denigrate women, denying them autonomy in this inferior role, by posing babies as penis substitutes. Freud's point is indirectly made but it seems pretty clearly to be about the unfair social overdetermination of the value of maleness in society. Millett opts for a deliberate mis-reading for the sake of a cheap flash: 'It somehow becomes the male prerogative even to give birth, as babies are but surrogate penises ... were she to deliver an entire orphanage of progeny, they would only be so many dildoes.'[7]

Millett's comments on Freud's deeply contradictory writings on women are frequently illuminating, but the whole attack is conducted with so much blinding vitriol, and is so determined not to salvage even a castrated version of Freudian theory that she weakens her case. Freud did not, after all, invent patriarchy; his chauvinism is of a very old-fashioned kind. It is hard to believe that 'penis envy', crude as its application has been, has smashed more female ambitions than its older common-sense cousin, which merely sneered that women who entered 'male' occupations were imitation men. Marxist-feminists, starting with Juliet Mitchell in *Psychoanalysis and Feminism*, feel that Freud and some modern members of his school have done more to enable understanding of gender construction in spite of the phallo-centric bias of their work than other psychoanalytic theorists seemingly more sympathetic to women. These feminists are now concerned with revision and reinterpretation of Freud's work, and an exploration of its uses for materialist theories of ideology. Millett, however, had to reject the unconscious, the pivotal concept in Freud, and something common to human subjects of both sexes, because she is committed to a view that patriarchal ideology is a conscious conspiratorial set of attitudes operated by men against all empirical evidence of women's equal status, in order to support patriarchal power in office. It must be imposed on an essential, but already social, female subject who is not tainted with femininity, passivity, penis envy, narcissism, and so on. Freud's understanding of the internalization of femininity is indeed conservative, even pessimistic from certain femininist perspectives, and Millett is out to prove that, though the con-spirators are formidable, the struggle is easier than we think. To this end she is not even afraid to misquote that most famous of

---

7. Millett, p. 185.

Freud's pronouncements on women which comes at the end of his essay on 'Femininity' where he warns his readers that he has discussed women 'only insofar as their nature is determined by their sexual function'.[8] (This reservation, of course, governs most of his discussions of men, as well.) Millett naughtily clips this sentence so that 'Freud warns that "their nature is determined by their sexual function"'.[9] Freud's destiny at Millett's hands is determined less by his anatomy than the 'cheap and chippy chopping' of his words.

Juliet Mitchell in *Psychoanalysis and Feminism*[10] refuses the simple homologies of Millett's analysis, and rehabilitates for English-speaking readers Freudian theory and its modern articulation, both as part of an analysis of femininity and as a way of introducing a more complex and comprehensible theory of ideology into Marxist–feminist thought. Her contribution is invaluable and has been widely influential in providing a powerful critique of Millett. But the integration of Marx and Freud, by Mitchell and others, has not proved easy. Mitchell, following Louis Althusser's use of Freud and Lacan, makes the unconscious central to the workings of ideology. She lays a heavy emphasis on the importance of oedipalization in the development of femininity. Ideology is endowed with a material existence and given a 'relative autonomy' from other determinations, thus avoiding a crudely economistic analysis of female subordination, but separating ideology from the mode of production so that their interrelation is hard to specify. For 'if the kinship system that defines matriarchy' (now redundant) is 'forced into the straightjacket of the nuclear family', the family in capitalism, how can it be forced out again?[11] The functionalist formulation of these problems may help to define the problem but it also tends towards the production of dualistic analyses of the economy and female socialization as they articulate women's subordination in modern industrial societies. Freudian theory, with its emphasis on repetition and reproduction of ideological positions, emphasises, perhaps too heavily, the unalterable distance between gender positions so that they remain rather like Marvell's 'Definition

---

8. Sigmund Freud, 'Femininity' in *New Introductory Lectures on Psychoanalysis*, James Strachey, ed., London 1973, p. 169.
9. Millett, p. 202.
10. Juliet Mitchell, *Psychoanalysis and Feminism*, London 1974.
11. Mitchell, p. 412.

of Love' stuck at distant poles, 'begotten by Despair/Upon
Impossibility'.

Moreover there is a peculiar congruence between Millett and
Mitchell which stems from their common preoccupation with
'ideology'. Millett's already constituted 'free' female subject, who
has only to throw off her ideological bondage, boards in the
same house where Mitchell's internally bound 'lady' lives her
ideological imprisonment in material ideology. Neither of them
really works for a living, or at least not in the sense in which
women who are considered more fully in terms of class *and*
gender work. For this establishment whether it goes under the
name of Relative Autonomy or Idealism is marked by its transhistorical and transclass character, and houses only the oldest
profession: its inmates are women who trade exclusively in their
sexuality.

The tendency both of Mitchell's Marxist–feminist structural-
ism and Millett's radical feminist idealism is to displace the
complex if mundane questions of women's subordination
through the sexual division of labour under different modes of
production. Mitchell poses the contradiction between patriarchy
and capitalism as a loophole through which feminism can view
the creation of the feminine unconscious, but like big Alice with
her eye to the keyhole there's not much she can do about it.
Patriarchy creates and recreates the psychic conditions for
women's subordination which are not the thin voile of false
consciousness, but rather the very flesh and blood of female
subjectivity. It must be hoped, given this analysis, that struggle
can take place where patriarchal ideology and capitalist ideology
and interests clash. This is certainly an argument worth having,
and one which certain Marxist–feminists are taking up.
Mitchell's own explorations of the problem run into difficulty
where she continues to use a very formalist description of 'levels'
in which women's work is the most remote and sketchy, and her
psychic processes the most prominent and solid. In Millett, on
the other hand, capitalism has disappeared except as an effect of
patriarchy. Ideology is the universal penile club that men of all
classes use to beat women. Women *do not* beat themselves. The
unconscious, both its formation and its effects, are denied and
'penis envy' has only to be exposed as the pathetic support to
patriarchal power that it is for women, the real women hidden
under male propaganda to be free in their individual conscious-

ness if not yet *en masse*. As a consequence of this optimistic view very few women speak for themselves in the pages of *Sexual Politics*, maybe because a real women is hard to find. Millett lets her male chauvinist social scientists and authors speak about them; even feminist fellow travellers like Mill and Engels are more prominent than nineteenth century feminist voices. Gender renegades, such as Mill and Engels, are allowed to espouse contradictions, but feminism itself must be positivistic, fully conscious, morally and politically correct. It must know what it wants, and since what many women wanted was full of contradictions and confusions, still entangled in what patriarchy wanted them to be or wanted for them, Millett does not let them reveal too much of their 'weakness'.

Ideology and Literature

In Millett's world weakness and masochism are male projections of women's character. She believes that Freud's theories and Lawrence's fictions are discourses of essentially the same order and type, except that one provides the scientific rationale for the other. Hardest to accept in Millett's literary analysis is the unproblematic identification of author, protagonist and point of view, and the unspoken assumption that literature is always a conscious rendering of an authorial ideology. Although this assumption slips now and then, it is always shoved back stage centre. For if the unconscious were allowed expression then the writer would be, like the dreamer, or the children with 'distorted' ideas about sexuality, off the hook. If he were, slyly, to disengage somewhat from his most monstrous creations then he would be like Freud, lying in the name of objectivity. Millett loves Lawrence, Mailer, Miller and Genet because they seem to be so autobiographically centred in their work.

Consequently Millett has more respect for MCP novelists than for their brother psychoanalysts or social scientists, for although literature is, in her view, a 'reflection' of the reality of patriarchal ideology it at least admits to being an imaginary tale of male potency. It accepts, in part, its status as a fiction. Moreover it takes the place of the revelations of psychoanalysts in that it discloses the relationship between sexuality and sociality without reference to objective knowledge of their real relationship, that is without the intervention of social science 'proofs'. Lawrence, Miller and Mailer are analyst and patient rolled into one, the onlie begetter of male fantasies that they themselves interpret. And since, in Millett's words, literature affords large insights 'into the life it describes, or interprets, or even distorts',[12] the critic can make 'a radical investigation which can demonstrate why Lawrence's analysis of a situation is inadequate, or biased, or his influence pernicious, without ever needing to imply that he is less than a great and original artist, and in many respects a man of distinguished moral and intellectual integrity'.[13] One does not have to quarrel with this judgement of Lawrence to wonder why it cannot be applied equally to Freud, why in the midst of this radical reordering of values only great art, of all the patriarchal discourses, survives the dust heap or the pyre. It would be easy, too easy, to call Millett's preference for the true art of lying, bourgeois humanism, to see its conversion in the too uncritical praise of other feminist critics for women's art, cultural feminism, and to criticize both attitudes as 'elitist' or sentimental. There is another more disturbing element in Millett's stay of execution. Phallocratic novelists can survive in Millett's brave new world because they have performed exactly as patriarchal ideologists are supposed to. Caught in the missionary position, in the act of 'describing, interpreting and distorting life simultaneously', the male novelist can only plead guilty to creating women consciously to do his bidding and fulfil his desires. Literature emerges, in this view, as having a formal homology with the working of patriarchy, except in literature the male writer can, presumably, have it all his own way. Millett reads *Sons and Lovers, Tropic of Cancer* or 'The Time of Her Time' as models of patriarchal power in action, sadistic, depersonalized sexuality and the subordination of women in full swing. But since the writing is fiction the author can be represented as telling the truth about his desires and gross falsehoods about cultural reality. Millett's contempt for Freud is based on her belief that he is doing the same thing behind the mask of science. Writers are confessed criminals, or better still, criminal informers; they have integrity because they admit to their lack of it. Ironically, this is also why Millett prefers her phallocratic authors to be reliable

---

12. Millett, p. xii.
13. Ibid.

narrators who identify wholly with their protagonists, although she recognizes uncomfortably that even these unregenerate chauvinists can occasionally act as double agents and project into their women characters. To fit her case they must be immersed, without contradiction, in their ideology of gender polarity and male dominance, so that their fictions become the ideal empirical verification of patriarchy's desired practice.

The consequence of this position is that Millett interrogates text and author simultaneously, using a popularized version of Freudian theory as it relates to male psychology as the major tool in her analysis. Discrete points are often sharp and revealing but since three different objects, author, text and social relations not to mention 'politics' have been collapsed into a single object the conclusions she draws from her readings are inevitably muddled. One can only look at a few examples of this process in action.

Millett has especial trouble in making *Lady Chatterley's Lover* fit her schema. She acknowledges that it is Lawrence's most sympathetic book about women, his 'attempt to make his peace with the female',[14] that it contains little of the sexual violence so prominent in Miller and Mailer, and even offers 'a program for social as well as sexual redemption'.[15] Generously, she reminds us that Lawrence's working title for the novel was 'Tenderness'.[16] Then she launches her attack on the book, using the crudest form of Freudian literary interpretation which reduces the author's work to his early familial relationships. As with penis envy, but with less justification, Millett assumes that the Oedipus complex is inevitably a pathological diagnosis instead of an essential process in human development which can under certain circumstances produce adult neurosis or pathology. She intimates somehow that Freud has invented it because he suffers from it, calling him 'another Oedipal son', like Lawrence.[17] As Millett deals with the relationship between author and character, the latter becomes transformed into a real historical figure.

We are frequently told that Lawrence made restitution to his father and the men of his father's condition in creating Mellors and others

14. Ibid., p. 238.
15. Ibid., p. 242.
16. Ibid., p. 238.
17. Ibid., p. 248.

like him. Such, alas, is not the case. Mellors is as one critic observes 'really a sort of gentleman in disguise', and if the portrait of the broken drunkard in *Sons and Lovers* is cruel, and it is undeniably, it is less cruel than converting the victim of industrial brutality into a blasé sexual superman who is too much of a snob to belong to either the working or the middle-classes. The late Lawrentian hero is clearly Lawrence's own fantasy of the father he might have preferred. In the same way, Lady Chatterley is a smartened-up version of his mother herself. Like his own wife Frieda von Richthofen, she is a real lady, not that disappointed little woman of the mining village with chapped red hands who fears her clothes are too shabby to be seen in Lincoln cathedral. Yet Mrs Morel is a brave, even a great woman, though waitresses in teahouses snub her when she can only order custard, too poor to pay for a full meal. *Sons and Lovers* gives us Lawrence's parents without the glamor with which his snobbishness later invested them. All the romances of his later fiction are a reworking of his parents' marriage, and of his own too, modeled on theirs, but a notable advance in social mobility. For Lawrence saw his course, saw it with a Calvinistic sense of election, as a vocation to rise and surpass his origins.[18]

Millett doesn't expand upon what could or ought to constitute literary 'restitution' to one's father. *Pace* Graham Hough, the most superficial reading of *Lady Chatterley* will show that Mellors is not drawn as a 'gentleman in disguise', but as a type still extant in British life, an embittered, educated man of working-class origins, unwilling quite to become a class renegade, but cut off from class identity.[19] He is not drawn as a blasé sexual superman, but rather as someone whose sexual experience has been bad enough to make him temporarily continent. Connie may owe something to Frieda, but the only thing that she has in common with Mrs Morel is her gender, though Millett is free to prefer the latter character. They are quite distinct portraits of two different women with different class backgrounds, psychology and experience. Millett's claim that writing about the aristocracy if you are not yourself of it is an attempt at class mobility makes a snob of everyone from Shakespeare — no, wait a minute, Chaucer — on upwards. If you're black and write about whites, or female and write about men or Irish and write about the English . . .?

These are all minor cavils however. What is worst about this

---

18. Ibid.
19. Graham Hough, *The Dark Sun, a Study of D.H. Lawrence*, London 1968, p.31.

passage is not its ad hominem attack on Lawrence's supposed regressive, snobbish and false use of his personal history, but Millett's wish to eat her Freud and castrate him too. She does not seem to see that you can't demolish a psychic schema of development for one sex and accept its linked application to the other without a much more elaborate and careful critique than she has presented. Thus she accepts Freud's assessment of masculinity — aggressive, sadistic, Oedipally bound, terrified of castration, fetishistic, and so on, but rejects the sexual bipolarity implied by identifying real men (admitted homosexuals excepted) with these attributes.

The whole of *Sexual Politics* is permeated by a coercive sexual morality, meant to replace those mores inscribed in patriarchy. Typical of the early years of the modern women's movement, it borrows from the sexual libertarianism of the alternative ideologies of the 1960s, which in turn reacted against the macho poses of the post-war fifties. It is marked, among other things, by an extreme distaste for the recrudescent sado-mas elements of sexuality, however 'playfully' practiced. Surprisingly it has very rigid notions of sexual health. Thus in spite of Millett's sympathy towards overt homosexuality she is clinically severe towards authors who seem to identify with their heroines. Tennyson is a case in point and she puts this tendency in his work down to his 'problems of sexual identity', unconsciously lining herself up with the very normative views she ascribes to Freud, Lawrence, Miller, Mailer.[20] Now that it has become less fashionable to promote a 'correct' feminist sexuality, so that it is no longer so important to be clitoral and/or gay as opposed to vaginal and straight, most of this moralizing comes over as specious and naive, especially in regard to literature. Millett comes close, but never close enough, to understanding that literature is the place where bisexuality is spoken even by the most consciously phallocratic authors.

A less positivistic but equally 'feminist' literary criticism would read not only *Lady Chatterley* but many of Millett's chosen texts quite differently. Mailer's 'The Time of Her Time', for instance, need not be read as a serious account of how Mailer-the-cocksman triumphs again, but rather as a Feiffer-like send up of the Greenwich Village macho scene, where Mailer's fake

---

20. Millett, pp. 76-7.

Irish bullfighter goads and gores his way through elaborate sexual games, in a parody of machismo and Hemingway. Mailer encourages such a reading by giving the girl the last word, allowing her to undermine with language the 'manhood' that had just been physically vindicated.[21] Mailer is hard to interpret because his writing about America identifies fascism and imperialism with male fantasies about power and sexuality. These are fantasies that Mailer shares: at certain points they seem to take over his work, as in *An American Dream*, a tendency that suggests the instability of the metaphor between sexuality and politics. Perhaps what these writers ought to have suggested to Millett is that the sociology of sex, particularly sexuality as expressed in literature, is not the key to or the symbol of power politics. (She does seem to lean towards this view somewhat in her treatment of Genet.) If there is a central conviction in Mailer it is his unshaken belief that the sexual is political and vice-versa. He keeps snapping away at the same view from every possible angle. In this belief Mailer and Millett are united and equally stubborn. *Flying*, Millett's feminist rewrite of Mailer, gets no closer to the relationship between sex, gender and politics than Mailer's work, though it contains as much coupling and campaigning.

Millett may take her authors seriously, but it is hard for her, given her rejection of formalist or structuralist methodologies of literary criticism, to stay with a single text long enough to let the contradictory elements in its ideological inscription play themselves out in her analysis. She tends to note them in passing as detours from the general coherence of her readings, but since these readings must support such literature as the vanguard of an ideological counter revolution with a well-planned, coherent, fully conscious attack on women it would be counterproductive of her to foreground conflict and sabotage, even fragging,[22] within the ranks. She looks for, and in most cases finds, a concrete reading, ties it to the text and heaves it over the side.

This method adds nothing to the development of a Marxist feminist literary criticism, which must look more carefully at the complex interrelation of class and gender ideologies in literature

---

21. Norman Mailer, *Advertisements for Myself*, New York 1959.
22. 'Fragging', slang word coined in the Vietnam war for attacks on US officers by their own men.

written by men and women, and must attempt to theorize imaginative writing as something more specific, strange and fragmented than a 'reflection' of either patriarchal ideology or real social relations. A socialist cultural criticism may wish to cut loose, finally, from feminism's overemphasis in the last decade on high culture as a leading influence, benign or vicious, on women's subordination or struggle. Millett's radical feminism is quite clear about culture's central place in the sexual revolution. Given the errors in her definition of patriarchy and the function of patriarchal ideology we should, as Marxists and feminists, be wary of placing all of our hopes and fears on the revision of culture. In her postscript, Millett concludes:

> The enormous social change involved in a sexual revolution is basically a matter of altered consciousness, the exposure and elimination of social and psychological realities underlining political and cultural structures. We are speaking then, of a cultural revolution, which, while it must necessarily involve the political and economic reorganization traditionally implied by the term revolution, must go far beyond this as well. And here it would seem that the most profound changes implied are ones accomplished by human growth and true re-education, rather than those arrived at through the theatrics of armed struggle — even should the latter become inevitable.[23]

Much of this statement is politically impeccable, but its emphasis, written as it was in the midst of the Vietnam war, is a little worrying. The realities of armed struggle are made to seem more distant and fictional than those of altered consciousness and human growth.

---

23. Millett, pp. 362-3.

2.
Wild Nights:
Pleasure/Sexuality/Feminism

... till women are led to exercise their understandings, they should not be satirized for their attachment to rakes; or even for being rakes at heart, when it appears to be the inevitable consequence of their education. They who live to please — must find their enjoyments, their happiness in pleasure!

Mary Wollstonecraft, 1792

Wild Nights — Wild Nights!
Were I with thee
Wild Nights should be
Our luxury!

Emily Dickinson 1861

I had been a hopeful radical. Now I am not. Pornography has infected me. Once I was a child and I dreamed of freedom. Now I am an adult and I see what my dreams have come to:

pornography. So, while I cannot help my sleeping nightmares, I have given up many waking dreams.

Andrea Dworkin 1981[1]

How difficult it is to uncouple the terms pleasure and sexuality. How much more difficult, once uncoupled, to re-imagine woman as the subject, pleasure as her object, if that object is *not* sexual. Almost two centuries of feminist activity and debate have passed, two hundred years in which women's understandings have been widely exercised, yet most of Mary Wollstonecraft's modest proposals for female emancipation are still demands on a feminist platform. Most distant, most utopian seems her hesitant plea that the social basis for woman's sexual pleasure be 'dignified' after 'some future revolution in time'.[2] Too near, too familiar, is her temporary expedient, the rejection of woman's pleasure as inextricably bound to her dependent and deferential status. Revolutions have come and gone, and sexuality is once more at the head of feminist agendas in the west, the wild card whose suit and value shifts provocatively with history. As dream or nightmare, or both at once, it reigns in our lives as an anarchic force, refusing to be chastened and tamed by sense or conscience to a sentence in a revolutionary manifesto.

In the 'right to choose' the women's movement has reasserted the tenets of liberal humanism, laying claim to its promise of individual civil rights for women, and acknowledging the difficulty of prescription in the area of sexual politics. Yet female sexuality remains one of the central contradictions within contemporary politics, causing as much anxiety to feminists and their sympathisers as to their opponents. Within feminist debate, radical and revolutionary feminists argue with their liberal and socialist sisters around definitions of a correct or politically acceptable sexual practice. The possible positions on this troubling issue that can be identified as feminist range from a pro-

---

1. Mary Wollstonecraft, *A Vindication of the Rights of Woman*, New York 1975, p. 119. Emily Dickinson, *The Complete Poems of Emily Dickinson*, Thomas H. Johnson ed., London 1977, p. 114. Andrea Dworkin, *Pornography: Men Possessing Women*, London, 1981, p. 304.
2. Wollstonecraft, p. 119.

pleasure, polymorphously perverse sexual radicalism, through cautious permissiveness, to anti-porn activism and a political lesbianism that de-emphasises genital sexuality. This muddy conflict on the site of feminism itself, suggests, among other things, how profoundly women's subjectivity is constructed through sexual categories.

The negative meanings historically associated with their sexuality have been a major impediment in women's fight for liberation. Historians suggest that the 'ideological division of women into two classes, the virtuous and the fallen, was already well developed' by the mid-eighteenth century. Certainly it received one of its major modern articulations at about this time in Rousseau's *Emile* (1762). In *Emile* the possibility of women's civil, economic and psychological independence is rejected because it would also enable the independent and licentious exercise of her supposedly insatiable sexual appetite. Woman's desire is seen by Rousseau as both regressive and disruptive of the new liberal social order he proposed; women's emancipation would mean a step backward for rational and egalitarian progress. It is important to remember that the notion of woman as politically enabled and independent is fatally linked to the unrestrained and vicious exercise of her sexuality, not just in the propaganda of the new right, but in a central and influential work of the very old left.

When feminists sought to appropriate liberal humanism for their own sex they had to contend with the double standard prominently inscribed within radical tradition, as well as with its suffocating and determining presence in dominant ideologies. Female sexuality is still the suppressed text of those liberal and left programmes that are silent on the issues of women's subordination. This silence has had its negative effect upon feminism itself, which must always speak into other political discourses. Where both right and left sexual ideologies converge, associating women's desire with weakness, unreason and materialism, it has been noticeably hard to insist on positive social and political meanings for female sexuality. Only its supposed disruptive force can be harnessed to revolutionary possibility, and then, perhaps, only for the moment of disruption itself. While most feminisms have recognized that the regulation of female sexuality and the ideological mobilization of its threat to order are part of women's subordination, it is not surprising that they have too often accepted the paradigm that insists that desire is a regressive force in women's lives, and have called for a sublimation of women's sexual pleasure to meet a passionless and rational ideal. Rousseau's formulation has cast a long shadow that cannot be dispersed by simple inversions of his argument. As long as the idea survives that a reformed libidinal economy for women is the precondition for a successful feminist politics, women can always be seen as unready for emancipation. This view, explicitly expressed in Mary Wollstonecraft's *A Vindication of the Rights of Woman* emerges in a different form in Adrienne Rich's radical feminist polemic, 'Compulsory Heterosexuality and Lesbian Existence' (1980). This article explores *A Vindication* at some length, and 'Compulsory Heterosexuality' very briefly, as part of a longer project to understand how the sexual politics of feminism has been shaped.

The Rights of Woman and Feminine Sexuality: Mary Wollstonecraft

The reputation of Mary Wollstonecraft's *A Vindication of the Rights of Woman* (1792), the founding text of Anglo–American feminism, generally precedes and in part constructs our reading of it. We are likely to look for, and privilege, its demands for educational, legal and political equality; these are, after all, the demands that link Wollstonecaft's feminism to our own. If we give ourselves up to *A Vindication*'s eloquent but somewhat rambling prose, we will also discover *passim* an unforgettable early account of the making of a lady, an acute, detailed analysis of the social construction of femininity, which appropriates the developmental psychology of enlightenment and romantic thought. It is certainly possible to engage with *A Vindication* so far and no farther, to let most of its troubling historical meanings and contradictions drop away, so that we may take away from it an unproblematic feminist inheritance. How much use can we make of this legacy without a sense of the history that produced it? Read *A Vindication* for its historical meanings and another text

---

3. Jeffrey Weeks, *Sex, Politics and Society*, London 1981, p. 30.
4. Adrienne Rich, 'Compulsory Heterosexuality and Lesbian Existence', in *Signs; Journal of Women in Culture and Society*, vol. 5, no. 4, 1980, pp. 631-60.

emerges, one that is arguably as interested in developing a class sexuality for a radical, reformed bourgeoisie as in producing an analysis of women's subordination and a manifesto of her rights.

This part of Wollstonecraft's project deserves our attention too, for only by understanding why Wollstonecraft wanted women to become full, independent members of the middle-class, can we make sense of the negative and prescriptive assault on female sexuality that is the *leitmotif* of *A Vindication* where it is not the overt subject of the text.

It is usual to see the French Revolution as the intellectual and political backdrop to *A Vindication*; it would be more useful to see it as the most important condition of its production. As Margaret Walters has pointed out, *A Vindication* sums up and rearticulates a century of feminist ideas,[5] but its immediate stake was in the political advance of a revolutionary vanguard — the middle-class itself, as Wollstonecraft and others imagined it. Every opinion in the text is written in the glare of this politically charged and convulsive moment, and the area of Wollstonecraft's thought most altered and illuminated by that glare is sexuality. In her two attempts at fiction, *Mary, a Fiction* and *Maria or The Wrongs of Woman*, one produced a few years before *A Vindication* and the other incomplete at her death in 1797, women's feelings and desires, as well as the importance of expressing them, are valorized. But in *A Vindication* Wollstonecraft turned against feeling, which is seen as reactionary and regressive, almost counter-revolutionary. Sexuality and pleasure are narcotic inducements to a life of lubricious slavery. Reason is the only human attribute appropriate to the revolutionary character, and women are impeded by their early and corrupt initiation in the sensual, from using theirs.

Why is *A Vindication* so suffused with the sexual, and so severe about it? This is the question that I will explore at some length below. Wollstonecraft's feminism and her positions on sexuality were, at this point in her life, directly bound up with her radical politics — they can only be understood through each other. In untangling the knotted meanings of the sexual in our own history, our own politics, it is useful to understand the

---

5.   Margaret Walters, 'The Rights and Wrongs of Women: Mary Wollstonecraft, Harriet Martineau, Simone de Beauvoir', in Juliet Mitchell and Ann Oakley eds., *The Rights and Wrongs of Women*, Harmondsworth, 1979, pp. 304-378.

different but recurring anxieties it has stirred for other feminisms, other times.

A Vindication of the Rights of Woman offers the reader a puritan sexual ethic with such passionate conviction that self-denial seems a libidinzed activity. And so it was, in the sense that a reform of sexual behaviour was Wollstonecraft's precondition for radical change in the condition of women; permitting the development of their reason and independence. The democratic imperatives — equality and liberty for all classes of persons — have been, for so long now, the well worn staples of liberal and left rhetoric that it is hard to remember that they were being invoked in new ways and with unprecedented exuberance in the 1790s. When we try to puzzle out the meanings of *A Vindication* it is the negative construction of the sexual in the midst of a positive and progressive construction of the social and political we must question. In that contradiction — if indeed it is a contradiction — our present conflict over sexual politics is still partly embedded.

Written in six weeks at the height of British left optimism about events in France, *A Vindication* came out early in 1792, the same year as the second part of Tom Paine's *Rights of Man*, a year before William Godwin's *Political Justice*. Each was, equally, a response to the political moment. All three were crucial statements about the social and political possibilities of a transformed Britain. An almost millenarial fervour moved British radicals in these years. Their political and philosophical ideas were being put into practice only a few hundred miles away; there were signs of reasoned and purposeful unrest at home among ordinary working people. The end of aristocratic privilege and autocratic rule in France was to be taken as a sign of universal change. The downfall of the Bastille, Thomas Paine exulted, included the idea of the downfall of despotism.

A Vindication engages with radical romantic politics at a moment when the practical realization of such a politics seemed as near as France itself. Wollstonecraft had already written one short pamphlet, *A Vindication of the Rights of Men* (1790), in support of the revolution, and was still to write a long piece on its behalf.[6] In *A Vindication of the Rights of Woman*, her most

---

6. Mary Wollstonecraft, *Historical and Moral View of the Origin and Progress of the French Revolution*, 1794.

important work, she took advantage of an open moment of political debate to intervene on behalf of women from inside the British left intelligentsia. Its message is urgent precisely because social and political reform seemed not just possible, but inevitable. The status of women as moral and political beings had become one fairly muted instance of the unresolved contradictions within the republican and democratic tendencies of the time. The overlapping tendencies of enlightenment and romantic thought emphasized the natural virtue rather than innate depravity of human beings, their equality before God, and the evils brought about by unequal laws and hereditary privilege. Arguments initially directed at a corrupt ruling class on behalf of a virtuous bourgeoisie inevitably opened up questions of intraclass power relations. With *A Vindication* Wollstonecraft challenged her own political camp, insisting that women's rights be put higher on the radical agenda. Addressed to Talleyrand, taking issue with Rousseau, speaking the political jargon of her English contemporaries, *A Vindication* invited the enlightenment heritage, the dead and the living, to extend the new humanism to the other half of the race. With a thriving revolution under way, the political and intellectual credit of republican sympathisers was as high as their morale. It seemed like the right moment to ask them to pay their debt to women.

The opening pages of *A Vindication* share the aggressive, confident mood and tone that had developed under the threat and promise of the revolutionary moment. Ridiculing the 'turgid bombast' and 'flowery diction' of aristocratic discourse, Wollstonecraft offers the reader instead, 'sincerity' and 'unaffected' prose, the style and standards of the class of men and women to whom she was speaking — 'I pay particular attention to those in the middle class, because they appear to be in the most natural [i.e. least corrupted] state.' Her unapologetic class bias was shared with her radical contemporaries — it is hardly surprising that idealized humanity as it appears in her text is a rational, plain speaking, bourgeois man. Denying any innate inequality between the sexes except physical strength, she promises to 'first consider women in the grand light of human creatures, who, in common with men, are placed on this earth to unfold their faculties', and addresses her sisters boldly as 'rational creatures' whose 'first object of laudable ambition' should be 'to obtain a character as a human being, regardless of the distinctions of sex....'[7]

How to attain this character? In Paine's *Rights of Man* the reader was told that inequality and oppression were the effects of culture rather than nature. The text itself is a politicizing event, first constructing and then working on an uncorrupted rational subject. Paine hoped, and his enemies feared, that some sort of direct political action to unseat despotic power would follow from a sympathetic reading of his pamphlet. The message and intention of *A Vindication* are very different. Nowhere does Wollstonecraft pose women, in their present 'degraded' condition, as either vanguard or revolutionary mass. Like the corrupt aristocracy, to whom they are frequently compared, they are, instead, a *lumpen* group who must undergo strenuous re-education in order that they might renounce the sensual, rid themselves of 'soft phrases, susceptibility of heart, delicacy of sentiment, and refinement of taste' ... 'libertine notions of beauty' and the single-minded 'desire of establishing themselves — the only way women can rise in the world — by marriage.'[8] Before the middle-class woman can join the middle-class man in advocating and advancing human progress she must be persuaded to become 'more masculine and respectable', by giving up her role both as 'insignificant objects of desire' and as desiring subject.[9]

Even in its own day *A Vindication* must have been a short, sharp shock for women readers. Men might be able to mobilize reason and passion, in them equitably combined, to change the world immediately; women, crippled and stunted by an education for dependence, must liberate themselves from a slavish addiction to the sensual before their 'understandings' could liberate anyone else. At later moments of political crisis feminists could, and would, portray women as vanguard figures, subordinated members of the propertied class who understood more about oppression, as a result, than their bourgeois male comrades. Not here. Read intertextually, heard against the polyphonic lyricism of Paine, Godwin and the dozens of ephemeral pamphleteers who were celebrating the fact and prospect of the revolution, *A Vindication* was a sobering read. Wollstonecraft sets out on an heroic mission to rescue women from a fate worse than

---

7.   Wollstonecraft, *A Vindication*, pp. 9-10.
8.   Ibid., p. 10.
9.   Ibid., p. 11.

death, which was, as she saw it, the malicious and simultaneous inscription of their sexuality and inferiority as innate, natural difference. This was how her political mentor and gender adversary Rousseau had placed them, too weak by nature to reach or be reached by sweet reason. Rousseau's influence was great, not least on Wollstonecraft herself. She accepts Rousseau's ascription of female inferiority and locates it even more firmly than he does in an excess of sensibility. Since lust and narcissism were evil they must belong to social relations rather than human nature; this was Rousseau's own position in relation to men. Accordingly, female sexuality insofar as it is vicious is inscribed in *A Vindication* as the effect of culture on an essentially ungendered nature. By tampering with the site of degrading sexuality without challenging the moralising description of sexuality itself, Wollstonecraft sets up heartbreaking conditions for women's liberation — a little death, the death of desire, the death of female pleasure.

Even if *A Vindication* is preoccupied with the sexual as the site and source of women's oppression, why is woman's love of pleasure so deeply stigmatized as the sign of her degradation? In refusing to interpret women's unbounded desire as a natural mark of sexual difference or the appropriate preoccupation of her mediated place in the social, Wollstonecraft is resisting a whole range of bourgeois positions around gender sexuality, positions rapidly hardening into the forms of bourgeois morality that would dominate nineteenth century ruling class gender relations. Her debate with Rousseau is central, because, like her, Rousseau wished to harness his gender ideologies to radical social and political theories. Rousseau's *Emile* is the place where he spells out the theoretical and socially expedient premises that excluded women from equal participation in the enlightenment projects for human liberation and individual transcendence. Arguing for the sexual assymetry of natural endowment, Rousseau insisted that women's 'first propensities' revealed an excess of sensibility, easily 'corrupted or perverted by too much indulgence.' In civil society women's amoral weakness must not be given its natural scope lest it lead, as it inevitably must, to adultery and its criminal consequence, the foisting of illegitimate heirs on bourgeois husbands. The remedy is borrowed back from the techniques of aristocratic despotism, elsewhere in Rousseau so violently condemned: women '... must be subject all their lives, to the most constant and severe restraint, which is that of decorum; it is therefore, necessary to accustom them early to such confinement that it may not afterwards cost them too dear.... We should teach them above all things to lay a due restraint on themselves.'[10]

Acknowledging, with crocodile tears, the artificiality of the social, while insisting on its necessity, Rousseau invokes a traditionally unregenerate Eve partnered to an Adam who has been given back his pre-lapsarian status. 'The life of a modest woman is reduced, by our absurd institutions, to a perpetual conflict with herself: but it is just that this sex should partake of the sufferings which arise from those evils it hath caused us.'[11] *Emile* lays out, in fascinating detail, the radical project for the education and adult gender relations of an enlightened bourgeoisie, a project that depended for its success on the location of affection and sexuality in the family, as well as the construction of the bourgeois individual as the agent of free will. The struggle between reason and passion has an internal and external expression in Rousseau, and the triumph of reason is ensured by the social nature of passion. Since male desire needs an object, and women are that infinitely provocative object, the social subordination of women to the will of men ensures the containment of passion. In this way Rousseau links the potential and freedom of the new middle class to the simultaneous suppression and exploitation of women's nature.

Rousseau plays on the already constructed sexual categorization of women into two groups — the virtuous and depraved. By insisting that these divisions are social rather than natural constructs — women are not depraved by nature — Rousseau can argue for social and civil restraints on women. Michel Foucault points out that the process of constructing women first and foremost as a sexual subject was in itself a class bound project: '... it was in the "bourgeois" or aristocratic family that the sexuality of children and adolescents was first problematized.... the first figure to be invested by the deployment of sexuality, one of the first to be "sexualized" was the "idle"

---

10. Jean-Jacques Rousseau, *Emile*, Barbara Foxley, tr., London, 1974, p. 332. Passages from *Emile* can all be found in Book V of this edition. However I have cited Rousseau as quoted by Wollstonecraft who comments on large chunks of Book V in *A Vindication*.

11. Ibid., pp. 332-3.

woman. She inhabited the outer edge of the "world", in which she always had to appear as value, and of the family, where she was assigned a new identity charged with conjugal and parental obligation.'[12]

Mary Wollstonecraft stood waist-deep in these already established and emergent sexual ideologies. At the time she was writing *A Vindication* she was neither willing nor able to mount a wholesale critique either of bourgeois sexual mores or the wider areas of gender relations. Her life was shortly to go through some very rapid changes, which would, ironically, mark her as one of the 'degraded' women so remorselessly pilloried in her text. A year and a half after her essay was published she was living with a young American, Gilbert Imlay, in France; two years later she was an unmarried mother. *A Vindication* is a watershed in her life and thought, but this crisis is marked in a curiously wilful way. The text expresses a violent antagonism to the sexual; it exaggerates the importance of the sensual in the everyday life of women, and betrays the most profound anxiety about the rupturing force of female sexuality. Both *Emile* and *A Vindication* share a deep ambivalence about sexuality. Images of dirt, disease, decay and anarchic power run as a symbolic undertext in both works, too frequently located in women's sexual being rather than in any heterosexual practice. This distaste is pervasively articulated in *A Vindication*, adumbrated on the first page with an arresting description of French gender relations as 'the very essence of sensuality' dominated by 'a kind of sentimental lust' which is set against the ideal of 'personal reserve, and sacred respect for cleanliness and delicacy in domestic life....'[13] The images of sexuality throughout are so gripping and compulsive that it is hard to tear oneself away to the less vivid analysis that insists, with commendable vigour, that these filthy habits are a social construction, foisted on each generation of women by male-dominated and male-orientated society.

The place of female sexuality in *A Vindication* is overdetermined by political as well as social history. Like many of the progressive voices of the late eighteenth century, Wollstonecraft had built her dreams of a new society on the foundation of

---

12. Michel Foucault, *The History of Sexuality: Volume 1: An Introduction*, London, 1979, p. 121.
13. Wollstonecraft, *A Vindication*, pp. 3–4.

Rousseau's *Social Contract* and *Essay on Inequality*. Rousseau's writings, insofar as they spoke about human beings rather than men, offered cold reason warmed with feeling in a mixture that was very attractive to the excitable radical temperaments of Wollstonecraft's generation. Rousseau, Paine wrote in 1791, expressed 'a loveliness of sentiment in favor of liberty, that excites respect and elevates the human faculties' — a judgement widely shared. How unlovely then, for Wollstonecraft to consider that in *Emile* Rousseau deliberately witholds from women because of the 'difference of sex' all that is promised to men. Rousseau's general prejudices and recommendations for women — functional, domestic education, nun-like socialization, restricted activity and virtual incarceration in the home — colluded with the gender bias and advice of more reactionary bourgeois authors, as well as society at large. The sense in which Rousseau's prescriptions were becoming the dominant view can be heard in the different imaginary readers addressed by the texts. In the section on women *Emile* slips in and out of a defensive posture, arguing, if only tactically, with an anonymous feminist opponent for the imposition of a stricter regime on women. Wollstonecraft too is on the defensive but her composite reader-antagonist was a society that believed in and followed Rousseau's novel advice to the letter. *Emile* offered its ideas as a reform of and reaction to liberal ideas on female education and behaviour. Thirty years on, *A Vindication* suggested that female sexual morality had become laxer, operating under just such a regime of restraint and coercion as Rousseau had laid out.

The project of *Emile* was to outline the social and sexual relations of an idealized bourgeois society by giving an account of the education and courtship of its youth. *A Vindication* appropriates part of this project, the elaborate set of distinctions between the manners and morals of the aristocracy and those of the new middle class. The anti-aristocratic critique is foregrounded and set in focus by the French Revolution: its early progress exposed the corruption of the ruling classes to a very wide and receptive audience. When Wollstonecraft suggests that vain, idle and sensuous middle-class women are to be compared with the whole of the hereditary aristocracy who live only for pleasure she strikes at two popular targets. When she identifies the aestheticized and artificial language of the ruling class — 'a deluge of false sentiments and overstretched feelings', 'dropping glibly from the tongue' as the language of novels and letters, she implies that it is also the language of women, or of the society adultress. At one level she is simply producing a gendered and eroticized version of Paine's famous attack on Burke's prose style and sentiments, in *Rights of Man, part 1*. At another, the massing of these metaphors of debased and disgusting female sexuality, even when they are ostensibly directed at the behaviour of a discredited class has the effect of doubling the sexual reference. Paine's comment — 'He pities the plumage and forgets the dying bird' — already carries sexual and gendered meanings. Because a naturally whorish and disrupting female sexuality was so profoundly a part of traditional symbol and reference, used to tarnish whatever object it was applied to, it became extremely difficult for Wollstonecraft to keep her use of such images tied to a social and environmental analysis. She herself is affected by the traditional association.

In *A Vindication* women's excessive interest in themselves as objects and subjects of desire is theorized as an effect of the ideological inscription of male desire on female subjects who, as a result, bear a doubled libidinal burden. But the language of that sober analysis is more innovatory, less secure, and less connotative than the metaphorical matrix used to point and illustrate it. As a consequence, there is a constant slippage back into a more naturalized and reactionary view of women, and a collapse of the two parts of the metaphors into each other. Thus, Wollstonecraft tries to argue *against* restraint and dependence by comparing the situation of women to slaves and lap-dogs — '. . . for servitude not only debases the individual, but its effects seem to be transmitted to posterity. Considering the length of time that women have been dependent, is it surprising that some of them hug their chains, and fawn like the spaniel.'[14]

But it is the metonymic association of 'slave,' 'women,' 'spaniel' that tends to linger, rather than the intended metaphoric distance, the likeness and unlikeness between them.

The same effect occurs when Wollstonecraft borrows a chunk of contemporary radical analysis of the mob to support her position that women need the same freedom and liberal education as men. In enlightenment theory a libidinal economy is brought to bear on subordinated groups: mass social violence is seen as the

---

14. Ibid., p. 82.

direct result of severe repression, which does not allow for the development of self-control or self governance. The mob's motive may be a quasi-rational vengeance against oppressors, but the trigger of that violence is the uncontrolled and irrational effect of sudden de-repression. Sexual symbolism is already prefigured in this analysis, so that when Wollstonecraft draws on it as a metaphor for women's uncontrolled sexual behaviour she reinforces the identification of loose women and mob violence. 'The bent bow recoils with violence, when the hand is suddenly relaxed that forcibly held it' — the sexual metaphor here, as elsewhere, is top-heavy, tumbling, out of control, like the imaginary force of female sexuality itself. Here, and at many other points in the text, *A Vindication* enhances rather than reduces the power of female sexuality, constructing it, unintentionally, as an intimate and immediate threat to social stability, nearer than the already uncomfortably near Parisian mob. It is no wonder that many nineteenth-century feminists, for whom the mob and the French Revolution were still potent symbols of disorder, found the book, for all its overt sexual puritanism, disturbing and dangerous.

The blurring of sexual and political metaphor so that sexuality is effectively smeared all over the social relations under discussion emphasises Wollstonecraft's deliberate privileging of sensibility and pleasure as the ideological weapons of patriarchy. Picking up on the negative vibes about female sexuality in *Emile*, she beats Rousseau with his own stick (as it seems) by making the sensual both viler and more pervasive in women's lives as a result of his philosophy of education put into practice. Wollstonecraft too wishes bourgeois women to be modest and respectable, honest wives and good mothers, though she wishes them to be other things as well. Yet only by imagining them *all*, or almost all, crippled and twisted into sexual monsters by society as it is can she hope to persuade her readers to abandon a gender specific and deforming education for femininity.

Yet the most incisive and innovative elements of *A Vindication* are deeply bound into its analysis of the construction of gender in childhood. The book gives us a complex and detailed account of the social and psychic processes by which gender ideologies become internalized adult subjectivity. This account is spread across the two-hundred-odd pages of the book and is extraordinary both as observation and as theory. Here is the childhood of little girls brought up, *à la* Rousseau, to be women only:

'Every thing they see or hear serves to fix impressions, call forth emotions, and associate ideas, that give a sexual character to the mind. False notions of beauty and delicacy stop the growth of their limbs and produce a sickly soreness, rather than delicacy of organs ... This cruel association of ideas, which every thing conspires to twist into all their habits of thinking, or, to speak with more precision, of feeling, receives new force when they begin to act a little for themselves; for they then perceive that it is only through their address to excite emotions in men that pleasure and power are to be obtained.'[15]

It is exaggerated; it is even fantasy up to a point. Yet reading this passage, I was both shaken by its eloquence and pricked by its accuracy.

Only an unusual 'native vigour' of mind can overturn such a vicious social construction, for: 'So ductile is the understanding, and yet so stubborn, that the associations which depend on adventitious circumstances, during the period that the body takes to arrive at maturity, can seldom be disentangled by reason. One idea calls up another, its old associate, and memory faithful to first impressions ... retraces them with mechanical exactness.'[16]

Here, in part, is the romantic theory of the unconscious, its operations laid bare to draw a particularly bleak conclusion about the fate of women.

The need to exaggerate the effects of a gender biased rearing and education led Wollstonecraft to overemphasize the importance of sexuality in women's lives. *A Vindication* is hardly a realistic reconstruction of the day to day activities and preoccupations of bourgeois women, the author herself not excepted. Rather it is an abstract formulation of the sort of social and psychic tendencies that a one-sided reactionary socialization could produce. It is unfortunate that Wollstonecraft chose to fight Rousseau in his own terms, accepting his paradigm of a debased, eroticized femininity as fact rather than ideological fiction. Woman's reason may be the psychic heroine of *A Vindication*, but its gothic villain, a polymorphous perverse sexuality, creeping out of every paragraph and worming its way into every

---

15. Ibid., p. 117.
16. Ibid., p. 116.

warm corner of the text, seems in the end to win out. It is again too easy to forget that this suffusing desire is a permanent male conspiracy to keep women panting and dependent as well as house-bound and pregnant. What the argument moves towards, but never quite arrives at, is the conclusion that it is male desire that must be controlled and contained if women are to be free and rational. This conclusion cannot be reached because an idealized bourgeois male is the standard towards which women are groping, as well as the reason they are on their knees. Male desire may be destructive to women, but it remains a part of positive male identity. A wider education and eros-blunting forays into the public world of work and politics keeps the rational in control of the sensual in men, and is the recommended remedy for women too. Wollstonecraft thought gender difference socially constructed but she found practically nothing to like in socially constructed femininity. With masculinity it was quite different — 'masculine' women are fine as long as they don't hunt and kill. Yet there could be nothing good about feminized men, since the definitions of the feminine available in A Vindication are shot through with dehumanizing and immoral sensuality. It's not surprising that women together — girls in boarding schools and women in the home — can only get up to unsavory personal familiarities, 'nasty, or immodest habits' This description backs up an argument, possibly forceful in its own time, for mixed education and a freer association of adult men and women; it rounds off the denigration of women's world in A Vindication.

Ironically, it is the revolutionary moment, with its euphoric faith in total social transformation that permits Wollstonecraft to obliterate women and femininity in their unreformed state. Although A Vindication outlines a liberal and unsegregated programme for female education and a wider scope for women's newly developed reason in the public and private world, it has nothing complimentary to say about women as they are. Their overheated sensibility is never seen as potentially creative. One can see how the moral analysis and the social description in A Vindication could be appropriated for a more conservative social theory, which might advocate a degree of exercise for women's adolescent bodies and minds, but would confine them to a desexualized domestic sphere as wives and mothers.

The novels of Jane Austen, Wollstonecraft's contemporary,

are the most obvious immediate example of a conservative recuperation of Wollstonecraft. *Northanger Abbey* paraphrases Wollstonecraft on the dangers to the young female reader of the gothic and sentimental novel, and *Mansfield Park* reads in many places like a fictional reworking of *A Vindication*. Possibly influence, partly mere convergence, the voices of the two women whose politics were deeply opposed, echo each other. It is Wollstonecraft who writes that 'while women live, as it were by their personal charms, how can we expect them to discharge those ennobling duties which equally require exertion and self-denial', but it might as easily be Austen on Mary Crawford. In the same sentence, and in much the same terms, Wollstonecraft denounces hereditary aristocracy. The appropriation of much of Wollstonecraft's writing for conservative social and political ideologies went unacknowledged because of her outcast social status and her revolutionary sympathies.

Nevertheless, mid-century women writers and feminists, looking for ways to legitimize their feminism and their sexuality, as well as their desire to write them both out together, found small comfort in *A Vindication*, where the creative and the affective self are split up and separated. In fiction and poetry, that discursive space open to women but sheltered from the harshest judgements of Victorian morality, late romantic women writers, as sick of Wollstonecraft's regime, if they knew it, as she had been sick of Rousseau's, tentatively began to construct the idea of a libidinized female imagination and, through it, women's right to reason and desire. Authority for such an unmediated and eroticized relation to art and life had to be sought in and stolen from male romantic manifestos. Nothing suggests more unequivocally how deep the effects of separate gender sexualities went, than a quick look at the 1802 introduction to *Lyrical Ballads* after a long look at *A Vindication*. The bourgeois poet was the romantic radical incarnated. Here is Wordsworth, like Mary Wollstonecraft a supporter of the revolution, telling the reader, as she never could, that the poet is a man 'endued with more lively sensibility, more enthusiasm and tenderness' than other men, 'a man pleased with his own passions and volitions, and who rejoices more than other men in the spirit of life that is in him.'[17] The

---

17. William Wordsworth and Samuel Taylor Coleridge, *Lyrical Ballads*, London, 1976, pp. 255-56.

appropriate, democratic subjects for his art were 'moral sentiments and animal sensations' as they existed in everyday life.[18]

We must remember to read *A Vindication* as its author has
instructed us, as a discourse addressed mainly to women of the
middle class. Most deeply class-bound is its emphasis on sexuality in its ideological expression, as a mental formation, as the
source of woman's oppression. The enchilding of women — their
relegation to the home, to domestic tasks and concerns, while
men's productive labour was located elsewhere — was a
developing phenomenon of middle-class life in the eighteenth
century. The separation of home and work in an industrial
culture affected the working class too, but it was not the men
only who worked outside the home: nor was the sexual division
of labour along these lines a working-class ideal until well on in
the nineteenth century. The romantic conception of childhood,
already naturalized in *A Vindication*, had no place in working-
class life. Nor did female narcissism and a passion for clothes
have the same meanings for, or about, working-class women,
who, as Wollstonecraft observes in *Maria*, were worked too hard
at 'severe manual labour' to have much time or thought for such
things. The ideal of education, opening up wider fields for the
exercise of the mind, was part of a bourgeois agenda for social
improvement that would 'lift' the poor as well as women.
Sequential pregnancies, exhausting child care in the grimmest
conditions, the double yoke of waged and unpaid domestic
labour, none of these are cited in *A Vindication* as the cause of
women's degradation. *Maria* includes an honorable if genteel
attempt to describe the realities of life for working class women.
A Vindication is more class bound and more obsessive; a brief,
though not unsympathetic passage on the horrors of prostitu-
tion, and a few references to the dirty backstairs habits that
female servants pass on to ladies is the selective and sexualized
attention that working class women get in *A Vindication*.

Most of Wollstonecraft's difficulties are with the obviously
binding power of the binary categories of class sexuality. Rather
than challenge them, she shifts her abstract women around
inside them or tries to reverse their symbolism. The middle-class
married adultress is magically transformed by liberty and educa-

---

18. Ibid., p. 261.

tion into the modest rational wife. If women in public and in promiscuous gatherings, whether schoolroom or workplace, were considered sexually endangered, Wollstonecraft would eroticize the safe home and the all-girls establishment, so that these harems and not the outside world are the places where modesty is at risk. It doesn't work, but it's a good try. It doesn't work because Wollstonecraft herself wishes to construct class differentiation through existing sexual categories. The negative effects of the text fell on the middle-class women which it is so eager to construct and instruct.

In *Sex, Politics and Society, The regulation of sexuality since 1800,* Jeffrey Weeks, summarizing and extending Foucault, reminds us that: '. . . the sexual apparatus and the nuclear family were produced by the bourgeoisie as an aspect of its own self-affirmation, not as a means of controlling the working class: . . . there are class sexualities (and different gender sexualities) not a single uniform sexuality. Sexuality is not a given that has to be controlled. It is an historical construct that has historical conditions of existence.'[19]

If we apply these comments, we can see that the negative gender sexuality Wollstonecraft constructs was one of several competing gender sexualities of the late eighteenth century. As Margaret Walters indicates, contemporary femininity grips Wollstonecraft even as she argues against it: a sexually purified femininity was equally a precondition for any optimistic, liberal re-ordering of intra-class gender relations, or female aspiration. But Walters is wrong in seeing this struggle as one between feminism and femininity. There is no feminism that can stand wholly outside femininity as it is posed in a given historical moment. All feminisms give some ideological hostage to femininities and are constructed through the gender sexuality of their day as well as standing in opposition to them. Wollstonecraft saw her middle class, for a few years at least, as a potentially revolutionary force. The men and women in it would exercise their understandings on behalf of all mankind. It was important to her that the whole of this class had access to reason, and that women's liberation was posed within a framework that was minimally acceptable to popular prejudices. That is why, perhaps, she finds herself

---

19. Weeks, p. 10.

promising the reader that the freedom of women was the key to their chastity. Within the enlightenment and romantic problematics, reason was always the responsible eldest son and sensibility — emotion, imagination, sensuality — the irresponsible rake, catalyst of change. Class differentiation through the redefinition of sexual mores was a process so deeply entrenched, in Wollstonecraft's time, that the moral positions around sexual behaviour seemed almost untouchable. Feminists of her generation did not dare to challenge them head on, although Wollstonecraft was beginning to work over this dangerous terrain, in her life and in her fiction at the time of her death. The combination of equal rights and self-abnegating sexuality in *A Vindication* has had special attractions for feminists who led very public lives, and found it terrifying and tactically difficult to challenge too many prejudices at once. As a liveable formula for independent female subjectivity though, it never had much going for it — not because an immanent and irrepressible sexuality broke through levels of female self-denial, but rather because the anti-erotic ethic itself foregrounded and constructed a sexualized subject.

As long as the double standard survives gender sexualities will be torn by these contradictions. When Wollstonecraft's ideas for mixed education and wider public participation for women began to be put into practice, women started to query and resist the gender ideologies in which they had been raised. With some help from a popularized psychoanalytic theory, pleasure and sexuality were written into a reworked version of female romantic individualism. Both individualism and these new gender sexualities are, quite properly, heavily contested areas within feminism. Wollstonecraft's project, with its contradictory implications, suggests some of the problems involved in the moralization of sexuality on behalf of any political programme, even a feminist one.

Feminism and Compulsory Heterosexuality: Adrienne Rich

Between the two texts I have chosen to discuss lie nearly two centuries in which successive feminisms have engaged with recalcitrant issues of women's sexuality. Yet while the specific issues have changed, many of the terms in which they are debated would be familiar to Mary Wollstonecraft. In the 1980s the independent sexuality that seems most threatening to the dominant culture as fact and symbol of women's escape from patriarchal control is lesbianism. Lesbian feminists, in the various political tendencies in the women's movement have for many years now been insisting that the cultural constraints on their sexual expression are central to women's subordination as a whole. Sexuality has never been a hidden issue in modern feminism, but its theorization has produced many painful if necessary disagreements, none more so than the place of lesbianism as a political stance within feminist practice. Adrienne Rich, the American poet and feminist theorist has developed a range of arguments about the meaning of female sexuality in our culture. Her position on the sexual politics of feminism is powerfully stated in an article first published in the feminist journal *Signs* in the summer of 1980, and widely available soon afterwards in pamphlet form. 'Compulsory Heterosexuality and Lesbian Existence' challenges the normative heterosexist values and repressive liberal tolerance of a large section of the women's movement, arguing that an acceptance of the virtue and centrality of historical and contemporary forms of lesbian experience is the base line for a feminist politics. Like Wollstonecraft, if a trifle more tentatively, Rich also poses a reformed libidinal economy for women as the precondition for the successful liberation of women. It is the common element in their thinking about women's sexuality that I wish briefly to examine in this last section.

The foregrounding of sexuality as the source of women's subordination is the element that most obviously links Wollstonecraft's analysis with radical and revolutionary feminism in the distinct but linked tendencies that have developed in Britain, France and the United States over the last fourteen years. These strands in feminism have taken the lead in privileging sexuality as the central fact and universal symbol of women's oppression. Radical feminism has built its theory and rhetoric around the ideological and actual violence done to women's bodies, while liberal and socialist feminism has been rather nervous of the sexual, working instead to define the specific forms taken by women's subordination in different class, cultural and racial groups, at discrete historical moments. These projects and strategies frequently overlap, but it is roughly fair to say that radical feminism emphasises the identity of gender oppression across history and culture. Revolutionary feminism pushes this analysis farther, posing a monolithic patriarchal tyranny, with sexuality as its weapon. Both tendencies have located the universal truth of gender oppression in a sadistic and insatiable male sexuality, which is empowered to humiliate and punish. Any pleasure that accrues to women who take part in heterosexual acts is therefore necessarily tainted; at the extreme end of this position, women who 'go with men' are considered collaborators — every man a fascist at heart. While Wollstonecraft acknowledged that a depraved sexual pleasure for both men and women was the effect of unequal power relations between them, radical feminism underlines the unpleasure of these relations for women. Where women have no choice over the aim and object of their sexuality, heterosexuality, in the words of Adrienne Rich, is 'compulsory' — an institution more comprehensive and sinister than the different relations and practices it constructs. Worse, compulsory heterosexuality is part of a chain of gender — specific tortures, both medical and conjugal: hysterectomy, cliterodectomy, battering, rape and imprisonment are all elaborations of the sadistic act of penetration itself, penetration the socially valorized symbol of violence against women. Men use these torments to shore up their own subjectivity. Their pleasure in them is a confirmation of male power. Pornography, in this analysis, is emblematic of all male sexuality, the violent fantasy behind the tenderest act of intercourse.

Rich defines heterosexuality as an institution 'forcibly and subliminally imposed on women' who have 'everywhere ... resisted it.' Although she admits that there are 'qualitative differences of experience' within heterosexuality, these differences cannot alter the corrupt nature of the institution, since a good partner is rather like a good master in slavery, a matter of luck not choice. While Wollstonecraft believed, cynically, that all women took pleasure in their slavery, Rich backs off from admitting that coercion, however subliminal, can produce pleasure. Binary categories, historically differentiated, are operating here. Bad women in 1792 experienced bad pleasure; good women in 1980 experience no pleasure. In both cases the effect is punitive.

Rich's abstract women — they are no nearer to real, historical women than the incredibly lascivious ladies of *A Vindication* —

are neither masochists nor nymphomaniacs, they are simply
women whose natural sexuality has been artificially diverted,
from their real object, other women. Women's long struggle
against heterosexuality took, according to Rich, a wide variety of
forms along what she calls the 'lesbian continuum', as distinct
from 'lesbian existence' — the natural sexuality of women. Rich
has shifted the terms in the nature/culture debate without really
altering the paradigm of women's sexuality. In her scenario
female heterosexuality is socially constructed and female homosexuality is natural. As in Wollstonecraft, what is bad goes on
the outside, what inheres is neutral or good. In Rich's formula,
women's libidinal drive is made central, transhistorical and
immanent where dominant sexual ideology had constructed it as
accidental and/or pathological. Political lesbianism becomes
more than a strategic position for feminism, it is a return to
nature. In this new interpretation of sexuality a fairly crude libidinal economy is asserted:

> Woman identification is a source of energy, a potential springhead of
> female power, violently curtailed and wasted under the institution of
> heterosexuality. The denial of reality and visibility to women's
> passion for women, women's choice of women as allies, life compan-
> ions, and community; the forcing of such relationships into dis-
> simulation, their disintegration under intense pressure, have meant
> an incalculable loss to the power of all women *to change the social
> relations of the sexes*, to liberate ourselves and each other. The lie of
> compulsory female heterosexuality today afflicts not just feminist
> scholarship, but every profession, every reference work, every curric-
> ulum, every organizing attempt, every relationship or conversation
> over which it hovers. It creates, specifically, a profound falseness,
> hypocrisy and hysteria in the heterosexual dialogue, for every heter-
> osexual relationship is lived in the queasy strobelight of that lie.
> However we choose to identify ourselves, however we find ourselves
> labelled, it flickers across and distorts our lives.[20]

The saturating power of this socially enforced — as opposed to
naturally lived — sexuality represses, in Rich's view, all creative
expression and all radical and revolutionary process. It is eerily
like Wollstonecraft's totalizing view of sexuality. Both Rich and
Wollstonecraft believe that heterosexuality as it is and has been

20. Rich, p. 657.

lived by women is an ideological distortion of the possibilities of female sexuality. At one level *A Vindication* is highly prescriptive: it asks women, at the very least, to resist the appeal of a pleasure that will put them at the sexual and emotional mercy of men. Wollstonecraft stopped short of defining an innate form of female sexuality — she understood after her encounter with *Emile* that arguing difference from nature was ultimately reactionary. Rich, on the other hand, has no qualms about constructing female sexuality as naturally different. She uses her analysis, in the passage cited above, to interpret conflicts within feminism today. The result is that these crucial differences, on whose working through the future of feminism depends, are collapsed into the denial of *some* women of the universal sexuality of *all* women. Any failure of energy or strategy can be reduced to the frustration and anxiety associated with a denied or feared sexuality. Difficulties between women are no longer about age, class, race or culture. All the legitimate problems inherent to an emergent politics are whittled down to a repressed but supracultural sexuality. In *Compulsory Heterosexuality* the solution for a better politics is contained in the appeal from bad culture back to good nature.

The theme of Rich's revision of female sexuality is the possible construction of a specifically *feminist* humanism. Benign nature is female — affectionate and sensual as well as creative, revolutionary and transcendent. In its political inflection it opposes an innately vicious male nature whose ascendency has produced the bad dream of phallocratic culture. According to Rich, '. . . heterosexuality as an institution has been organized and maintained through the female wage scale, the enforcement of middle-class women's leisure, the glamorization of so-called sexual liberation, the withholding of education from women, the image of "high art" and popular culture, the mystification of the "personal" sphere and much else.'[21] These rather heterogeneous, class–specific and ethnocentric devices support heterosexuality rather than capitalism or patriarchal relations. Take away these and other cultural supports and heterosexuality would presumably wither away. Destroy heterosexist culture at any historical moment and lesbian/feminism would emerge triumphant

---

21. Rich, p. 659.

from its ashes. Rich's simple belief in the all-embracing political possibilities of lesbian existence, her rejection of the political integrity of heterosexual feminism constitutes a denial both of the specificity and variety of female sexuality and the specificity and variety of feminism.

The identification of the sources of social good or evil in the sexual drive of either sex, or in any socially specific sexual practice is a way of foreclosing our still imperfect understanding of the histories of sexuality. The moralization of desire that inevitably follows from such an analysis colludes with those dominant practices that construct human sexuality through categories of class, race and gender in order to divide and rule. The sexuality constructed by a feminist revolution will be a new social relation, with new contradictions and constraints. The dream of an autonomous sexuality, not constructed through the desire of the other, male or female, is a transcendental fantasy of bourgeois individualism. It poses a subject who can stand outside the social. Perhaps, considering its political difficulties in the past, feminism should resist appropriating such a subject, or at least refuse to hang our hopes for sexual pleasure round its neck.

The walls and doors of the women's toilets at the University of Sussex library were, and are, covered with women's writing. From this lowest seat of high learning a polylogic testament to women's entry into discourse can be read in the round. There is, inevitably, a euphoric temptation to read too much out of these expressive inscriptions. For if young women can shit *and* write, not for some patriarchal pedant, but for each other's eyes only, what vestiges of Victorian constraints remain? It is true, of course, that the vast majority of contributors to this particular public/private debate are young, white and middle-class, but not all women's loos so decorated are quite so class and race bound. In the smallest rooms of this academy politics and intellectual matters are informally debated, but sex as the preferred topic wins hands down.

'How do I get an orgasm?' prompted a booth-full of replies and commentary in the early mid-seventies, showing off the range and ingenuity of women's sexual practices and theories. Advice included detailed instructions to be relayed to a male partner as well as the succinct, laconic recommendation to 'Try Women'. There was an address for suppliers of vibrators and an illustration, definitely not erotic, to help one find the elusive clitoris. In the wide variety of responses one was noticeably absent — no contributor contested the importance of the question. No one queried the centrality of orgasm for women's sexual practice or the importance of sexual pleasure itself. No anachronistic bluestocking suggested that intellectual and sensual pursuits were incompatible. No devout Christian was moved to tell her sisters to wait until marriage. Only now, from a different time and place in the feminist debate over sexuality does that apparently unanimous agreement among young educated women that sexual pleasure, however achieved, was an unproblematic desire seem curious. About the means of arriving at pleasure there was plenty of disagreement; if anything that cubicle was a telling reminder that there has never been a single femininity, and that within feminism sexuality and the meaning of pleasure have most frequently been the site of anger, contradiction and confusion, too often illuminating class, cultural and racial division between women. Now, when female sexuality is indisputably centre-stage in feminist debates but pleasure is too rarely its subject and eros rampant is more likely to conjure up a snuff movie than multiple orgasm, that loo wall remains with me as an important event in the history of feminism, a moment whose appearance and significance we must work to understand.

3.

The Feminist Politics of
Literary Theory

About ten years ago, during the high point of feminist activism
in Britain you could find a new-minted piece of folk wisdom
inscribed on the walls of women's loos throughout the country,
and quoted endlessly in the literature of the movement: 'A
Woman Without a Man is Like a Fish Without a Bicycle.' As a
defiant slogan of independence and autonomy it has always irritated me, not only for its 'separatist' implications or its disturbing, Dali-esque juxtaposition of selves and things but also for its
complacent essentialism and the false (in-)congruities of its
metaphor. Women aren't like fish, supplied with a natural
element and equipped for easy passage through it. The 'revolutionary' choice for them will never be for a streamlined new
identity in harmony with an environment in which rust-prone,
male-designed transport technology is redundant. At many
points in the Institute of Contemporary Arts weekend 'Crossing
the Channel'[1] writers and critics proudly maintained the useless-
ness of 'theory' for their practices, and as several of them
disavowed both the present and historical connection between
literature and politics I found my least favorite feminist epigram
swimming into view suitably revamped for the occasion —
'A critic without a theory of representation is like ... a writer
without a politics is like ....'

The aesthetic, as either art practice or as commentary was

---

1. A weekend conference in December 1984 in which French and English writers
and critics considered the uses of critical theory.

slowly glassed in, a lonely fish in a pure element, safe from that wobbly, effortful journey through twentieth century terrains of catastrophe and contradiction that some of us had thought was the point and process both of writing and reading. 'Theory', which I hardly recognized in the denatured and reified form in which it was used by both French and English participants, had been for me, and, I know, for many other feminist readers, writers and cultural critics a way of understanding that grim and comic conjunction of self 'in' and 'out' of society that the literary inscribes by offering us both a theory of representation and of gender as constructed rather than natural meanings.

As the weekend wore on I could see other feminists in the audience (which was, as is usual at cultural events, at least half female while the platform sported two token women) becoming more and more restive. It wasn't simply that they were disturbed by the neo-neo-formalism of so many of the contributions which privileged the 'writer' and 'critic' as men of genius ('Let's face it', Frank Kermode had said in a related event some few weeks before, 'There are a few really great critics and everyone knows who they are.') whose best work must be above the heads of and apart from the concerns of the masses. It was that the negative history of the engagement between French theory and British and French literary practice being sketched out by most of the speakers bore no relationship to the realities of that engagement for women over the last fifteen years. Because gender was never introduced by any of the invited participants as a meaningful variable in the Anglo–French cultural development, and feminist theory or imaginative writing was barely mentioned, large and significant chunks of the cultural history of the past couple of decades were simply omitted from the discussion.

For the engagement of feminism with 'theory' in France, Britain and the United States has had a major impact on writing and criticism both inside and outside academia, and has been one of the main forces that has kept French structuralist, psycho-analytic, linguistic and political analysis from being wholly denatured and depoliticized as it crossed various waters.

Althusser, Lacan, Barthes, Derrida, Macherey, Foucault have been appropriated by English speaking feminists as part of their analysis of sexual difference, of the persistence of femininity and of the crucial place of visual and written representation in the construction, maintenance and subversion of sexual ideologies.

The critiques and innovations of French feminists, such as Luce Irigaray, Michèle Montrelay, Helene Cixous, Catherine Clément and the manifestos and texts of the new feminist avant-garde writers have been relatively widely translated and circulated. The work of Julia Kristeva has been especially influential and important. In particular Irigaray and Wittig have suggested to aspiring anglophone feminist novelists and poets that imaginative writing can elide the space between a theory of difference and an art practice.

Literature, as a cultural object has a different place in feminist cultural and historical analysis than it does in androcentric criticism. One of the central historical discourses in which sexual difference is represented as both a social and psychic reality, it is also one of the few public genres in which women themselves spoke about these questions. For feminist critics, the literary is always/already political in very obvious and common sense ways. For this reason, much feminist criticism of the late sixties and early seventies worked on literary texts by women as if they were 'true' accounts of the socially real, and on literary texts by men as if they were fantasies saturated with dominant and biased sexual meaning. This 'common sense' approach to the literary, which did not have a theory of representation or of the specificity of imaginative writing, and which assumed a curious psychic separatism about the processes of writing by men and women, was soon seen to be of somewhat limited use in understanding how sexual ideologies are constructed and circulated so that they assume 'natural' meaning for both men and women as writers and readers. Feminist critics began to look around for more adequate explanations of ideology, writing and sexual difference than were available in the liberal humanist approaches, or the new critical formalism in which most of them had been trained. While male critics in Britain had as a main spur to the development of Marxist criticism the need to dismantle the hegemony of Leavisite notions of culture, and behind them, a conservative nineteenth-century romanticism, feminist critics, who were very much on the margins of the tertiary teaching of literature — though women form the majority of students of literature — were intervening to overthrow both these older humanisms and to criticize the androcentric assumptions of the new male Marxist critics. Literature, film, and the visual arts were central objects of feminist analysis of women's subordination, for it was in these practices, together with the critical consensus that supported them and constructed their canons, that the languages and images through which subordinate female identities were naturalized could be identified. Moreover both the visual and written text demonstrate the connection between our fantasies of sexual difference (the psychic structure of difference) and its social meanings. Marxist literary criticism has always been somewhat nervous and tentative in its handling of the construction of social hierarchy in literary texts, as if class were only really meaningful as a lived relation, or an economic fact. Feminism on the contrary has insisted from Mary Wollstonecraft onwards that representations of sexual identity as well as its social articulation are both crucial elements in the subordination of women. It was Wollstonecraft too who identified the novel as the popular literary genre directed at women readers that would feed and reinforce denigrating, 'sentimental' definitions of femininity. Both in the nineteenth century and today, feminism has seen the question of the representation of women, sexual difference and gender relations as a 'political' question. Since the literary was one of the primary sites of that representation it could never, whatever its didactic purpose, wholly assume for the woman reader a universalizing function that obscured the real relations of social hierarchy and difference. The 'stuff' of the literary, its narratives and its poetics, is steeped (one might say mired) in the contemplation and elaboration of sexual difference and inequalities — and this is as true of most imaginative writing by women as it is of most men's writing. Thus no feminist critic, writer or artist today could assert with the bland assurance of some of the men on the platform of 'Crossing the Channel' that art was the 'other' of politics, or that some knowledge of contemporary theories of the psyche and of language were not a useful part of the equipment of both writer or cultural critic.

I would like to argue that the feminist intervention into cultural practice has, in the last fifteen years, actually transformed dominant ideas about culture, and has made greater inroads on the notion of art as only good where it speaks for a general humanity than any cultural intervention except the renaissance of Black American writing from the late fifties onwards. An inroad is by no means a victory, as any glance at the frequently spiteful and partisan reviews that feminist writing gets in the newspaper and periodical press can easily confirm.

But even the most mischievous and spiteful review points to an arena of public confrontation over these questions and usually reflects a more sophisticated form of combat than was around ten years ago. The ICA weekend, which so angered the feminists in the audience, revealed another sort of resistance to the combined intervention of specifically political cultural practice and the socialist and feminist criticism that supports it — a denial, a disavowal of the terms of that art practice, and a retreat to familiar positions of elitism and aestheticism. While women weren't mentioned, the 'crowd' as reader was despised, with only Salman Rushdie and Raphael Samuel to defend political art, politicized artists and the idea of a broad readership. (One of the best moments of the weekend occurred when one of the French participants, in a burst of post-lunch hyperbole, insisted that none of the hundreds of thousands of French people who followed Sartre's bier had read a word he had written, proof positive that the multitude were swinish illiterates, and left-wing writers, even when dead, dangerous demagogues. 'How do you know', inquired Rushdie with bitter politeness, 'Did you ask them?') Women were, I guess, virtually included in this discussion as feminism was one of the unarticulated targets of the defenders of formalist art. The question of theory was more difficult, since Rushdie together with other writers tended to see its uses in imaginative writing as marginal, pointing out that he took his models and examples from the popular storytellers still practicing in the sub-continent.

Perhaps, in order to point out the specific uses of 'theory' for feminism in general and feminist criticism in particular I should also tell a story, one that places those uses in concrete historical context, rather than asserting a general influence.

From 1976 until 1978 or 1979 I was a member of a group called unaesthetically but accurately The Marxist–Feminist Literature Collective. When I joined it had been going for some months, and its membership hovered around twelve for its duration as a group. It was formed initially as a reading group of feminists interested in developing a Marxist feminist analysis of literature and most, though not quite all of the members were students or teachers of literature in higher education. We ranged in age from under twenty to over forty, and there were always some Americans (either expatriates like myself, or temporary members) among us. The group met in London but its members came from all over the bottom half of Britain, from Brighton, Oxford, Reading, Hull, Birmingham and Bristol. Our early reading list contained classical Marxist writing on literature, and French theory — Barthes, Saussure, Macherey, Kristeva, Lacan and others. We met quite often, every two or three weeks, and attendance was regular. Our aim was first to understand the theory we were reading, and it was interesting that even the most professionally experienced members of the group approached the theoretical texts with some nervousness, and it was often the younger members who were initially most confident in dealing with them. In the second place we wanted to appropriate what we read for an analysis of literature that took account of both class and gender but saw them as separate and equal determinants. We were moderately confident that we could integrate Marxism and feminism, and some of us believed that we could also successfully integrate psychoanalytic theory with both, but we were aware from the beginning of the considerable difficulties of such syntheses, and our discussions continued to raise new problems. I still have some of the papers from the group, especially from the year 1976-1977 and it is clear we worked hard, regularly writing and circulating short papers for discussion.

At some point we decided to offer a collective paper to the 1977 Sociology of Literature Conference at Essex which took as its topic the year 1848.[2] We read therefore texts from that period — the Brontes, Elizabeth Barrett Browning, and tried out our tentative critical syntheses on these nineteenth century writings. A whole weekend was given up to putting together the bits of the paper, editing sections down to size, writing transitions and whole sections, agreeing the final copy. It was painful, time consuming, humbling, instructive and exhilarating. Ten of us appeared at the conference and we gave the paper a dramatic performance, all of us reading parts of it out, ten women on the platform. Even at a conference of socialist literary critics, our presentation and the paper itself caused a mild sensation. Very few of the men at the conference had any experience of collective writing of an intellectual as opposed to an agit-prop, political

2. Marxist Feminist Literature Collective, 'Women's Writing: *Jane Eyre, Shirley, Villette, Aurora Leigh*' in *1848: The Sociology of Literature: Proceedings of the Essex conference on the Sociology of Literature, July 1977*, F. Barker, J. Coombes, P. Hulme, C. Mercer and D. Musselwhite, eds., University of Essex 1978

kind, and I suspect that we were challenging more than a male Marxist hegemony of criticism and theory but, equally important, the 'individualist' notion of criticism as the work of single intellects, something that Marxist critical practice as opposed to theory had not really confronted. Looking back too, I think the obvious differences in the group in terms of age and status were shocking, breaking down for a few minutes at least the institutional barriers between students and tutors, not in the 'acceptable' social way over a drink but via a democratic, intellectual practice. (This was made easier because we were not students and teachers at the same institutions, but it did help to provide a better model for intra-institutional relations.) For me that group was absolutely formative for my work. I had written one big piece of feminist criticism before I joined, but working on the conference paper confirmed my interest in the mid-nineteenth century and dictated the course of my writing for many years after. My fear of theory as an alien and impenetrable discourse — something felt by many of us trained in the humanities — was permanently dissolved and my sense of its political uses, in analysing representation and relating that analysis to wider socialist and feminist questions was clarified and confirmed. The group continued for at least a year after the Essex event and contributed in a collective way to other venues, though never as spectacularly.

Throughout the life of the group we debated the politics of accessibility and discussed the different ways of arguing the questions of culture and politics with which we were all concerned. What was the audience we wished mainly to address? We wanted to find out how could we talk to more women, and not only middle-class university educated white women. We discussed the ways in which it was appropriate to use our collective work to aid our careers which were at very different stages. We learned a great deal about the contradictions and difficulties of working collectively in a field that prized the individual and original insight above any other, learning how hard it was to 'let go' of a private property in ideas and language. We did not entirely let go. Rather more of us are now working as lecturers in polytechnics and universities — many of the younger women are now in those jobs, but a few are working in further education and community projects. A good number of us, perhaps most of us would still see ourselves as socialist feminists, or at any rate, socialists and feminists. As well as changing the direction of our own writing, the collective experience was very important to me in thinking about the function of criticism in the seventies and eighties, and it is with these thoughts that I want to close this piece.

In recent male Marxist criticism 'friendly' to feminism it has become common to find the women's movement of the last fifteen years, and the cultural practice that has emerged from it as a model for a revitalized, political, even revolutionary relationship between art and society. Terry Eagleton in both *Literary Theory* (1983) and in *The Function of Criticism* (1984) has made interesting points along these lines, and Francis Mulhern has also talked about the renaissance of the political novel in the utopian writing of American feminist writers, both Black and white.[3] I suppose I have been saying something like this myself in the above discussion, posing the intrinsically political and progressive nature of feminist cultural analysis against a resurgent reactionary aesthetic shared by too many of the writers and critics on the ICA platform at the weekend in question, but symptomatic of a larger movement to the right in the USA and Britain under Reagan and Thatcher, and the related shifts away from a left analysis of cultural practice in France in recent years. It is important however not to idealize or reify the gains of the women's movement or its present effects around a cultural politics, for it too is dispersed and in many ways demoralized in all these countries, and if its cultural interventions are still strong, their base in a social movement with a public profile and an agreed political agenda and strategy has significantly weakened. A cultural politics without a strong political culture behind it is condemned to reminisce (note the increasing number of feminist autobiographies that have appeared in the last few years). However powerful its literary voice it will not have an ongoing social movement to criticize and encourage it. Without that critique, it can, like all cultural movements that outlive their immediate political moment become smug, institutionalized, reflexive and stale. Cultural practice is rarely exactly in synch with the political moments that produce it, but equally they will not be as vital a part of a 'counterpublic sphere' (Eagleton's phrase) or a 'revolutionary literary culture' (Mulhern's) without

---

3. See the *New Statesman*, March 22, 1985.

them. It is one of those semi-tragic ironies that feminist criticism has become legitimate within the academy in Britain at a moment when education is contracting. There are no new jobs for the new feminist scholars our graduate programs have produced, and while the disproportion between men and women in English studies continues to make it a 'woman's subject' the demands of these women to be taught feminist texts and feminist forms of analysis cannot be met by existing faculty staff. In the discussion that I chaired between Terry Eagleton and Frank Kermode the ostensible topic was the uses of French theory (Barthes in particular) for literary criticism. Kermode gave a pessimistic and depressed account of the influence or efficacy of such theory. He thought that there were few Marxist critics teaching in institutions of higher learning in Britain, fewer still who were any good at it. Barthes's influence had been negligible, and Barthes's importance anyway was not as a radical thinker or theorist, but as an intellectual in a more elitist and literary mode. Eagleton was optimistic, and looked to the spread of new ideas even to the secondary schools; he certainly asserted the vital connection between theory and politics, and saw a potential triumph of the new English teaching against an older reactionary humanism. In the way they spoke however I sensed a still shared notion of 'the critic' as a rather isolated academic figure (like older romantic notions of the writer). Kermode and Eagleton differed importantly on the question of text and canon, and on the possibility or desirability of politicizing the teaching of litera-ture in the academy. What was missing from their discourse was any notion of a dialectical relationship between the critic–tutor and her students, a relationship that has been enormously important for feminist critics, for it is in and through their women students that they have to a great extent developed and expanded their critique of male-dominated culture. If a genera-tion of students is coming into polytechnics and universities who have no experience of left social movements then the role of tutor–critic shifts again — the agenda, reading-lists and discus-sions must be rewritten to give them an historical grounding in the progressive literature and cultural analysis they are still asking to study, and the tutor/critic must engage with their sense of the present political moment, not only his or her own. The setting up of women's studies in the seventies and early eighties in higher and further education was a most important development for it now provides a fragile but still intact infrastructure for the development of new political ideas. Women are channelled into literary studies for all the wrong reasons, to do with reactionary and essentialist notions of female character and skills, but they also choose that area quite consciously as one in which the psychic and social aspects of sexuality, difference and gender relations will be studied. It is no use trying to create an ideal model of cultural intervention out of a social movement whose character has changed with the changing times. But it is worth trying to make sure that a feminist and socialist politics of culture is not eclipsed, and that its continuing vitality in art practice and cultural analysis be used to get men and women who have come to adulthood in the last six years to construct a progressive cultural politics for the eighties. Time for us fish to get on our bikes.

II

Literature and Feminism

4.

Language and Gender*

Poetry is a privileged metalanguage in western patriarchal culture. Although other written forms of high culture — theology, philosophy, political theory, drama, prose fiction — are also, in part, language about language, in poetry this introverted or doubled relation is thrust at us as the very reason-for-being of the genre. Perhaps because poetry seems, more than any other sort of imaginative writing, to imitate a closed linguistic system it is presented to us as invitingly accessible to our understanding once we have pushed past its formal difficulties. Oddly we still seem to expect poetry to produce universal meanings. The bourgeois novel is comfortably established as a genre produced by and about a particular class, but there is an uneasy feel about the bourgeois poem. Poetry is increasingly written by members of oppressed groups, but its popular appeal is so small in western society today that its shrinking audience may make its elitism or lack of it a non-issue. Its appeal may have diminished in relation to other literary forms but its status and function in high culture

---

*This essay was written for a conference on patriarchy held in London in the spring of 1976. It is the earliest piece in this collection and represents my first enthusiastic attempts to use psychoanalytic theory in cultural criticism. The theoretical sections of the essay are, not surprisingly, fairly rough, a congested paraphrase of my sources. But the application of the theory, which has been better synthesized by others, seems to me still useful, especially since poetry is still a field much neglected by feminist critics. I have updated the theoretical references.

69

continues to be important. This paper examines women's poetry as part of an investigation of women's use of high language, that is, the language, public, political and literary, of patriarchal societies.

A study of women's writing will not get us any closer to an enclosed critical practice, a 'feminist literary criticism'. There can in one sense be no feminist literary criticism, for any new theoretical approach to literature that uses gender difference as an important category involves a profoundly altered view of the relation of both sexes to language, speech, writing and culture. For this reason I have called my paper Language and Gender rather than Women and Poetry, although it grew out of work on a critical anthology of English and American women's poetry that I introduced and edited a few years ago.[1] Some of the problems raised there still seem central to me — the insertion of female centred subject matter into a male literary tradition, the attendant problems of expressing this matter in a formal symbolic language, the contradictions between the romantic notion of the poet as the transcendent speaker of a unified culture and the dependent and oppressed place of women within that culture. New problems have occurred to me as equally important. The difficulty women have in writing seems to me to be linked very closely to the rupture between childhood and adolescence, when, in western societies (and in other cultures as well) public speech is a male privilege and women's speech restricted by custom in mixed sex gatherings, or, if permitted, still characterized by its private nature, an extension of the trivial domestic discourse of women. For male speakers after puberty, the distinction between public and private speech is not made in nearly such a strong way, if at all. Obviously, in the twentieth century and earlier, such distinctions have been challenged and in some cases seem to be broken down, but the distinction is still made. The prejudice seems persistent and irrational unless we acknowledge that control of high language is a crucial part of the power of dominant groups, and understand that the refusal of access to public language is one of the major forms of the oppression of women within a social class as well as in trans-class situations.

---

1. Cora Kaplan, *Salt and Bitter and Good: Three Centuries of English and American Women Poets*, London and New York 1975.

A very high proportion of women's poems are about the right to speak and write. The desire to write imaginative poetry and prose was and is a demand for access to and parity within the law and myth-making groups in society. The decision to storm the walls and occupy the forbidden place is a recognition of the value and importance of high language, and often contradicts and undercuts a more radical critique in women's poetry of the values embedded in formal symbolic language itself. To be a woman and a poet presents many women poets with such a profound split between their social, sexual identity (their 'human' identity) and their artistic practice that the split becomes the insistent subject, sometimes overt, often hidden or displaced, of much women's poetry.

The first part of my paper will try out a theoretical account of the process by which women come to internalize the suppression and restriction of their speech. The second part demonstrates how the struggle to overcome the taboo is presented as the hidden subject in poems that seem deliberately difficult and opaque.

Do men and women in patriarchal societies have different relationships to the language they speak and write? Statements of such a difference, questions about its source, persistence and meaning run through western writing since Greek times. Often buried in that larger subject, the exploration and definition of gender difference in culture, it becomes a distinct issue when women speak or write, and men protest, not only or primarily at what they say, but at the act itself. Recently left feminists have used work on ideology by the French political philosopher, Louis Althusser, together with the psychoanalytic theories of Freud and his modern French interpreter, Jacques Lacan, to clarify their understanding of the construction of femininity.[2] Contemporary work on ideology in France accepts Freud's theory of the unconscious and is concerned, among other things, with the construction of the subject in culture. Language is the most important of all the forms of human communication. Through the acquisition

---

2.   Louis Althusser, 'Ideology and Ideological State Apparatus', and 'Freud and Lacan' in *Lenin, and Philosophy and Other Essays*, London 1971. Jacques Lacan, *Ecrits: A Selection*, London 1977. Jacques Lacan *The Four Fundamentals of Psycho-Analysis*, London 1977. See also *Feminine Sexuality: Jacques Lacan and the ecole freudienne*, Juliet Mitchell and Jacqueline Rose, eds., London 1982.

of language we become human and social beings: the words we speak situate us in our gender and our class. Through language we come to 'know' who we are. In elaborating and extending Freud's work, Lacan emphasizes the crucial importance of language as the signifying practice in and through which the subject is made into a social being. Social entry into patriarchal culture is made in language, through speech. Our individual speech does not, therefore, free us in any simple way from the ideological constraints of our culture since it is through the forms that articulate those constraints that we speak in the first place.

The account that follows here is necessarily very schematized, designed simply to show the crucial nexus between the acquisition of subjectivity through language and the recognition of the social nature of female identity.[3]

Every human child, according to Lacan, goes through an encounter with his own image in the mirror, somewhere between six and eighteen months, which is particularly significant and a precondition of the acquisition of subjectivity. For in that encounter the image is misrecognized as an ideal whole — a counterpart, an Other, of the fragmented, feeling being. During this period the child is angrily conscious of the capricious comings and goings, which he is helpless to control, of persons on whom he relies for physical care and emotional comfort. The perception of the image in the mirror as both self and other, as the same and different, the projection of an ideal form of the self through a spatial relation acts as the basis for the acquisition of subjectivity, and is, as well, the crude form, self and other for all intersubjective relations. Although the child may learn words quite early, during the first year and a half of life, the mastery of language succeeds the mirror stage and is the true point at which subjectivity is attained. Nevertheless even the early use of very simple abstractions show how the child gains some small form of control over the absence and presence of his caretaker. The

---

3.   Useful introductory syntheses of the Lacanian account of the construction of the subject in language are Chris Weedon, Andrew Tolson, Frank Mort 'Theories of Language and Subjectivity' in *Culture, Media, Language*, Stuart Hall, Dorothy Hobson, Andrew Lowe and Paul Willis, eds., London 1980 and Terry Eagleton, 'Psychoanalysis' in *Literary Theory*, London 1984. The substantial introductions by Juliet Mitchell and Jacqueline Rose to *Feminine Sexuality* situate the work of Freud and Lacan in relation to femininity.

classic example, taken from Freud, is the *fort/da* game, in which the child in the mother's absence, throws away an abject *'fort'* and retrieves it *'da'* to symbolize and, in part, control, her absence and presence. As the child acquires more linguistic competence, for example the correct use of names and pronouns to differentiate self from others, he moves from the omnipotence implicit in the pre-linguistic fantasy when he and the mirror image are one, to the necessary limitation of his own desires and powers when he acceded to language, to subjectivity and the world of social relations. In language the child acquires the necessary abstractions to situate himself in relation to others and to speak the particular meanings of his own experience in a public, socially understood discourse.[4]

For Lacan, language, adult or competent speech, is the Symbolic order. It embodies the abstracted relations of the laws of a particular culture. Language only exists through individual speech, so in each speech act the self and the culture speak simultaneously or, to put it another way, each time we speak we are also spoken: This formulation is abstract, but is not meant to be understood as a mechanical operation in which a ventriloquist culture moves our lips. Lacan uses and transforms the linguistic theories of Ferdinand de Saussure who makes the basic distinction between language and speech. Saussure also suggests that meanings, words, can only be understood as differences from other meanings. Meanings — signifiers — are part of chains — think of a sentence as a chain — and refer not to some fixed phenomenological object but to the meanings, either present or implied in the chain, which therefore make up the sense of the chain. To the extent that the words we choose have meanings other than the particular ones that an individual speech act intends, these absent but still invoked relations of meaning are responsible for a 'veering off of meaning' or 'the sliding of the signified under the signifier', of sense under meaning in any given signifying chain.[5] It will become clear quite soon how the distinction between language and speech, the definition of meanings as relations of difference and the crucial role of language in

---

4. Lacan, 'The Mirror Stage as Formative of the Function of the I', *Ecrits*, pp. 1-7.
5. Lacan, 'The Agency of the Letter in the Unconscious or Reason Since Freud', *Ecrits*, pp. 146-78.

the development of the child's consciousness of self, relates to women's use of language.

Symbolic language, which includes everyday speech as well as written or imaginative forms, uses two basic tropes, metaphor and metonymy. These tropes 'present the most condensed expression of two basic modes of relation; the internal relation of similarity (and contrast) underlies the metaphor; the external relation of contiguity (and remoteness) determines the metonymy'.[6] While metaphor and metonymy are the stuff of poetry (Roman Jakobson, who I have quoted here, sees metaphor as the principal mode in romantic and symbolic poetry and metonymy the mode of the epic), these linguistic tropes are the modes through which we come to perceive all relations of difference, such as gender difference and the separation of the self from others. Lacan has identified these figures of speech with Freud's concept of the modes that occur in dreams. Metaphor equals condensation; metonymy equals displacement. Language like the unconscious resists interpretation even as, through dreams and in ordinary discourse it invites us to interpret it. We ought not to think of the use of metaphor and metonymy in imaginative genres as uniquely isolated or sophisticated. How men and women come to speak at all, how they see each other through speech, the social taboos on speech for children and women, all these relations bear upon the way in which individual poets are seen to 'create' new symbolic identifications and relations.

Having gone so deep into language we must now go back to the construction of the subject in culture, and pick up our child at what Freud and Lacan designate the oedipal stage which is also the point at which the child's competence in speaking means that he has virtually entered the Symbolic order. Entry into the Symbolic order is necessary, says Lacan, for mental stability. If the subject cannot be located in linguistic abstraction, then in extreme cases, as observed in the broad disorder termed schizophrenia, words cannot be constructed in an individual discourse. The dislocated subject treats them as things, sounds, associations, and does not use them in a logical pattern to situate herself in her intersubjective (social) situation. The difference between male and female entry into the Symbolic has to do with

---

6. Roman Jakobson, *Studies in Child Language and Aphasia*, The Hague 1971.

the stage of development which overlaps the full acquisition of language, and through which the child accepts his or her gender identity — the oedipal phase. In Lacan, the phallus (not to be confused with the actual penis) is the 'missing' signifier to which both sexes must reconcile their relationship. Full entry into the Symbolic does not depend on having or not having a penis, but on the symbolic interpretation a child places on its absence or presence in his/herself and in the two powerful figures of the mother and father. In order for women to identify finally with their mothers and take their place as female in culture they must accept the missing phallus as a permanent loss in themselves. According to Freud's account of the oedipal resolution, the lack of a phallus in the mother is a nasty shock for both boys and girls. Boys repress their incestuous feelings for their mothers and their anger with their fathers as a result of the implied threat of castration — seen as already accomplished in the mother. At this point they accede to an identification with the father, which seals their gender identity and holds out the promise of a future align- ment with authority, the Symbolic order, or law of the Father in place of the lost identification with the mother. Little girls, who must position themselves very differently in relation to the missing phallus, accept, sometimes reluctantly and with ongoing hostility, their likeness to the mother. The introduction of the father/phallus as the third term in the child's social world, breaks the early mother-child relationship for both sexes and brings on all the ensuing crises of identity through gender differ- entiation, so that all children lose the dyadic relation to the mother as they enter a wider society. Girls, as Freudian theory would have it, have a particular relation to loss or lack in that they must substitute for it, not the possession of the phallus but babies and/or an intersubjective relation with men (who are necessary for the production of babies).[7]

The phallus as a signifier has a central, crucial position in language, for if language embodies the patriarchal law of the culture, its basic meanings refer to the recurring process by which sexual difference and subjectivity are acquired. All human desire is, in Lacan's view, mediated through language, through the 'defiles of the signifier' and is expressed through the desire

---

7.   Lacan, 'The Signification of the Phallus', *Ecrits*, pp. 282-91.

of the other — the projected ideal form of the imago (remember the model of the mirror phase) which becomes dispersed through our entry into the Symbolic in our real relation to others. Only if we accept the phallus as a privileged signification (a meaning which *does* relate to something outside itself) do we see that the little girl's access to the Symbolic, that is to language as the embodiment of cultural law, is always negative, or more neutrally, eccentric.

Even if we do accept the phallus as a privileged meaning, the concept of negative entry, as it has been posed so far seems at once too easy and too difficult to grasp. It is a convenient way of describing a phenomenon not yet fully understood or articulated in psychoanalytic theory. I would prefer, cautiously, to call the entry into the Symbolic 'different' rather than 'negative' for girls, since lack, in Lacanian theory, is as much an experience for men as for women. Also the production of subject as the place and origin of meanings (the entry into language) is necessary for both men and women. The formation of the unconscious in the first instance occurs when the child substitutes language for drives, demand for need, duplicating in the unconscious the prelinguistic arrangement of drives. A second stage of formation can be noted when abstractions, even those as simple but central as the fort/da game allow the child to produce itself as the subject who controls absence. All of language can then be seen as an extended system of mastery over primary need which can never entirely succeed, since the repressed material 'escapes' through dreams, through slips of the tongue, and so on. Why should women whatever the relation of difference through which they enter the Symbolic be less adept at this system than men? Empirical studies that I have seen don't suggest that there is that much significant variation between male and female speech until puberty, if ever, although it is a subject only recently taken up in linguistics. I will return to this problem briefly in the next section, but I want to suggest tentatively here that it is at puberty, the second determining stage of gender identity in culture, that a distinction between male and female speakers is confirmed.

At puberty female social identity is sealed by the onset of menstruation and fertility, and here, in western culture, is where the bar against the public speech of females is made. Puberty and adolescence fulfill the promises of the oedipal resolution. The male is gradually released from the restrictions of childhood, which include the restriction of his speech among adults. The girl's different relation to the phallus as signifier is made clear by a continued taboo against her speech among men. Male privilege and freedom can now be seen by the adult female to be allied with male use of public and symbolic language. In many cultures there is a strong taboo against women telling jokes. If we think of jokes as the derepressed symbolic discourse of common speech, we can see why jokes, particularly obscene ones, are rarely spoken from the perspective of femininity. Adult femininity thus requires (at least in Western culture) an extension of the injunction: 'Children should be seen but not heard'. A sexual division of labour in the reproduction of ideology thus appears. Men reproduce it directly through the control of public speech, and women indirectly through the reproduction of children in the institution of the family. Since women have spoken and learned speech up to and through adolescence they continue to speak among themselves, and to their men in the domestic situation. It is a taboo which seems, in modern society, made to be broken by the demands of women themselves. When women are freed from constant reproduction, when they are educated equally with men in childhood, when they join the labour force at his side, when wealth gives them leisure, when they are necessary and instrumental in effecting profound social change through revolution — at these points women will protest and break down the taboo.

It should be clear to the reader that what I have produced so far is an account of a process by which women become segregated speakers, not an explanation of why this process should take place. Nor have I claimed for it a universal application, but limited myself to western societies. If we assume for the sake of the rest of my argument that the segregation of male and female speech, although apparent to little girls as they observe the social relations of adults and interact with them, is crucially and traumatically confirmed in adolescence, then we may say that the predominance of expressed male perspectives in common and high speech stems from the taboo after childhood. There are therefore two very important and distinct stages at which women's apparently weaker position in language is set. The first is at the oedipal stage where the child, constructed as a speaking subject, must acknowledge social sex difference and align herself with women and restricted speech — a distinction blurred by the restrictions on children's speech. The second stage, puberty, further distinguishes girls from boys by the appearance of adult sex difference and access to public discourse for men.

This account makes some sense in psychic terms of the significant but statistically small presence of women as makers of high culture, of their anxiety about their precarious position, about their difficulties (which are often made into strengths) when using what is clearly in many ways a 'common' language. It is not an alternative to other sorts of social and political analysis of the oppression of women in patriarchal culture through more brutal means, and in other ideological forms.

The seventeenth century in England produced a number of important women poets whose first task seemed to be to challenge the bar against women as speakers and writers. Anne Bradstreet (1612-1672) says

> I am obnoxious to each carping tongue
> Who sayes, my hand a needle better fits

and looks back towards a golden age when there was no bias

> But sure the antique Greeks were far more mild
> Else of our sex, why feigned they those nine
> And poesy made Calliope's own child;[8]

Anne Finch, Countess of Winchelsea (1661-1720) attacks with more vigour and subtlety symbolic associations as spoken from the masculine position. For example, a rose, a cupped flower has no gender in English but to male poets it often represents the female. Its metaphorical associations are with the female sexual organs, its metonymic associations are with muteness, frailty. In asserting her right to an original poetic gift Anne Finch rejects both the rose/woman image and woman's approved leisure occupation, embroidery.

> My hand delights to trace unusual things,
> And deviates from the known and common way;
> Nor will in fading silks compose
> Faintly the inimitable rose ...[9]

8. Kaplan, *Salt and Bitter and Good*, p. 29.
9. Ibid., p. 61.

The use of 'deviates' and 'inimitable' in this passage seem especially suggestive. She uses deviate when she might use wander or swerve or some softer verb. For women to write at all was to be deviant. The poet refuses to be positioned in mute nature. The rose is therefore 'inimitable'. 'Trace' and 'compose' are reversed and ironised; 'trace' used for creative writing and 'compose' for embroidery. It is a brave and largely successful attempt at challenging metaphor through the subtle inversion of a traditional poetic image, but it strikes me as damned hard work. And the sliding of meaning, the effect of metonymy, is obvious. In defying traditional male-centred associations she reminds us of them; they assert themselves as meanings in spite of her skill and care. The ghosts of the meanings she wishes to resist, shadow her words.

There is a haunting painting by Odilon Redon of a woman's face in ivory cameo, further enclosed in a green oval mist. A wraithlike madonna, still, and at the same time full of intense activity, she holds two fingers to her lips, and, perhaps, a cupped paw to her ear. The picture is titled *Silence*. Enjoining silence, she is its material image. A speaking silence — image and injunction joined — she is herself spoken, twice spoken we might say — once by the artist who has located *his* silence in a female figure, and once again by the viewer who accepts as natural this abstract identification of woman=silence and the complementary imaging of women's speech as whispered, subvocal, the mere escape of trapped air ... shhhhhhhh.

More, her speech seems limited by some function in which she is wrapped as deeply as in the embryonic mist. Mother or nurse, the silence she enjoins and enacts is on behalf of some sleeping other. In enforcing our silence and her own she seems to protect someone else's speech. Her silence and muted speech, as I interpret it, is both chosen and imposed by her acceptance of her femininity. It has none of the illusory freedom of choice that we associate with a taciturn male. It is not the silence of chosen isolation either, for even in a painting significantly without other figures it is an inextricably social silence.

Redon's Madonna trails meanings behind it like the milky way. *Silence* makes a point central to my argument that it is perhaps difficult to make with any literary epigraph. Social silence as part of the constitution of female identity — i.e., subjectivity — is a crucial factor in her handling of written language. In an as yet almost unresearched area there is very little evidence to suggest that women's common, everyday speech is in any way less complex than men's and some evidence to suggest that girls not only speak earlier than boys but develop linguistic complexity earlier too. It has been tentatively suggested that although girls are more 'verbal' (whatever that may mean) by the age of eleven or twelve, there is less meaning in their speech, though the phonemic complexity is greater. Robin Lakoff, in *Language and Woman's Place*[10] does not adduce any particular evidence for her ideas or locate her women speakers in any class, race or locale, but suggests that women do speak a sort of second class English which is more interrogatory, more full of 'empty' qualifiers ('lovely', 'kind of') and, because vulgarity is censored, is super-genteel and grammatically more correct than men's speech. It is by no means clear that these observations would be true (if at all) of any group of women except perhaps upwardly mobile middle class white American women, and if true of this group it seems much more likely to be related to a class plus gender instability than to be a particular quality of women's speech. In any case, recent debates over the language of class and of Black English has produced persuasive evidence that a restricted or alternative code does not necessarily produce restricted meanings. The variations that Lakoff lists as being special to women's speech seem very slight when compared to the variations of grammatical structure in Black English compared to standard English. Obviously the subject has barely been opened much less closed, but one might hazard that women speak the language of their class, caste, or race and that any common variants, which are in any case never fully observed, do not in themselves limit the meanings their speech can have. The sanction against female obscenity can have a particular application in the sanction against the telling of jokes and the use of wit by women, since dirty jokes are forms of common speech in which the repressed meanings of early sexual feelings are expressed in tight symbolic narratives.

It is the intra- and trans-class prejudice against women as speakers at all which seems most likely to erode women's use of

---

10. Robin Lakoff, *Language and Woman's Place*, New York 1975.

'high' language. This preference is connected with the patriarchal definition of ideal femininity. 'Silence gives the proper grace to women', Sophocles writes in *Ajax*. Its contradictions are expressed succinctly in the play, 'The Man who Married a Dumb Wife'. A famous physician is called in to cure the beautiful mute. He succeeds, she speaks, and immediately begins to prattle compulsively, until the husband bitterly regrets his humane gesture. His only wish is to have her dumb again so that he might love her as before. Women speak on sufferance in the patriarchal order. Yet although the culture may prefer them to be silent, they must have the faculty of speech in order that they may be recognised as human. One reading of the Dumb Wife, whose speech is her only flaw, is that the physician's alchemy was necessary to reassure the husband that he had married a human woman, although her unrestrained, trivial speech destroys his ability to see her as the ideal love object.

Elizabeth Barrett Browning comments bitterly on the prohibition against women as speakers of public language in her long feminist poem *Aurora Leigh*. Aurora, who defies society to become a major poet, recounts her education at the hands of her aunt who was a model of all that was 'womanly':

> I read a score of books on womanhood ... — books that
>   boldly assert
> Their right of comprehending husband's talk
> When not too deep, and even of answering
> With pretty 'may it please you', or 'so it is', —
> Their rapid insight and fine aptitude,
> Particular worth and general missionariness,
> As long as they keep quiet by the fire
> And never say 'no' when the world says 'ay', ... their,
>   in brief,
> Potential faculty in everything
> Of abdicating power in it.

Aurora calls 'those years of education' a kind of water torture, 'flood succeeding flood/To drench the incapable throat ...' The imposed silence is described as intersubjective, a silence whose effort is bent towards 'comprehending husband's talk'.[11] Women

---

11. Elizabeth Barrett Browning, *Aurora Leigh and Other Poems*, Cora Kaplan ed., London 1978, First Book, pp. 51-2.

writers from the seventeenth century onwards (when women first entered the literary ranks in any numbers) comment in moods which range from abnegation to outright anger on the culture's prohibition against women's writing, often generalizing it to women's speech. They compare their situation to that of 'state prisoners, pen and ink denied' and their suppressed or faulty speech to the child's or the 'lisping boy's'. Emily Dickinson's 'They shut me up in Prose/As when a little Girl/They put me in the Closet — / Because they liked me "still" — '[12] condenses all these metaphors by connecting verbal imprisonment to the real restrictions of female childhood, and adds the point that the language most emphatically denied to women is the most concentrated form of symbolic language — poetry.

The consciousness of the taboo and its weight seemed to press heavily on the women who disobeyed it, and some form of apology, though tinged with irony, occurs in almost all of the women poets, as well as in many prose writers, whether avowed feminists or not, as an urgent perhaps propitiating preface to their speech. In the introduction to the anthology I ascribed this compulsion to an anticipatory response to male prejudice against women writers, and so it was. But it now seems to me that it goes much deeper, and is intimately connected as I have said with the way in which women become social beings in the first place, so that the very condition of their accession to their own subjectivity, to the consciousness of a self which is both personal and public is their unwitting acceptance of the law which limits their speech. This condition places them in a special relation to language which becomes theirs as a consequence of becoming human, and at the same time not theirs as a consequence of becoming female.

The best writing by women about women writing has been about fiction; the weakest about poetry. Fiction, whether gothic, sentimental or realistic has a narrative structure and gendered characters in which the author can locate and distance her own speech. One might say that the narrative discourse itself provides a sort of third term for the woman author by locating (even, and perhaps especially, in a first person narrative) the loss or absence of power anywhere but in her own voice. If fiction

---

12. Kaplan, *Salt and Bitter and Good*, p. 154.

has been the most successful genre for women writers it is not, as has been often suggested, because the novel makes use of the domestic scene, or the life of the feelings, or 'trivial' observation, all those things supposedly close to women's experience, but because its scene is that world of social relations, of inter-subjectivity, in which the author can reconcile to some extent her speech and her silence and be the first to explore and expose her bisexuality without the threat of losing her feminine identity.

Lyric poetry from the romantic movement onwards had an imperative and a structure that was different from that of fiction. Anne Finch, Countess of Winchelsea (much admired by Words-worth who saw her poems as prefiguring romantic verse) wrote in the late seventeenth and early eighteenth centuries. She noted that women were both tempted to try their hand at poetry and inhibited from doing so by the development of a critical canon in which 'Poetry has been of late so explain'd, the laws of itt being putt into familiar languages, that even those of my sex (if they will be so presumptious as to write) are very accountable for their transgressions against them.' These 'laws' about diction, metre, figure and subject had a certain impersonal force, although Anne Finch forebore to write about love lest such writ-ing by a woman give offence. The romantic aesthetic rejected the neo-classical critical standards. The poet was required first and foremost to speak in his own voice. The power of that individual voice was identified with the freedom and transcendence of the individual, and, in its most radical formulation, with the libera-tion of humanity.

In the 1800 and 1802 Prefaces to *Lyrical Ballads*, the manifesto of early romanticism, Wordsworth rejects artificial diction, and asks the poet to use 'as far as is possible, a selection of the language really spoken by men ... the very language of men'. The poet is 'a man speaking to men; a man ... pleased with his own passions and volitions, and who rejoices more than other men in the spirit of life that is in him ...', who has 'acquired a greater readiness and power in expressing what he thinks and feels', who must speak his own truth 'for where the understand-ing of an Author is not convinced, or his feelings altered, this cannot be done without great injury to himself: for his own feel-ings are his stay and support, and if he sets them aside in one instance, he may be induced to repeat this act till his mind loses all confidence in itself and becomes utterly debilitated.' '. . . all good poetry is the spontaneous overflow of powerful feelings . . .' expressed (in tranquillity) 'by a man who has also thought long and deeply.' Children's perceptions are important subjects. The poet is 'affected more than other men by absent things as if they were present . . .' 'He is the rock of defence of human nature; an upholder and preserver, carrying everywhere with him relationship and love.' In asking the poet to use the language of men Wordsworth de-emphasises the importance of metre and rhyme in poetry and places central importance on 'natural' metaphor, pointing out that pleasure in poetry as in all the arts stems chiefly from 'the perception of similitude in dissimilitude. This principle is the great spring of the activity of our minds and their chief feeder. From this principle the direction of the sexual appetite, and all our passions connected with it take their origin; it is the life of our ordinary conversation; and upon the accuracy with which similitude in dissimilitude and dissimilitude in similitude are perceived, depend our taste and our moral feelings.'[13]

If we now think back to the Lacanian account of the constitution of subjectivity that has been presented we see that Wordsworth's poet resembles in certain ways (though not in all respects) the successfully achieved subject who has located himself and his own meanings, particularly those relating to absence and difference, through 'the language really spoken by men', which ought to be prosaic in its naturalness but without losing its symbolic and abstract status. The poet's ability to symbolise through the use of metonymy and metaphor makes him 'the rock of defence of human nature; an upholder and preserver, carrying everywhere with him, relationship and love.' These symbolic forms are not merely verbal tricks, but the very matrix of our human experience. The poet's own feelings are his 'stay and support' but through them he upholds and preserves the essential laws of the culture as they are expressed in human nature, 'our moral feelings'. Our ability to discern difference in similarity and similarity in difference is part of the same faculty that locates us in our gender identity 'the direction of the sexual appetite, and all the passions connected with it.' It is a brilliant exposition of the connections between symbolic language,

13. William Wordsworth and Samuel Taylor Coleridge, *Lyrical Ballads*, London 1976.

cultural law, masculine identity and the self. In this analysis 'the child is father to the man.' Wordsworth sees all these aspects of the poet not in tension or contradiction but as aligned and complementary. He stresses the mastery of absence and difference through the control of language. Early romantic optimism did not recognize the resistance to meaning of language or the disjunction between language and speech which makes it difficult for present meanings to account wholly for absent ones. There is, of course, no theory of the unconscious or repression — common language is the demystified discourse of the self; the poet's voice, freed from the artificial control of the neo-classical aesthetic soars upwards on the full warm current of natural meanings.

Wordsworth was one of many romantics who believed in the transforming power of natural language. Political romantics like Thomas Paine saw democratic language as a radical political force, where aristocratic language had been instrumental in reproducing the mystifications that kept men in chains. If the poet or philosopher could appropriate speech he could transform culture. In this way the romantics actually moved towards a notion of the materiality of language while building an individualist, idealist ethic with it.

'Men' and 'man' is, of course, used by Wordsworth in its innocent, if ideologized sense — as 'human'. How lacking in universal resonance his description of the lyric poet is can be judged by reading the poetry written by women in the late eighteenth and early nineteenth century, poetry which tried in many cases to meet the definitions offered in the Preface to Lyrical Ballads. (Wordsworth may have been more appealing to them than Coleridge's colder anatomy of the imagination.) Yet in the late 1860s young Alice Thompson, yet to become the feminist poet, critic and editor Alice Meynell, looked back on more than a half century of women's writing in the romantic lyric tradition and complained of her own 'rhyming faculty' that 'whatever I write will be melancholy and self-conscious, as are all women's poems.'[14] While only a minority of male poets might see themselves as fitting Wordsworth's hyperbolic description of a man 'pleased with his own passions and volitions, and who rejoices more than other men in the spirit of life that is in him', it was

---

14. Kaplan, *Salt and Bitter and Good*, p. 181.

certainly true that women poets, if not sad in themselves, produced poetry in which melancholy was a dominant mood. Of the poets Alice Meynell would have read, from Charlotte Smith, born in 1749, whose long poem *Beachy Head* celebrates the influence of 'wild nature' on the soul, through Anne Radcliffe, Joanna Baillie, Felicia Hemans, the Bronte sisters, Dora Greenwell, and Christina Rossetti, the melancholy muse is in ascendance. (Only Elizabeth Browning escapes this description.) Their poetry reflects, throughout the period, late romantic disillusion without early romantic mania. It might be true to say that women poets queried the terms of romantic optimism without ever experiencing it, or at worst, imitated it in poems that rang false. The pressure of the early romantic aesthetic was towards the affirmation not the interrogation of states of feeling. This latter activity could be better done in prose where the narrative structure could explain as well as project emotion.

Charlotte Smith speaks longingly of a childhood identification with 'Nature's rudest scenes', but points out that for herself and for all women this happiness vanishes after the onset of puberty — 'The village girl is happy, who sets forth/To distant fair' but after believing 'half' her 'rural lovers' oaths/Of constant faith, and still increasing love ... Her happiness is vanished.'[15] Trite as this schematized poetic account of melancholy seems it points the way towards the problem faced by all women poets who accepted some part of romantic doctrine. Puberty sealed femininity. The pre-pubescent girl might wander happily, like a boy, in 'upland solitude' but women, grown women, were tied by their maternal function and could only identify with nature in the shape of the controlling moon significantly 'mute arbitress of tides'. Following the injunction to express what she 'thinks and feels' women produced poems describing states of feeling characterized by loss and emptiness, often induced at least conventionally, by contemplation of the same wild nature that gave male poets visions of a more interesting and upbeat variety.

Nineteenth century middle-class women found themselves writing poetry in their spare time; as with men's amateur verse most of it is awful at a very basic level, imitative and unimaginative, though it appealed to other women readers, for it was published in surprising quantity and anthologized at mid-

---

15. In an excerpt from her long poem 'Beachy Head' in Kaplan, pp. 76-81.

century in vast compilations of women's verse. Even this 'bad' poetry is worth reading, for it suggests a pattern of difficulty with the handling of language and subject and the achievement of an individual 'voice' that does seem to relate to the structuring of femininity through language that I have described.

Dora Greenwell (1821-82) provides an interesting example. In a poem titled *Bring Me Word How Tall She Is*, which takes its theme from the leader 'How tall is your Rosalind?/Just as high as my heart', she writes about two childhood friends, 'he was/ for God, and she for him', thrown out of the garden (Eden). They grow up in a fallen world in conflict but interdependent.

> At length, in stature grown
> He stands erect and free,
> Yet stands he not alone
> For his beloved be
> Like him she loveth wise, like him she loveth free.
>
> So wins she her desire
> Yet stand they not apart;
> For as *she* doth aspire
> He grows, nor stands she higher
> Than her Beloved's heart.

The surface of the poem seems to describe the model of women's achieved desire through relationship to the man; she becomes wise and free through her subordination; her location is no higher than the heart. There *is* a tension and dislocation in the metaphor, for she is, in their adolescent companionship, a huntress, and her wisdom and freedom do owe as much to mimicry as to subjugation. The missing meanings are much clearer in another much better poem which avoids the Adam/Eve metaphor for the relationship she is describing and thus overcomes the resistance to her meaning which the patriarchal structure of the original myth imposes.

The Sun-Flower

> Till the slow daylight pale,
>   A willing slave, fast bound to one above,
> I wait; he seems to speed, and change, and fail;
>   I know he will not move.

I lift my golden orb
    To his, unsmitten when the roses die,
And in my broad and burning disk absorb
    The splendours of his eye.

His eye is like a clear
    Keen flame that searches through me; I must droop
Upon my stalk, I cannot reach his sphere;
    To mine he cannot stoop.

I win not my desire,
    And yet I fail not of my guerdon; lo!
A thousand flickering darts and tongues of fire
    Around me spread and glow.

All rayed and crowned, I miss
    No queenly state until the summer wane,
The hours flit by; none knoweth of my bliss,
    And none has guessed my pain.

I follow one above,
    I track the shadow of his steps, I grow
Most like to him I love
    Of all that shines below.

The sun-flower is deliberately contrasted here to the female flower symbol, the dying rose. Yet the speaker is female; she misses 'No queenly state'. The master/slave dualism is kept, and indeed the sexual imagery of the poem is masturbatory since the flower and the sun never touch. But the transexual symbol of the sunflower and the way in which it imitates and follows the sun seems more like a figuring of an imaginary relationship with the sun as the ideal, wholly conceived mirror image which 'will not move'. Though the desire for and of the Other cannot be finally achieved through total identification, it does produce a gratification which suggests the child's pregenital polymorphous pleasure. The adult knowledge of difference is present but the fantasy is that the queenly state and identification with the male primacy can both be had through imitation/identification. I don't pretend to understand the poem fully though I have been pondering it for a long time. It seems to me a peculiarly forceful lyric with a coherent set of images and one in which the speaker has unquestionably achieved her own voice. It certainly is not a melancholy voice, and indeed the poem seems to refer the reader to a set of feelings that are familiar and powerful — what is repressed, missing, is the whole scene of the poem, and no wonder, for under the master/slave image that Victorian readers might immediately read as man/woman lies a fantasy of masculine identity which is profoundly subversive and therefore repressed in language and culture.

In saying this much about the poem in psychoanalytic terms I am very emphatically *not* attempting to interrogate the personal unconscious of the poet, but only the poem itself from the perspective of femininity. The poet has cleverly chosen a figure and a structure that does not require or want the intervention of a 'human' voice; in fact it is essential that the sense of the poem is not internally deciphered by the poet. Women's poems where certain transexual gender identifications are made but not internally decoded are not uncommon in this period. Compare the much more famous poem of Emily Dickinson, 'My life has stood a loaded gun —', which uses the same overt image of master and slave but where object and subject merge in a fantasy of masculine identity and power. These poems are deliberately hard to understand, and some of our satisfaction in them is that we accept the metonymic force without wanting to look too hard for the missing signification, which is located *inside* the symbolized fantasy, without needing to be raised to full consciousness.

Another way in which women and men poets represent desire and experience suppressed in patriarchal culture is through structuring the poem as a dream. Dream form frees the poet from a logical progression of images and, perhaps, disassociates the speaker from the content so that he is less 'responsible' for any of its meanings. Some of Emily Dickinson's best poems are in dream form though they are not identified as dreams. Christina Rossetti, Emily Dickinson's exact contempory (both born 1830) uses the dream very successfully:

> Once in a dream (for once I dreamed of you)
>   We stood together in an open field;
>   Above our heads two swift-winged pigeons wheeled,
> Sporting at ease and courting full in view:—
> When loftier still a broadening darkness flew,

Down-swooping, and a ravenous hawk revealed;
Too weak to fight, too fond to fly, they yield;
So farewell life and love and pleasures new.
Then as their plumes fell fluttering to the ground,
Their snow-white plumage flecked with crimson
drops,
I wept, and thought I turned towards you to weep:
But you were gone; while rustling hedgerow tops
Bent in a wind which bore to me a sound
Of far-off piteous bleat of lambs and sheep.[18]

Here there is one line of explanation, 'So farewell life and love and pleasures new'. The female reference — lambs and sheep are often used as metaphors for the helpless, weakminded, voiceless world of women and children — is left open. Except for that final image the poem could refer to an oedipal or adolescent crisis of either sex, but the fact that the poet must join the world of lambs and sheep locates the symbolic experience of the speaker in the realm of femininity. The poem does not *necessarily* have to be read as heterosexual. The recognition of gender difference also means separation from the mother, and adolescence as separation from sisters, but the unashamed courting pigeons suggest heterosexual love as surface, controlling meaning.

A list of typical female references would be misleading since their meaning depends on the whole poem, the signifying chain. Christina Rossetti and Emily Dickinson both image the speaking female as a song bird, but male poets use this image as well for themselves, which suggests that when women take it over it has transexual connotations. It is an apt image of escape from female limitations, for birds' maternal duties don't keep them from flying or singing. In a brilliant, but neglected poem by Christina Rossetti the dream form or rather the dream-waking state is used again. *In an Old World Thicket* picks up, deliberately I think, on several poems of Tennyson's, who frequently uses the dream to express censored feelings. In Christina Rossetti's poem the speaker finds herself in a wood 'Where every mother bird brought up her brood/Safe in some leafy niche'.

Such birds they seemed as challenged each desire;

16. 'On The Wing', Kaplan, p. 139.

> Like spots of azure heaven upon the wing,
> Like downy emeralds that alight and sing,
>> Like actual coals on fire,
> Like anything they seemed, and everything.

> Such mirth they made, such warblings and such chat
>> With tongue of music in a well-turned beak,
> They seemed to speak more wisdom that we speak,
>> To make our music flat
> And all our subtlest reasonings wild or weak.

These mother-birds transcend and vanquish our human speech, but the speaker cannot join them. In fact 'Bird ceased to answer bird', her vision dies and she is left in

> ... the bitterness of such revolt,
>> All impotent, all hateful, and all hate,
> That kicks and breaks itself against the bolt
>> Of an imprisoning fate.
> And vainly shakes and cannot shake the gate.

> Out of the deep I called of my desire;
> My strength was weakness and my heart was fire;

The poem as a whole seems a symbolic narrative of the conflict between femininity and the attempt to achieve a voice through a more direct relationship to the Symbolic order. The speaker's 'rebellious soul' is

> A random thing I seemed without a mark
>> Racing without a goal
> Adrift upon life's sea without an ark.[17]

A mark, literally a missing meaning, would attach her to goals; so of course would an ark in which the whole culture, male and female, is contained — although this image of cultural unity presents the conflict once again, and prefigures the poem's resolution. At the peak of her crisis the speaker asks how to face the perpetual Now? '...' Void of repentance, void of hope and fear.

---

17. Kaplan, pp. 139-43.

Of possibility, alternative ... Of promise even which has no gift to give.' Sense is made of this passage if we attach it to the permanent, eternal lack and absence to which women are to become reconciled, or else live in constant mourning and self-pity. At the end of the poem the speaker proposes a sort of compromise in which the moon, rising, lights up the vision of the mother-bird and the setting sun illuminates the 'meek, mild faces' of a 'homeward flock, at peace/With one another and with every one' and led, wait for it, by 'A patriarchal ram'. Birds tomorrow, sheep today. The poem is a sustained lyric attempt, and a poetically well-realized one, to produce a symbolic representation of the crisis of women who cannot accept or be sealed by their femininity, just as *Goblin Market* is an allegorical attempt to project a female sisterhood that protects each other from a poisonous male sensuality. *Goblin Market* can stand on its own as a fairy story although it too should be read metonymically rather than metaphorically, but 'In an Old World Thicket' only hangs together as a sustained symbolic attempt if the missing meanings are related to female experience. Universalized, they seem dislocated and weak.

This paper itself can only make a very small scratch on a very large subject. When I delivered the paper in an earlier form at the Patriarchy Conference women seemed happier with the readings of specific poems than with the theoretical frame, which I have enlarged and altered. Some women expressed dismay at the negative implications of my conclusions for the writing of poetry. Let me state them more positively this time round: at the pole of difficulty we have the construction of female subjects as speakers presented with a taboo against public speech, the price of and the effects of that repression, a male centred linguistic tradition which, in an extreme form, is their female (and therefore human) identity. At the other pole is the field of language itself, open to invasion and subversion by female speakers. The overt and hidden subject of women's poetry is often a dialectic between those two poles. Women's poetry also suggests that language cannot be conquered or taken over simply by itself. We must re-understand poetry by introducing gender, of the poet and the 'speaker' as crucial categories which deny it a universalizing suturing place in high culture. Lacan states the contradiction women face in writing poetry as a means of doing battle against their linguistic oppression in culture, when, in another context he asks, 'what do we have in metonymy other than the power to bypass the obstacles of social censure? This form which lends itself to the truth under oppression, doesn't it show the very servitude inherent in its presentation?' I have suggested that metonymy is a dominant trope in women's poetry, since it is a way of referring to experience suppressed in public discourse. Perhaps that is why so much of the most resonant female poetry has been written with a full and bitter self-consciousness of the resistance of all patriarchal culture to the female voice. Sylvia Plath's poetry works towards a gothic symbolization of the ineluctable patterning of literary language to express patriarchal law:

> Love is the uniform of my bald nurse
> Love is the bone and sinew of my curse
> The vase, reconstructed houses the elusive rose.[18]

This understanding should, simultaneously, make women better poets and point them towards wider remedies for the cultural conditions that impede their speech.

---

18. Sylvia Plath, 'The Stones', *The Colossus and other Poems*, New York 1968.

5.

The Indefinite Disclosed:
Christina Rossetti and
Emily Dickinson

To fill a Gap
Insert the Thing that caused it —
Block it up
With Other — and 'twill yawn the more —
You cannot solder an Abyss
With Air.

Emily Dickinson, c. 1862[1]

This curious, compacted lyric is one of a group of poems that form a distinct category in the work of two Victorian women poets, Emily Dickinson and Christina Rossetti. Such lyrics speak directly to and about the psyche, expressing and querying feelings that are deliberately abstracted from any reference to, or analysis of, the social causes of psychological states. They attempt to escape immediate or specific social determination, a project that cannot be finally realized since all representation as such must exist within a cultural discourse. Most of Dickinson's verse, and the larger part of Rossetti's, exclude the social in this way; but in this particular sub-genre their poetry also employs atypical forms of imagery. Instead of straightforward metaphorical constructions, comparisons of like to unlike (as in the metaphysical mode for which Dickinson is famous, or the more traditional late Romantic style preferred by Rossetti), these lyrics are marked by their use of synecdoche, where the part stands for the whole, and metonymy, where the images are narratively or

---

1. Emily Dickinson, *The Complete Poems of Emily Dickinson*, Thomas H. Johnson, ed., London, 1975, p. 266.

associatively related rather than expressly compared.[2] Images and their meanings are left dangling, as in 'To fill a Gap' where 'Gap', 'Other', 'Abyss' and 'Air' are not meant as metaphors for each other but as substitutes. 'Gaps' are caused by absence and loss and can only be described through an articulation which opens rather than blocks the 'Abyss'.

Such strategies were not vulnerable to the type of textual explication used by Victorian critics, which depended on a text susceptible to paraphrase. Similarly, their richness of reference makes them texts puzzling to modern critics intent on extracting a single or definitive interpretation; dream-form, too, either directly stated or implied, becomes an important means of presenting distorted or unclear images with impunity. While these modes are idiosyncratic to Dickinson and Rossetti, conveying powerful ideas and feelings past internal and external censors, they are by no means the monopoly of women writers. But they deserve the special attention of feminist critics because they seem to 'fill a Gap' in our understanding of women's subjectivity — their sense of themselves — and because their very openness renders the poems at once problematic and vulnerable to particular kinds of misreading. It is too easy to bind them into biographical interpretations of the poets' lives or build them into additional 'literary' evidence to buttress interpretations of women's experience drawn from their prose fiction. Worst of all, because these lyrics are so clearly 'about' the psychological, they can be used to substantiate specific psychoanalytic theories of femininity. The use of psychoanalysis in literary criticism as a way of exploring the conjunction between specific historical ideologies and individual literary works has become popular in recent years, partly in response to the attempt to integrate Marxism and psychoanalytic theory. Feminists have supported and added substantially to such integration, and my reservations about interpretation are intended, not to denounce this enterprise as such, but to serve as a critique of its least useful tendencies.

Why should such common uses of the lyric of feeling, particularly when its meaning is difficult or obscure, be inappropriate? These texts speak to and about psychic phenomena in ways that

2. My use of these distinctions is largely drawn from Roman Jakobson, *Studies on Child Language and Aphasia*, The Hague 1971, pp.44-45 and *passim*.

are unique in women's writing of the period. However formal their presentation, they are, by virtue of their fragmentary and opaque language, torn away from a chain of meaning that would bind them to larger interpretations. Their sybilline quality means that they can be inserted into almost any theory about women as social subjects and about high culture as an expression of women's suppressed and distorted subjectivity. Most of the poems that follow, would, for example support either a phallocentric theory of women's psychological development as espoused by Freud and some of his modern followers, or a concentric theory, lately in vogue in feminist psychoanalysis and already popularized in feminist literary criticism as the concept of 'inner space'.[3] Phallocentric theories see language and gender-socialization organised around the phallus as a privileged signifier of 'difference'; concentric theory sees the vagina as an equally powerful force in the organization of women's social, psychic and sexual being, also expressed through their use of language. These theories are still in the early stages of development, and although I am myself tentatively aligned with neo-Freudians such as Lacan, I cannot see the lyrics I am examining as decisive witness for either side. Their real strength, in relation to the casual reader and the critical theorist alike, is that they are shapes, like ink-blots, from which to decipher related images in our own experience and intellectual orientation. These poems interrogate states for which the poets themselves had no ready explanations; in turn they interrogate our own theory and politics. The symbolic strategies that they employ ensure that this is their main effect, making them stand apart from other lyrics by the same poets, which are more precisely metaphorical and more immediately didactic, as well as standing in opposition to narrative, the dominant genre of women's prose writing.

In focusing on the work of two poets who were exact contemporaries (both born in 1830) certain ironic anomalies are apparent. Emily Dickinson's verse, unpublished in her lifetime, has been much more fully worked over by modern critics than

---

3. For phallocentric theory see Jacques Lacan, *Ecrits*, London 1977. For concentric theory see Karen Horney, *Feminine Psychology*, London, 1967. More recent feminist discussion of 'phallocentric' versus 'concentric' include Luce Irigary, 'Women's Exile', *Ideology and Consciousness*, vol. 1, 1977, pp. 62-76; Parveen Adams, 'Representation and Sexuality', *m/f*, vol. 1, 1978, pp. 66-82 and Michèle Montrelay, 'Inquiry into Femininity', *m/f*, vol. 1, 1978, pp. 83-101.

Christina Rossetti's, which enjoyed considerable popularity until the turn of the century. Rossetti belongs to the pre-Raphaelite school; her poetry has an obvious niche in English literature, but the twentieth century has virtually ignored her, and for this reason I shall devote more of my attention to her. On the other hand, Dickinson's thousands of short lyrics, as edited by Thomas H. Johnson, have proved a scholar's gift to scholars, a virgin oeuvre on which to make their mark. Yet even though Dickinson's poetry has been tackled from almost every critical position, she, like Christina Rossetti, figures much less prominently in the new feminist literary criticism than women novelists of the same period.

One can only suggest some reasons why their work has been slighted by feminists. A large portion of both poets' writing is devotional, it is true; but so is much well-thought-of poetry. More important, perhaps, is the reflexive nature of the verse, its concentration on the inner life, its virtual exclusion of the contemporary or social. Emily Dickinson's approach is analytic, intellectual even; she read more widely than her urban British contemporary. Her lyrics most typically seek to analyse emotions through analogy; that is the way in which she uses the metaphysical. Rossetti's poems offer a sensuous appreciation of emotion. A conscious preoccupation with the constricting demands of femininity does not often surface in the poetry of either. Even in life their protests against the constraints of gender were muted at the social level, where they presented exaggerated examples of retiring women. Unlike contemporary women novelists, many of whom were also perfect Victorian gentlewomen, they hardly ever make combative social relations with lovers or family the subject of their poetry. Instead, their verse is preoccupied with a melancholy inner struggle for peace of mind. This introspective, almost morbid preoccupation marked not only their verse but also that of many lesser women poets of the century — so much so that in the mid-1890s the young Alice Thompson, who would become the poet and feminist Alice Meynell, wrote bitterly of her 'rhyming faculty' that 'whatever I write will be melancholy and self-conscious, as are all women's poems'.[4]

---

4. See *Salt and Bitter and Good: Three Centuries of English and American Women Poets*, Coa Kaplan ed., New York and London 1975, p. 181.

Dickinson's and Rossetti's lyrics are so meagre in description of their cultural surroundings that they do not date, except in certain turns of speech, and therefore withhold the crucial historical distance that places the nineteenth-century novel in a convenient conceptual past; the modern reader cannot see them through the wrong end of the binoculars, from a progressive present in which a better world for women is implicit. Such poetry accentuates the way in which the female psyche has a recalcitrant tendency to remain recognizable in its supposedly 'weaker' aspects, despite a variety of ostensible improvements in women's social and political status. This emphasis may suggest the difficulty they present for a new feminist criticism. The women's movement today — Marxist, bourgeois or radical feminist — tends to endorse women's struggle through social and political action and to resist as weakening those psychoanalytic interpretations of femininity that seem to confirm or eternalize women's passive and masochistic behaviour. Both Rossetti and Dickinson represented very fully the internal struggles of women of their day as well as ours, without the comforting assurance that their spiritual malaise would be cured by egalitarian marriage, revision of the laws of inheritance, education, employment, a more equitable division of labour, the loosening of sexual prohibitions, or the curtailment of parental authority.

Since the most intractable problem facing feminists today is the relationship between the psychological components of femininity, and the social and political elements of women's subordination, it is not surprising that the writing of Dickinson and Rossetti should provide much thought but small comfort. Their poetry — particularly at its most arcane and difficult points — does, however, help us to understand the relationship between the imaginative act and the dominant ideology. Despite considerable prejudice against women writers in the nineteenth century, imaginative writing was, of all forms of public discourse, the one in which women were most able to participate and, in England, become prominent. Perhaps it was thought to be the least dangerous to bourgeois hegemony and hence to patriarchal power. This being so (and it is, of course, open to debate), we might come to their poetry in a new way, understanding that even when its overt intention is revolutionary it is only rarely a force that ruptures or alters existing social and political forms. In their most radical sallies it may be said that Rossetti and Dickinson conformed to the judgement of an approving contemporary critic who compared Christina Rossetti favourably with Elizabeth Barrett Browning because Rossetti accepted 'the burden of womanhood'. Where their strategies of subversion are subtle, even subliminal, the effect may still be to confirm traditional arrangements by substituting fantasy for anger. Both a clearer definition of the place of literary discourse in women's oppression and the place of literature in resistance to it is needed. Such an approach would begin by accepting the contradiction posed by women's writing as simultaneously an historical record of their oppression and a definitive mark of their defiance, hence making the conservative implications of the work of these two major poets less embarrassing for feminist criticism.

Christina Rossetti

Two recent feminist readings of Christina Rossetti's *Goblin Market* (1862) may help to distinguish between useful and misleading analyses of such poetry. *Goblin Market* has for some years had an underground reputation as a forgotten feminist classic. Christina Rossetti adamantly resisted attempts to press an interpretation on the poem, insisting that it was what its surface suggests — a fairy story. It unquestionably belongs to the genre of 'faery' which had a long tradition in English and underwent a late-nineteenth-century revival. A narrative (like many of Rossetti's longer poems), it is the story of two sisters, Laura and Lizzie, who live alone together. Wilful Laura looks at and listens to the fairy men, then buys and sucks the goblins' magical fruit which produces a violent addiction. The goblins sell only once to each buyer and Lizzie, older and more careful, watches her sister waste away in 'baulked desire'. Finally she takes a silver penny and seeks out the goblins who literally assault her with their wares, but cannot make her open her lips to eat the fruit herself. The sexual analogy is quite explicit:

> Like a royal virgin town
> Topped with gilded dome and spire

> Close beleaguered by a fleet
> Mad to tug her standard down.[5]

Finally they toss back her penny and, covered in juice, 'In a smart, ache, tingle', Lizzie rushes back to Laura crying 'Hug me, kiss me, suck my juices'.[6] Laura obeys and recovers; Lizzie does not suffer, and the two sisters live to marry and tell their tale to their own children, both as cautionary and as heroic, with the moral that 'there is no friend like a sister'.[7]

My first example, Maureen Duffy's interpretation in *The Erotic World of Faery*, is full of suggestive insights culled from psychoanalytic theory; but it is never clear how the text is being defined in relation to her analysis. It is not just that the text is left unspecified as a product of Christina Rossetti's conscious intention or as unconscious displacement — the problem of conscious or unconscious production of images is never taken up. Sometimes it seems as if Duffy views the poem as a loose but evocative series of representations in which each reader can find a metaphor to suit his or her fantasy; at other points the poem is seen to be grounded in Victorian sexual taboos; at still others the text is used as a 'timeless' example of the way in which the unconscious displaces and condenses sexual meanings. We might start by asking what conscious sexual under- and overtones Rossetti meant the poem to carry. To the extent that it is allegorical, the goblins' fruit and the serpent's apple are constant, implied metaphors. The lines already quoted about the 'virgin town' make clear Rossetti's basic analogy between goblins-with-fruit and sexual temptation. But the last thing *Goblin Market* intends is a recapitulation of Eve's fall. The analogy is there to set up a different, contradictory set of relations to the story of Adam and Eve. While the snake's apple produces sensations of shame in the Edenic couple, the goblins' fruit gives Laura knowledge of desire but not shame. This, and the fact that Laura and Lizzie are sisters instead of mates, constitutes the deliberate contrast Rossetti establishes between her fairy tale and the Edenic myth.

---

5.   Christina Rossetti, *The Poetical Works of Christina Rossetti with Memoir and Notes etc.*, William Michael Rossetti, ed., London 1904, p. 6.
6.   Ibid., p.7.
7.   Ibid., p.8.

Duffy's basic assumption is that the poem concerns fantasy sex, desire and masturbation. But read as an allegory (bad thoughts equal bad fairies, forbidden fruit is the female body itself), the narrative breaks down; the point about the goblins is that they represent — whether consciously, unconsciously, or as a result of ambiguity — both real tempters of the other sex (i.e. males) and paranoid projections of temptation. Duffy sees Laura devouring the fruit as 'a powerful masturbatory fantasy of feeding at the breast', quoting Rossetti in support: 'She sucked until her lips were sore.'[8] But even this simple image is too condensed to be reduced to a single connotation; childish greed and undifferentiated sensual pleasure may be indicated, but a contradiction remains: children can get sore lips from eating too much tart fruit, but babies don't get sore lips from breast-feeding. *Mothers* do, however, get sore nipples from being sucked, and if we are to pursue the masturbatory implications of Duffy's reading then presumably sore lips must be transposed from mouth to vagina. But what is important about the passage is not the physical site or source of sensual excitement, but the moral overtone: you can hurt from too much pleasure, oral or genital. As with Duffy's suggestion that the goblins' invitation to Lizzie to 'Bob at our cherries/Bite at our peaches' is a temptation closer to fellatio (surely the sexual practice least likely to have been known to the author?), we are confronted by the poem's ability to induce fantasy, its power to stir further erotic association in the reader.

Duffy's attempt to historicize the poem produces further difficulties. Quoting William Acton's *The Functions and Disorders of the Reproductive Organs* (1857), she suggests that the symptoms of Laura's decline are those which Acton ascribes to the habitual masturbator. Although Acton's text conveniently precedes the poem's writing by a few years, it is highly unlikely that Christina Rossetti, who refused to dip into a racy novel, would have read it. True, Acton simply repeats and gives spurious scientific valorization to current beliefs about masturbation, but his symptoms are punitive projection rather than medical reality. If one wanted to look for a 'real' medical analogy for Laura's decline, and one moreover that Christina Rossetti might have witnessed, one could point to drug addiction, of course, but possibly to anorexia, now commonly thought to be associated with pubescent crises at

---

8.   Maureen Duffy, *The Erotic World of Faery*, London 1972, p. 290.

the onset of adult female sexuality. This explanation is equally hypothetical; its only advantage is that it is less specific and coincides both with the mysterious ailments of adolescence and with the traditional malaise following fairy curses on either sex. But pursuit of Laura's disease distracts from what is really important: its place in the moral narrative. Laura is ill with 'baulked desire', not guilt; Lizzie goes out determined to cure, not absolve, her, by getting her sister more of what she wants. Most important for the structure of the poem, Laura's illness is an excuse for the next 'erotic' episode in the poem, Lizzie's assault by the goblins.

Finally, Duffy sees in Laura and Lizzie 'the sisters who appear repeatedly in paintings and drawings from Millais to Sargent. This double female image is an interesting component of the period's eroticism akin to the heterosexual desire to see blue films about lesbians.'[9] The sisterly relationship in the poem has definite and unsuppressed sensuous elements, but are we really to believe that Christina Rossetti produced a representation of female eroticism pandering to male taste? Blue films about lesbians are made for and by men, as distinct from represent-ations by lesbians about lesbian relationships made by and for women. Both may satisfy the erotic fantasies of either sex in different ways, but it is hardly useful to talk about a 'period's eroticism' as if it were a unified phenomenon. In addition, the 'erotic' encounter between Laura and LIzzie is far more daring than any scene, however suggestive, portrayed in the high art of the period. It is protected from censure through its enclosure in fairy tale and through the pain and anguish of the cure (Lizzie's embrace) which now tastes of bitterest wormwood. The poem operates its own internal censorship by making joint motifs of pleasure and punishment strongest at the most significant erotic moments. What such historicizing in relation to Victorian sexual attitudes and high art may locate is the site of contradiction within a poem that struggles to represent female sexual fantasy while being constrained nevertheless by the guilt inherent in even the most displaced expression of such fantasy.

Ellen Moers, in *Literary Women*, provides a much tauter commentary on the poem. More careful in her use of psycho-analytic interpretations, she contributes to our understanding of

---

9.   Ibid., pp. 288-9.

the punitive elements in *Goblin Market* by examining the mixed elements of sensuality, sadism and violence in the sisters' confrontation with the goblins. Moers places the poem within her discussion of female Gothic, a genre in which violence to women in supernatural settings is a leading trope. However, Moers' argument for the prominence of hand-to-hand sadism, pinching and plaguing is based on her assessment of the limited heterosexual experience open to single women writers in the nineteenth century. Their sexual experience and subsequent sexual fantasy are linked to the night side of Victorian nursery, where siblings, cousins and friends were allowed a pre-pubescent freedom denied to young men and women: 'Women authors of Gothic fantasies appear to testify that the physical teasing they received from their brothers — the pinching, mauling, and scratching we dismiss as the most unimportant of children's games — took on outsize proportions and powerful erotic overtones in their adult imaginations ... (it was not only sexual play but *any* kind of physical play for middle-class women that fell under the Victorian ban)'.[10]

Moers extends her argument by pointing to the prominence of the nursery-tussle motif in the writing of many other Victorian women. Her clear and cautious use of the relation between socialization, fantasy and literature is a model for feminist critic-ism. She does not attempt to prove anything about Christina Rossetti's individual experience; rather, she generalizes illumin-atingly about the social components of women's sexual imagina-tion. She is, if anything, a little too eager to clean up the poem by locating its more disturbing elements in a harmless practice that demonstrates the poverty rather than the richness of women's sexual fantasy.

While *Goblin Market* cannot be decoded as an elaborate adult sexual scenario, it undoubtedly remains an exploration of women's sexual fantasy that includes suggestions of masochism, homoeroticism, rape or incest. The images are incomplete and blurred for several possible reasons. Most obviously the blurring can be seen as a form of both conscious and unconscious censor-ship; it is also (perhaps primarily) the result of sexual ignorance. Christina Rossetti was sexually uninitiated, and while we may not have to fix her imagination at the level of a ten-year-old, we

---

10. Ellen Moers, *Literary Women*, New York 1976, p. 105.

may legitimately see transformed fantasies as indistinct, referring characteristically to sensations rather than particular practices. Blurring occurs typically in fantasy anyway, where images condense and overlay each other, while condensed images often contract pleasure and punishment into a single act. The most interesting element of the poem remains this obscure level of internal reference combined with its very precise form. The narrative shape of the poem signals the primacy of erotic fantasy. The two sisters are given to the reader without social context. The absence of all social detail except their apparently orphaned state fits in well with the conventional frame of the fairy or folk tale as well as that of sexual fantasy, where too much specificity can impede the erotic message. The encounters with the goblins, and Laura's and Lizzie's embrace at the end of the poem, are presented within a surprisingly threadbare narrative scheme; the poet's words and attention are lavished instead on the 'erotic' incidents.

This rich concentration on the sensuous moment is typical of erotic fantasy; but the fairy story or folk tale similarly often contains irrelevant narrative elements that have little direct bearing on the dramatic crises. Thus the closing of the poem, like its opening, is compatible with both. Rather than leaving the girls locked in the annealing embrace, Rossetti projects them forwards into marriage and motherhood. This social ending — traditional in many narrative forms — is odd here only because the poem does not begin with a typical fairy story introduction. Instead it dives right into the heart of the matter: 'Morning and evening/ Maids heard the goblins' cry ...' My analysis of the poem does not attempt to refute Duffy and Moers by going one better. Rather, it attempts to locate the poem within Christina Rossetti's work, and to identify particular strategies, conscious or unconscious, for conveying the pleasurable but forbidden past the Victorian censor. More important, I have tried to suggest the difficulty of disentangling the text as an historical structure of meaning and the text as read by the critic at any point after its production. Most simply, I suppose, *Goblin Market* can be seen as a comical-tragical view of the erotic from the women's position with conscious and unconscious elements inextricably mingled. A brief funny-sad lyric of *c.* 1861 by Emily Dickinson reads like a marginal gloss on Rossetti's poem:

> Over the fence —
> Strawberries — grow —
> Over the fence —
> I could climb — if I tried, I know —
> Berries are nice!
>
> But — if I stained my Apron —
> God would certainly scold!
> Oh dear — I guess if He were a Boy —
> He'd — climb — if He could![11]

Like a number of Victorian poets, Christina Rossetti used dream-form as a favourite device when she wanted to exempt her poems from the demands of clarity. Poetry did not have to be very difficult to be thought obscure — witness contemporary verdicts on Robert Browning. Fancy, faery, dream-form and the absurd, as in Edward Lear's verse, were acceptable ways round the expectation that each metaphor be complete in itself, not too far-fetched, and related to the one that followed. For Tennyson, too, dream-form was a means of introducing irrational, private states of being into a canon built round a literature concerned with socially conventional ideas and feelings. Such alien psychic levels find their representation elsewhere in Victorian writing not only through the convention of the dream (both Alice's adventures are dreams), but through methods of displacement such as setting poem or novel in the past or in another country where things can be ordered differently. English writers themselves (the Brownings are perhaps the most celebrated example) went abroad in order to be released from the claustrophobic mores of their class and culture. The other scenes — Wonderland, the world of Tennyson's *The Princess, Goblin Market,* Arthur's Court — are all in part used to suspend social rules; the dream-state, as one of these other worlds, permits the expression of feelings and the enactment of dramas taboo in genteel households.

Christina Rossetti's work represents part of this movement away from the Victorian ideal of the socialized and accessible poet, but the evolution of an alternate aesthetic was very gradual as well as being practised well in advance of any theory to

---

11. Dickinson, p. 115.

defend it. Midway between the fantasy world of *Goblin Market* and the stated dream-form of 'My Dream' and 'On the Wing' is *An Old-World Thicket*, another long poem by Rossetti that uses reverie, the state between sleep and waking. *An Old-World Thicket* has Dante's *una selva oscura* as its epigraph, and its scene and structure are meant to remind the reader of the opening of *The Divine Comedy*:

> Midway this way of life we're bound upon,
> I woke to find myself in a dark wood,
> Where the right road was wholly lost and gone.[12]

For Christina Rossetti, Dante was a deeper poet even than Tennyson, one of the few contemporaries to whom she gave whole-hearted admiration.[13] *An Old-World Thicket* is about her own mid-life crisis, but for English readers not familiar with Dante, Rossetti's opening lines — 'Awake or sleeping (for I know not which)/I was or was not mazed within a wood' — might also recall Tennyson's 'A Dream of Fair Women', where reverie gives way to dream so that the poet 'At last methought that I had wandered far/In an old wood' (11.53-4). Dante's dark wood and Tennyson's 'old wood', peopled with tragic heroines from the past, are brought together in Rossetti's poem, where the tragedy's queen is the poet-speaker herself. Tennyson's wood, like Dante's, is dark and menacing —

> There was no motion in the dumb dead air,
> Not any song of bird or sound of rill;
> Gross darkness of the inner sepulchre
> Is not so deadly still ... ('A Dream of Fair Women',
> 11.65-8)

---

12. Dante, *The Divine Comedy, I: Hell*, London 1977, Canto I, 11. 1-3.
13. She was not, however, above parodying him. I suspect that Rossetti's 'The Prince's Progress', in which a wayward prince lets his betrothed die of grief and old age while he dawdles Ulysses-like through a series of adventures, is in part an impish send-up of Tennyson's 'The Princess'. Tennyson's prince rescues his reluctant fiancée by breaking into her women-only university, an enclave of Victorian radical feminists. Rossetti counters this paranoid fantasy of female power with a mythic version of passive femininity and errant masculinity; her prince arrives 'Too late for love, too late for joy', Rossetti, p. 34.

There are forests and forests; Rossetti's wood is full of mother-birds and their broods in a shade that 'danced and twinkled to the unseen sun', a world where

> Branches and leaves cast shadows one by one,
>> And all their shadows swayed
> In breaths of air that rustled and that played.

Her birds 'challenged each desire ... Like anything they seemed, and everything'.[14] Tennyson's fair women are legendary figures, doomed and sexually active phantoms from the past brought, at their moment of grief and trauma, to the dead forest. Rossetti presents a single active female consciousness, the poet's own, in an alive, feminine and sensualized forest.

The future of this modern female psyche is unresolved, sometimes in harmony with, occasionally in counterpoint to, the mood of the surrounding nature. Often it is rebellious — 'Such revolt ... That kicks and breaks itself against the bolt ... And vainly shakes, and cannot shake the gate.'[15] *An Old-World Thicket* concerns anger, depression, resignation, loss of faith, represented in a deliberately abstracted form relieved by natural symbol — the birds, the aspens and the 'widening waters'. It is bracketed by two significant and comprehensible images, the 'mother-bird' and her brood of the opening lines, and 'A patri-archal ram' and 'all his kin' whose moonlit figures represent the final peace and resignation of the poet-speaker. Tennyson's poem (in which the poet-dreamer is a passive observer) looks at women as archetypal representations; Dante's journey is into the self. Rossetti's self-conscious use of the two frames is a daring sleight of hand by which the reader is tricked into accepting a female Dante as an appropriate epic searcher for inner truth and peace. Tennyson's poem is almost a self-parody of male dreams about female sexual power: Rossetti's is a moody evocation of female impotence. Yet, as in *Goblin Market*, the images of *An Old-World Thicket* can no more be made to fit a coherent psychic schema than translated into social or autobiographical narrative. The poem seems to move from the fantasy world of magical birds who 'speak more wisdom than we speak' to the social

---

14. Rossetti, p. 64.
15. Ibid., p. 65.

symbol of the ram's tinkling bell that controls the flock, from forest to farm. But within the poem the imagery is wilder; the fluctuating mood of the poet-speaker, 'Adrift upon life's sea without an ark', is all contradiction and conflict, in revolt against a life in which 'habit trains us not to break but bend'. The 'mazed' world of the forest orchestrates the speaker's mood; the dream state indicates that the poet sees the ram's control as illusory. The Gothic shifts from outer scene to inner feeling are not metaphorical but metonymic, contiguous statements about the positioning of the self in relation to the scene. Though these shifts are contained within an overarching metaphor (the belief that man's submission to God brings salvation and relief) we need not follow Christina Rossetti's ram all the way home, responding instead to the multiple meanings projected through the dreamer and her forest.

The dream-state poem allows a suspension of the real and a representation of mood rather than narrative. Dream-form gives the writer still more permission, for it disclaims all conscious responsibility for the statement in the poem, and repels an interpretation of its content. There is a witty example of the ability to deflect analysis in Christina Rossetti's 'My Dream', written in about 1855. The poem is a delicious fantasy about a 'crew' of royal crocodiles who emerge from the Euphrates and are eaten by their king, represented as a sort of natural monarch —

> His punier brethren quaked before his tail,
> Broad as a rafter, potent as a flail.
> . . . .
> He knew no law, he feared no binding law,
> But ground them with inexorable jaw.

The cannibal crocodile sleeps, and in sleep dwindles 'to the common size'. Reduced, he watches a 'wingèd vessel' tame the wild waters and sheds 'appropriate tears':

> What can it mean? you ask. I answer not
> For meaning, but myself must echo, What?
> And tell it as I saw it on the spot.[16]

---

16. Ibid., pp. 315-16.

Christina Rossetti is wickedly proprietary about this 'dream'; its
first line ('Hear now a curious dream I dreamed last night')
mimics the sort of breakfast-table clarion that submits the rest of
the family to the dreamer's monologue. The 'dream' itself is
overloaded with symbols — heathen, phallic and patriarchal —
but they are as elusive as a gnomic folk tale. The poem irritated
William Rossetti, for he could make little of it. As long as he was
convinced his sister was writing up a real dream he was content
to leave it as an example of

> the exceptional turn of mind of Christina Rossetti — the odd freak-
> ishness which flecked the extreme and almost excessive seriousness
> of her thought ... It looks like the narration of a true dream; and
> nothing seems as if it could account for so eccentric a train of
> notions, except that she in fact dreamed them. And yet she did not;
> for, in a copy of her collected edition of 1875, I find that she has
> marked the piece 'not a real dream.' As it was not a real dream, and
> she chose nevertheless to give it verbal form, one seeks for a mean-
> ing in it, and I for one cannot find any that bears development. She
> certainly liked the poem, and in this I and others quite agreed with
> her; I possess a little bit of paper, containing three illustrations of her
> own to *The Dream*, and bearing the date 16 March '55. There is (1) the
> dreamer slumbering under a tree, from which the monarch crocodile
> dangles; (2) the crocodile sleeping with 'unstrung claw', as the
> 'wingèd vessel' approaches; and (3) the crocodile as he reared up in
> front of the vessel and 'wrung his hands.'[17]

Christina Rossetti's choice of passages for illustration is
almost as tantalising as the poem itself. 'My Dream' is a joky
lesson to critical head-hunters tracking either phalluses, patriarchs or oppressors, or all three; Christina Rossetti's illustrations
suggest that she 'did it to annoy' because she knew it teased.

'My Dream' teases, but it also gives pleasure, as William
Rossetti ruefully admits. So too does a much more intense lyric
in dream-form, 'On the Wing' (1862), which reiterates the
themes of love and loss so familiar in Rossetti's poetry:

> Once in a dream (for once I dreamed of you)
>   We stood together in an open field;
>   Above our heads two swift-winged pigeons wheeled,
> Sporting at ease and courting full in view:—

---

17. Ibid., p. 479.

When loftier still a broadening darkness flew,
  Down-swooping, and a ravenous hawk revealed;
  Too weak to fight, too fond to fly, they yield;
So farewell life and love and pleasures new.
Then as their plumes fell fluttering to the ground,
  Their snow-white plumage flecked with crimson drops,
    I wept, and thought I turned towards you to weep:
  But you were gone; while rustling hedgerow tops
Bent in a wind which bore to me a sound
  Of far-off piteous bleat of lambs and sheep.[18]

As in *Goblin Market*, the speaker is careful not to confuse punishment (the loss of 'life and love and pleasures new') with guilt, which remains deliberately unassigned. The poem contains a series of highly condensed visual images in which the supposed lovers are both participants and witnesses of a roughly sketched primal scene, but one which contains pre-lapsarian innocence too. The hawk is the agent of vengeance for the 'open', 'full in view' courting in which birds and bird-watchers are engaged. Caught in the act by father, fate, authority, the birds are too 'weak' and too 'fond' to fly. Death and lost virginity mingle in the crimson drops on white plumage. Memory and prophecy are bound up in the vision; how or why the dream-lover is excised from the scene we do not know. Without his presence, the piteous bleat of 'lambs and sheep' (the mother-child dyad), calls the dreamer back to the lonely world of women and children to which all unwedded females are consigned.

Both the dream-form and the allegorical scene release the poem from a conventionally moral conclusion. The dreamer and her lover are spectators of, not actors in, a drama which enacts a 'natural' tragedy. The pigeons' fate is connected to the dreamer's largely through narrative contiguity: they watch the fate of others. The interpolated conclusion, 'So farewell life and love and pleasures new', is ambiguously related to both human and animal couples. But the 'ravenous hawk' is the poem's villain — emphasized, even over-emphasized, as a natural, not divine, avenger. No sexual or social transgression is implied by the words of the poem, so that we have no means of connecting the

18. Ibid., pp. 352-3.

traumatic scene in the air with the history of loss attributed to the dreamer. Dreamer and lover remain in a metonymic relation to the pigeons and hawk; unspecified, incomplete. Although 'On the Wing' is more coherent in its internal narrative, potentially easier to reduce to a psychological analogue, it too is essentially a fragment snipped out of a fuller social or psychological history. Since the dreamer is not 'responsible' for developed meaning the reader is free to fill up the space between the field and the air with her own connotative meaning. One might ask why such a poem requires a feminist reading. Although the images may evoke memories and fears in either sex, the closing link between dreamer, lambs and sheep makes it clear that it is spoken from the female position. Women readers may thus find it a particularly poignant focus around which to organise their own emotions. I came across a comment of William Rossetti's in his memoir of Christina which is in no way a gloss on any particular poem, but suggests one determining factor among others on all of them. Rossetti wrote that Christina had 'a rather unusual feeling of deference for "the head of the family," whoever he might be — my father, Dante Gabriel, and finally myself.'[19]

Emily Dickinson

Christina Rossetti's verse offers up the dream-scene as fantasy in bursts of rich sensuous confusion. Emily Dickinson only rarely uses indirect or 'permissive' forms when she wishes to project sensuous or lascivious images. She is more likely to go for overt statement, as in 'Wild Nights'. The dream-state, rarely signalled by the expressed convention of dreaming, is used to emphasise the dislocation between the poem's images — shifts from inner to outer representation, from realism to fantasy. Perhaps because she did not anticipate a wide reading public for her verse she had little hesitation about using metonymic or synecdochic tropes such as 'If end I gained/It ends beyond/Indefinite disclosed —.'[20] Queries about the 'Indefinite disclosed' are common in her work, applying equally to the human and to the divine condition. The use of the word 'blank' to signify an unrepresentable emotion or

---

19. Ibid., p. lxvi.
20. Dickinson, p. 345.

position is typical — 'From Blank to Blank — /A Threadless Way/I pushed Mechanic feet —' or 'Pain has an element of blank.'[21] The dream scene is, however, implicitly invoked in certain poems, not all of them within the sub-genre of 'difficult' verse discussed here. The famous lyric 'Because I could not stop for Death'[22] is an instance where the dream is a secondary frame for a poem in which the primary convention is a classical or medieval reference to death as driver, boatman or charioteer — here, in genteel bourgeois disguise as the carriage-man. Within the poem the landscapes of school, fields and cemetery seem arbitrary choices, laconic milestones viewed as in a dream. The final thrust of the poem turns in part on the distortion of time as it might be experienced in a dream-state: the moment of recognition of death is longer than the centuries of eternity themselves. Here a traditional metaphor brackets a more eccentric and obscure series of events.

Two other poems in unstated dream-form are more ambitious and less easily understood. Both are well known. 'I started Early — Took my Dog —' moves from a realistic opening to a deliberately fantastic centre. 'The Mermaids in the Basement ... And Frigates — in the Upper Floor' invite the speaker as grounded mouse into a Gothic sea mansion. In the last section, Gothic, fantasy and reality are elided and the 'Tide' as man engulfs 'Shoe', 'Apron', 'Belt' and 'Bodice' until the speaker starts and heads back towards the 'Solid Town' where 'with a Mighty look —/At me — The Sea withdrew —.'[23] The overt formalized allegory in this poem notifies us that it is a daytime fantasy, on the surface a comic one. The inversion of the looker and the looked-at is funny; the mermaids stare at the conventionally dressed speaker, the frigate invites the land mouse on board. The 'Tide' — nature, lover, rapist, gentleman — strands the retreating speaker in her safe social world. Because both sex and death are incorporated in the sea as symbol, as an unstable reference, and because the dreamer's desire in relation to this lover-destroyer is also unstable, the mermaids and the frigate act is displacing images to decoy the reader away from the more erotic and unnerving implications of the poem, joking up its tragic

---

21. Ibid., pp. 373, 323.
22. Ibid. p. 350.
23. Ibid., pp. 254-5.

overtones. The strategies of disguise here bear a strong resemblance to those used by Christina Rossetti in both 'My Dream' and 'On the Wing'.

Much more powerful and unpleasant is 'My Life had stood — a Loaded Gun.'[24] Surely we are at least safe in the land of metaphor: the speaker is the gun; God/lover/man is represented in the 'master' as the omnipotent figure who will shoot the gun. Indeed he is all of these. But wait a moment, guns? Guns and bullets, the 'Yellow Eye', 'emphatic Thumb', are phallic objects. The Victorian model marriage, where masters are men and slaves are obedient women, is broken up in this poem. Master and gun, hunter and weapon are hardly God and his servant Emily, lover and mistress. Instead they are two parts of the phallic actor, the speaking gun and the silent but ambulatory gun-toter. It is unclear throughout the poem who is in command, and the bullet-gun-master are welded into an androgynous fantasy — violent, fetishistic and atavistic. The poem toys with omnipotence, banishes femininity. The 'Life' that had 'stood' 'in Corners' is decoded into something quite other than the familiar poet-speaker whose bodice and apron mark both her subjectivity and subjection.

Anne Sexton, talking about her own poetry in an interview some years ago, supports the concept that the poet herself may not want to know too much of what's going on in a poem. 'An image might come to me, a line — you don't know where it's going to go. It goes its own way.' She asks that a poem 'be what it means to its *readers*' as well as to the army of critics. 'I feel that the poems I love by other people belong to *me*. I don't need to hear what these poems mean, because they may have a meaning so deep I don't *want* to know.'[25] To accept Sexton's point as poet and reader is not to beg the question of meaning, to return literature to a purely subjective relationship between text and audience, or to valorize all individual interpretations. But it may be that these complex lyrics of Rossetti and Dickinson were designed to circumvent the resistance of writer and reader as well as to defy contemporary critical reduction. Female lyric poets of the last century, I would argue, chose to cut out the

24. Ibid., p. 369.
25. Gregory FitzGerald, 'The Choir from the Soul: A Conversation with Anne Sexton', *The Massachusetts Review*, vol. xix 1978, pp. 69-88.

social in order to foreground the psychic subject, though they were often without a traditional language with which to describe its antics. It is tempting to see their poetry as historical verification of the theories about femininity and the unconscious available to us — even, to credit them with a barely suppressed, subversive anticipation of Freud. But while these poems do throw psychological states into sharp relief and avoid realistic reconstructions of social relations, they cannot transcend the ideological orientation of their authors; the very absence of the ideologies of social realism in the texts signals the binding strength of their presence in the material world of the poem's creation. Further, it signals women's difficulty in speaking their psychological conflicts through rational discourse. Writing criticism, like writing poetry, is — among other things — a political act; and the writing of Marxist-feminist literary criticism is not a neutral activity, but speaks from within a specifically defined political dialectic. This group of lyrics pierces to the root of a particularly painful, unresolved contradiction in feminist theory — the contradiction between progressive social struggle and the recalcitrant female psyche — and so moves us further towards an interrogation of our own positions.

6.
The Thorn Birds:
Fiction, Fantasy, Femininity

Autobiography

Reading, dear reader, is a sexual and sexually divided practice, a fact I discovered in puberty when the erotic possibilities of an already compulsive activity began to appear. Narrative pleasure lost its innocence; adult fictions with their gripping scenarios of seduction and betrayal held me captive. I read with heart pounding and hands straying, reducing the respectable and the popular to a basic set of scenarios. *Peyton Place, Jane Eyre, Bleak House, Nana*: in my teens they were all the same to me, part of my sexual and emotional initiation, confirming, constructing my femininity, making plain the psychic form of sexual difference. In my bookish, left wing but rather puritanical household I kept the secret of my reading practice pretty well; after all it was precocious and respectable, was it not, to read all of Dickens at thirteen, to have a passion for Zola a year later? Only I knew that I read them for the sentimental and sexual hype. Physically I developed late; before I swelled, curved or bled I had, psychically speaking, read myself into womanhood. The difference in me as a *reader* was perhaps the first and most significant sign of the social and psychic implications of being female. And it was confirmed through an incident when I was at least fourteen when I read Margaret Mitchell's *Gone With the Wind*. Like many readers of this early blockbuster romance I read it in one bout, too engaged with the story to eat or to sleep. I was a fast reader, but it must have taken me two days; no skipping here for the romance takes up most of the text. My compulsion was observed for the book itself was not approved of; pro-Southern and unashamedly racist, as well as without literary merit in my parents' eyes, it brought together a reactionary political narrative with a reactionary emotional one. I finished the book late in the night and the ending left me in despair and near hysteria. How could the author refuse a happy resolution? How could Scarlet's moral, sexual and emotional awakening 'come too late'. In the register of psychic melodrama *Gone With the Wind* brought home to me what I already knew at a social and political level, had felt powerfully the day the Rosenbergs were executed that life was, could be, unfair and I met this realization with howls of rage and pain.

My mother took me into the bathroom, and in my memory, though not in hers, threw cold water over me to stop my sobs. And I was ashamed at being so uncontrolled, so held by such a 'bad' book, for this was America in the mid-fifties and my passion for social justice, my political loyalties were well developed. As a political subject I knew what side I was on; in these same years I came home in the afternoon from school and listened to the Army-McCarthy hearings on the radio with my milk and cookies, cheering when the Right was challenged and lost points. I was an optimistic child; I believed even in those dark years that progressive forces would triumph eventually, and in the same way I hoped for the future realization of my sexual and emotional fantasies, though this reward seemed as distant as the revolution. Both my parents found my slavish addiction to fifties femininity, its fashions that harnessed thrust and spiked us and its macho-femme versions of sexual difference, regressive and worrying. For me however my political and sexual desires, utopian and transgressive, were bound together, which made my passionate response to *Gone With the Wind* even more contradictory, for it was not only, not even primarily Scarlet that drew me to the book, but the whole scenario of lost causes, sexual and political, and Rhett Butler above all as the knowing and desiring protagonist. I loved the book, I think, because it was a transgressive read in a house where there was no censorship, only waves of disappointment. The deep South and its fake aristocracy, imitation feudalism (which Mitchell both deplores and celebrates) was an imaginary historic site where traditional femininity could be lived in an unashamed way, at one level at least. It probably met my fantasy that in less politically radical households fifties female adolescence was given more space and approval.

Yet *Gone With the Wind* is not a conventional piece of romance fiction, or Scarlet a conventional heroine. Her femininity is masquerade, for behind it lies a scheming active masculine ambition to survive and get ahead. Only her hopeless passion for the hopeless Ashley Wilkes marks her out as conventionally feminine. Unsentimental and asexual in most of her dealings with men, an unwilling mother, Rhett must convert her to sexuality, and by taking the child away, to some measure of maternal feeling. For all his macho qualities it is Rhett, not Ashley who is the maternal man, taking over when Scarlett's parents die and the social relations of the South disintegrate, educating and protecting Scarlet, proud involved father to his daughter, a man who values women more than men. When he abandons her she is truly abandoned, and must go back to her childhood, to Tara, to start again.

For me personally it was a resonant and painful text, for I was engaged in a long and bitter struggle with my father in these years, for my autonomy, for his love and approval. But it spoke I think to a much wider audience of American women readers for whom the pre-Civil War South did serve as a sort of pre-capitalist site of family romance, a mythical moment of settled traditional social relations that the Civil War destroyed forever. In terms of its connotations for twentieth century readers both North and South, that imaginary historical landscape was both Edenic and poisoned — by slavery, by illusion — and its violent disruption necessary so that the South could enter modern industrial capitalist society. Sherman's rape of Georgia, Rhett's violent seduction of Scarlet are analogous events in the text, progressive events if you like, which take place in a world tinged with unbearable emotional nostalgia. *Gone With the Wind* encourages the reader to regress, insists that she moves on. As a parable of Southern history and as a romantic narrative with incestuous overtones it is history and fantasy spoken from the position of the women. It remains so today.

My reading of romance didn't stop of course with the cold slosh of maternal reality. But I was internally cautious about being so profoundly 'carried away' by my romance reading after that. I regularly read and reread certain texts that spoke to me in the same register of desire as *Gone With the Wind* and these significant fictions crossed the boundaries of high and popular genres. So the two other books I remember from my teens as affecting me in similar ways were Anya Seton's historical novel *Katherine* and *Anna Karenina*. It was over twenty-five years before a novel triggered the uncontrolled level of fantasy response that I had experienced with *Gone With the Wind* and, not surprisingly I encountered it first as a television serial. Colleen McCullough's *The Thorn Birds*[1] seduced me away from a more respectable piece of viewing — *The Raj Quartet* — and so profoundly affected was I by the first episode I saw (not the first in the series) that I rushed out to buy the paperback. A matriarchal family saga starting in Australia between the wars, it is overtly transgressive where *Gone With the Wind* is subtle. The first two thirds of the book centre on the growing attachment for and eventual seduction of a Catholic priest, Ralph, by a much younger woman, Meggie, whom he meets when she is only nine. Incest is the only slightly displaced theme of the book; in the character of Ralph the author constructs an ideal maternal man, even a feminine man, to whom sexual access is of course taboo. Deeply conservative politically in ways I shall go into later, the book appropriates contemporary feminist discourses on sexuality in interesting ways. I don't know a single man who has read it except to engage with it professionally; yet like *Gone With the Wind* it has broken sales records internationally. Like *Gone With the Wind* it is a fantasy about both history and sexuality imagined from the woman's position and it speaks powerfully to the contradictory and unreconciled feelings about femininity, feminism and fantasy which mark out that position for, at the very least, first world white female readers. Unlike mass market romance, Mills and Boon and Harlequin, these long blockbuster romances do not solicit the reader to identify with a single female protagonist. Rather they evoke powerful overlapping scenarios in which the relation of reader to character is often deliciously blurred. They invite, I would argue, the female reader to identify across sexual difference and to engage with narrative fantasy from a variety of subject positions and at various levels. *The Thorn Birds* confirms not a conventional femininity but women's contradictory and ambiguous place within sexual difference. Feminist cultural criticism has engaged in a very

---

1. Colleen McCullough, *The Thorn Birds*, London, 1977.

interesting debate about the meaning of reading, and watching, romance. What follows is a contribution to that discussion which tries to see how, in historical, political and psychoanalytic terms, texts like *Gone With the Wind* and *The Thorn Birds* come to have such a broad appeal for women, centering the female reader in a particular way, and reworking the contradictory elements that make female subjectivity such a vertiginous social and psychic experience.

History

Fiction, fantasy and femininity. Since the rise of the popular novel directed at a female audience the relationship between these three terms has troubled both progressive and conservative analysts of sexual difference, not least those who were themselves writers of narrative. The terms of the debate about the relationship between 'reading romance' and the construction of femininity have remained surprisingly constant in the two hundred years since Mary Wollstonecraft and Jane Austen first engaged with the issue as a response to the expansion of sensational literature directed at the woman reader.[2] Both Wollstonecraft and Austen agreed that the 'stale tales' and 'meretricious scenes' of the sentimental and gothic novel triggered and structured female fantasy, stirring up the erotic and romantic at the expense of the rational, moral and maternal. Both thought that such reading could directly influence behaviour — inflamed and disturbed readers might, in Wollstonecraft's evocative phrase 'plump into actual vice.' But Wollstonecraft's main concern was not with junk reading as the route to adultery but as the path to conventional, dependent, degenerate femininity — to the positioning of the female self in the degraded, dependent role as 'object of desire'. At the time she was writing *A Vindication of the Rights of Woman* Wollstonecraft was defending a relatively conventional sexual morality. Even so she was much less concerned with the danger to women's sexual virtue that

---

2. Mary Wollstonecraft, *A Vindication of the Rights of Woman*, Carol H. Poston ed., New York, 1975, pp. 183-186. Jane Austen, *Northanger Abbey* and *Mansfield Park*. The following discussion of gendered reading in the late eighteenth and early nineteenth century is drawn from the above texts.

romance reading might breed than with the far reaching political effects of such indulgence. As the narrative of desire washed over the reader, the thirst for reason was quenched, and the essential bridge to female autonomy and emancipation, a strengthened 'understanding', was washed out. The female psyche could not, it seemed, sustain or combine two mental agendas; for them it must be either reason or passion, pleasure or knowledge. Austen's version of this libidinal economy was perhaps slightly less punitive, but this was only because her ambitions for her heroine/reader were a less radical and limited moral autonomy within the dominant convention as wife, mother and lover. Moral and spiritual integrity, and to some extent independence for women was essential, but an independent life and a productive life combined were not thinkable within her novels. Both Wollstonecraft and Austen assumed, as most analysts of romance reading do today, that romance narrative works on the reader through rather simple forms of identification. The reader aligns herself with the heroine and suffers her perils, passions and triumphs. The narrative structure of the fiction then 'takes over' everyday life, and gender relations are read through its temptations, seductions and betrayals. Alternatively, romance provides an escape from the everyday realities; the pleasure of fantasy numbs the nerve of resistance to oppression.

Wollstonecraft's implicit theory of reading assumes the reader will identify herself with the female heroine. The reading of popular fiction and the fantasy induced by it depend at one level on the identification of reader and heroine, and the subsequent acting-out of a related narrative trajectory. Late eighteenth century theories of reading, as they appeared in both aesthetic and political discourses, assumed a fairly direct relationship between reading and action, especially in the naive reader, the barely literate, uneducated working-class person — and women. In this period of expanding literacy and political turmoil, the question of the ability to read is at the center both of progressive programmes that sought to radicalize the mass of the people, and conservative resistance to revolution. A great deal of attention was given not only to the dynamic effects of reading on the unschooled subject but also to the distinction between reading as a social act (a pamphlet read to others in a coffee house or village square, books read at the family hearth) and reading as a private act, unregulated and unsupervised by authority. Both forms of reading can be subversive, but the latter, less open to surveillance and control, more defiantly announcing the mental autonomy of individual subjects whose 'independence' is not acknowledged by the dominant social and political order, offers a particularly insidious form of subversion. The question of women's reading as it is understood in the 1790s is situated within these wider anxieties about reading and revolution, literacy and subjectivity.[3] Accordingly both Wollstonecraft and Austen knew women must read to achieve even minimal independent status as subjects and are, in somewhat different ways, concerned more with something intangible and complex that sensational novels may produce than a simple incitement to misbehave. Private reading is already, in itself, an act of autonomy; in turn it sets up, or enables space for reflective thought. Fiction gives that reflection a narrative shape and sensational fiction produces a sort of general excitation, the 'romantic twist of the mind' that concerned Wollstonecraft. The desire to inhabit that provocative landscape and live its stories mentally rather than those of the supposed social real was as worrying as any specific identification with romantic female protagonists. In fact Wollstonecraft's analysis of the construction of a degraded and dependent femininity in *A Vindication* insists that although female children have no innate sexuality — she bitterly rejected Rousseau's insistence that they did — women come to see themselves narcissistically through the eyes of men; through the gaze of the male rake, they become 'rakes themselves'. Female subjectivity was characterized in this account by its retrograde tendency to take up other subject positions and identify self as object. It is this already unstable, degraded subject (constructed in childhood and early adolescence) that read romance and fantasized about it. For Wollstonecraft and Austen popular sensational literature both reinforced and evoked a set of romantic scenarios that the reader will use at once to interpret, act through and escape

---

3. The debates about reading appear *passim* in the extended pamphlet exchange over the French revolution and its effects in Britain. See especially the writings of Thomas Paine and Hannah More, the trials of booksellers and publishers in the 1790s as well as letters and papers of various radical figures. E.P. Thompson, *The Making of the English Working Class*, London 1968, Part One, pp. 19-293 contains a general discussion of these issues, and cf. Olivia Smith, *The Politics of Language*, 1791-1819, Oxford 1984.

from ordinary life. Each part of this reading effect is 'bad'; each involves different elements of projection and displacement and constitute together the negative effect of fiction and fantasy.

There was very little possibility in late eighteenth century progressive or conservative thought for a positive account of fantasy for women, the lower classes or colonial peoples. For all of these lesser subjectives the exercise of the imagination was problematic; for the untutored, 'primitive' psyche was easily excited and had no strategies of sublimation; a provocative narrative induced imitation and disruptive actions, political or social. When radicals supported the subjective equality of any of these groups they generally insisted that their reasoning capacity was equal to that of a bourgeois male. The psyche of the educated middle class male was the balanced psyche of the period; reason and passion in a productive symbiosis. Men of this class were felt to have a fixed positionality; radical discourses presented them as the origin of their own identities, as developing independent subjects, the makers and controllers of narrative rather than its enthralled and captive audience. This capacity to produce a master narrative, like their rational capacity to take civic, political actions, remained latent in them as readers. Men of the ruling class, so went the dominant mythology, read critically, read not to imitate but to engage productively with argument and with narrative. They understood the difference between fiction and fact, between imagination and reason. The normative male reader could read a gothic novel for amusement and pleasure unlike his credulous female counterparts. Like the poet whose writing practice used 'emotion recollected in tranquility' the two modes of reason and passion were ever open to him; in the same way he could inhabit both a public and private sphere and move between them. The enlightenment asked man to subordinate passion to reason; romanticism argued for a productive interaction between them, assuming optimistically that the rational would act as a check to passion, and that passion itself would be transformed, sublimated through the imagination. As literacy spreads and reading becomes one of the crucial practices through which human capacity, integrity, autonomy and psychic balance can be assessed, reading habits and reading response are increasingly used to differentiate readers by class and sex. By the 1790s reading by the mass is argued *for* as a necessary route to individual and group advancement, both as the crucial preparation for social and political revolution, and as the significant activity to stem the revolutionary tide. Thomas Paine pushes the polemic farthest, conflating reading with civil liberty itself — prophesying that censorship will breed its own revenge — that it would become dangerous to tell a whole people that 'they shall not read'. Reading both as an activity and as a sign of activities it may engender becomes a metonymic reference to forms of good and bad subjectivity, of present and potential social and psychic being. So Wollstonecraft in 1792 ends her diatribe against romance reading on an uncertain note, insisting that it is better that women read novels than not read at all.

Fantasy

In the previous two sections I have been deliberately using the term fantasy in its contemporary everyday sense: as a conscious construction of an imaginary scene in which, it is invariably assumed, the fantasist places him/herself in an easily identified and constant role in the narrative. This common sense working definition has been undermined at various points in the discussion of autobiography and history, but it is more or less adequate for a preliminary account of fantasy as 'daydream', as a conscious, written narrative construction, or as an historical account of the gendered imagination. Yet fantasy used solely or unreflectedly in this way invokes the relation between dream and fiction, without actually theorizing that connection. Unless we actually work through that relationship, and distinguish between fantasy as an unconscious structure and as a form of social narrative we are unlikely to break free of the stigmatizing moralism that taints most accounts of romantic fantasy and gender, representing romance as a 'social disease' that affects the weaker constitution of the female psyche. Psychoanalytic discussions of fantasy are not wholly free of elements of moralization, but as Alison Light has commented in her illuminating discussion of romance fiction, sexuality and class, psychoanalysis at least 'takes the question of pleasure seriously, both in its relation to gender and in its understanding of fiction as fantasies, as the explorations and productions of desires which may be in excess of the socially possible or acceptable'.[4]

Freud began his work on fantasy by appealing to the relation-ship between fantasy and day-dream — 'scenes, episodes, romances or fictions which the subject creates and recounts to himself in the waking state.'[5] But as he develops his concept of fantasy, it becomes clear that fantasy operates at three different registers at least — at unconscious, subliminal and conscious levels. At each level fantasy expresses social content, but is, at the same time separate from it. Indeed Juliet Mitchell, in an interesting discussion of the origins of fantasy specifies its moment of genesis as the moment when the baby deprived of the breast fantasies sucking, transforming the external world and its '"things"' — the people, sounds, sights and smells and so on' into representation. This moment is identified in psychoanalysis as the moment of the foundation of desire, and according to Mitchell again the moment when the 'human animal' becomes a 'human being'. Thus the experience of the external world provides 'the support (or underpin) for the phantasy scenario which comes into being with their absence.'[6]

Sexuality, representation, fantasy and subjectivity. In psycho-analytic theory, the infant's fantasy is the mode through which sexuality (desire) is constituted, and equally the ability to repre-sent the missing activity or pleasure is the process through which subjectivity — social and psychic identity — is formed. A psychoanalytic theory of fantasy not only takes 'pleasure seriously' but places the ability to think about pleasure at the center of what constitutes us as human subjects. If we accept that fantasy has this crucial place in mental life, and if we emphasise it for the moment as a process rather than a particular scenario or set of scenarios, then perhaps we can make more sense of the problem it has posed for feminism. For the advocacy of stern prophylactic measures to 'cure' women of romantic

---

4. Alison Light '"Returning to Manderley" Romance Fiction, Female Sexuality and Class', *Feminist Review*, no. 16, Summer, 1984, p. 7.

5. J. Laplanche and J-B Pontalis, 'Phantasy (or Fantasy),' *The Language of Psycho-analysis*, London, 1983, p.316. I have chosen to follow the general American usage, and have used a single spelling 'fantasy' for both conscious and unconscious fantasy.

6. Juliet Mitchell, 'Psychoanalysis: A Humanist Humanity or a Linguistic Science?', in *Women: The Longest Revolution: Essays in Feminism, Literature and Psychoanalysis*, London, 1984, pp. 233-47.

fantasy, has, in this recent wave of feminism as in the ones that have preceded it, produced its own backlash and internal unease. Letting go of romantic and sexual fantasies of an 'incorrect' kind has proved very difficult; perhaps because their obstinate presence in women's imaginative life can never simply be a sign of their psychic subordination to patriarchal relations, but always, simultaneously the mark of their humanity.

In a few pages we will look at *The Thorn Birds* as an example of how fictions written in the last fifteen years for and by women can remap the insistent scenarios of fantasy in relation to feminist discourse. First more needs to be said about the specifically Freudian elaboration of a theory of fantasy. It is helpful to isolate three important elements of Freud's use of fantasy: first, how it specifies the relationship of the classic fantasy scenario to the place of the subject within it; second, how it describes the relationship between the different psychic registers in which fantasy occurs and third, its problematic perspective on the origins of primal or unconscious fantasy.

My understanding of Freud's deployment of fantasy is heavily dependent on two interpretative texts, the entry on 'Phantasy (or Fantasy)' in J. Laplanche and J-B. Pontalis's *The Language of Psycho-Analysis* and the essay by the same authors 'Fantasy and the Origins of Sexuality' (1968).[7] The latter piece in particular explores the question of the positionality of the subject in fantasy. The authors begin by emphasizing that 'the primary function of fantasy' is to provide 'a setting for desire'.[8] Scenario thus takes precedent over any fixed identification of the subject with any one character in the scene, and indeed such indentification may shift in the course of a fantasy scenario (the example from Freud is his brief and suggestive essay 'A Child is Being Beaten').[9] More radically Laplanche and Pontalis suggest that the 'fixing' of subject identification is not the point of fantasy anyway. Insisting on the close relationship between the initiation of desire in the psychic subject and the origin of fantasy they argue that

---

7. J. Laplanche and J-B. Pontalis, 'Fantasy and the Origins of Sexuality', *International Journal of Psychoanalysis*, 49, Part 1, 1968, pp. 1-17.
8. Ibid., p. 17.
9. Sigmund Freud, 'A Child is Being Beaten', *The Standard Edition of the Complete Psychoanalytic Works of Sigmund Freud*, London 1953-73, XVII, p. 177.

> Fantasy is not the object of desire, but its setting. In fantasy the subject does not pursue the object or its sign: he appears caught up himself in the sequence of images. He forms no representation of the desired object, but is himself represented as participating in the scene although, in the earliest forms of fantasy, he cannot be assigned any fixed place in it ... As a result, the subject, although always present in the fantasy, may be so in a desubjectivized form, that is to say, in the very syntax of the sequence in question.[10]

Moreover the point at which desire originates, the point of separation of the subject from the sensory objects of satisfaction, becomes soon enough in psychic development a point of prohibition. Fantasy thus becomes the 'favoured spot' for the articulation of those defensive mechanisms through which the psyche deals with such prohibition. Fantasy scenarios are rarely straightforward narratives in which the 'wish' is simply represented in the pursuit of an object by a subject-protagonist. Yet this is, on the whole, how it is assumed fantasy works when it is induced or provoked by visual or written fictions. In particular, analyses of mass-market romance of the Mills and Boon and Harlequin type have emphasized the congruence between reader and heroine and the coherence between socially normative models of heterosexual romance and romance narrative. Moreover mass-market romance is frequently assumed to embody the basic schema or scenario of romantic fantasy which is then elaborated in more sophisticated or complex narratives. These latter may be novels in the high art canons, like Ann Radcliffe's gothic masterpiece *Mysteries of Udolpho* or Brontë's *Jane Eyre* or they may be slightly upmarket modern popular texts — blockbusters, bodice-rippers, historical romance, family saga. However as Tania Modleski convincingly argues in *Loving with a Vengeance: Mass-produced Fantasies for Women* — which focuses on three genres of mass-market fantasy, Harlequins, Gothics and soap-operas — it is useful to distinguish between types of romance in thinking about the relationship of different kinds of narrative to female subjectivity.[11] Modleski however sees the lack of an easy identification of reader to protagonist in the text as a 'problem' and one that points towards a critique not of the

---

10. 'Fantasy and the Origins of Sexuality', p. 17.
11. Tania Modleski, *Loving With a Vengeance: Mass-produced Fantasies for Women*, New York, 1984.

novels but 'the conditions which made them necessary.'[12] Her analysis of the revenge narrative, beneath the narrative of seduction contests in persuasive ways the notion of the simple scenario of mass-market romance. Nevertheless her discussion of the identification of the reader with the heroine is disappointing, for her strategy is to associate the 'schizophrenic' and 'apersonal' effect of reading Harlequins (where the reader is always more knowledgeable and in control than the heroine) with the situation of the hysteric, as if seeing oneself from outside in the dramatic script were only a sign of female distress about femininity, a form of splitting that a reformed social world could and ought to remedy.[13] In a similar way her comparison of the gothic formula with paranoia, while not falling into the trap of pathologizing either reader or text, tends to set up certain narrative elements — the use of the feminine man in gothics — as subject/object relations. *Loving with a Vengeance* uses Freud, but tends to read him through a feminist appropriation of psychoanalytic theory that emphasizes 'object relations' in the formation of subjectivity, rather than through a notion of fantasy as a scenario in which the shifting place of the subject and desubjectification is a characteristic part of the activity.[14] Accordingly her analysis is quite gender bound; the female subject/reader has, as she suggests, an active psychic relation to the texts in which heroines are posed as passive, but she must be situated in the text *as* female subject. Crossing the boundaries of gender as part of the acts of reading and fantasizing plays no significant part in her analysis.

For Laplanche and Pontalis however the variability of the subject's place in fantasy is a key to the heterogeneous nature of fantasy itself, the mixed form in which it mostly appears to us in reverie, reminiscence and dream. The lack of subjectivization of fantasy in original fantasy scenarios — the primal scene, seduction and castration — cannot be clearly contrasted with the presumed place of the subject in daydream as a 'first person'

---

12. Ibid., p. 57.
13. Ibid. There are however many instances other than hysteria of psychic states where subjects see themselves from outside. See, for example Freud's discussion in 'Screen Memory', *Standard Edition*.
14. As in the work of Melanie Klein and others. Nancy Chodorow, *The Reproduction of Mothering*, Berkeley and Los Angeles 1978 is an example of one kind of feminist appropriation of 'object relations' theory.

narration in which the subject's place is 'clear and invariable.' For although 'the work of our waking thought' that organizes and makes dream scenes coherent may impose a daydream form on the incoherence of dream, and so rationalize the material in relation to a fixed subject position, certain characteristic fantasies of a waking kind refuse the imposition of this kind of narrative realism. To support their argument Laplanche and Pontalis cite especially 'A Child is Being Beaten' in which Freud notes that both the sex of the child and the figure of the beater oscillate in the course of the fantasy, and his 'Screen Memory' where the subject sees the self as a character in the narrative reconstruction. They go even further in analyzing the instability of subject position in seduction fantasy: '"A father seduces a daughter" might perhaps be the summarized version of the seduction fantasy . . . it is a scenario with multiple entries, in which nothing shows whether the subject will be immediately located as *daughter*: it can as well be fixed as *father*, or even in the term *seduces*.'[15]

Freud asserts the 'profound kinship' of original, unconscious fantasy and conscious fantasy and their persistence through very different modes and stages of psychic life by emphasizing that

> The contents of the clearly conscious fantasies of perverts (which in favourable circumstances can be transformed into manifest behaviour), of the delusional fears of paranoics which are projected in a hostile sense on to other people), and of the unconscious fantasies of hysterics (which psychoanalysis reveals behind their symptoms) — all these coincide with one another even down to their details.[16]

The persistence and repetition of certain fantasy scenarios in the psychic life of men and women with very different psychological disturbance, and the ambiguity of subject positions in the elements of original fantasy that are supplied in dream, acting-out, and waking reverie, these aspects of Freud's work on fantasy (highlighted by Laplanche and Pontalis) can lead to a very different 'take' on both the textual fantasy inscribed in romance fiction and the reader's mode of appropriating such fantasy. Freud's development of his ideas about fantasy, were, as Laplanche and Pontalis suggest marked by an 'ambiguity of

---

15. 'Fantasy and the Origins of Sexuality', p. 14.
16. Ibid., p. 11.

conceptions as new avenues open out to him with each new stage in his ideas.'[17] However if we follow Laplanche and Pontalis's way through this conceptual underbrush it is clear we are moving away from fantasy as an activity that serves to fix subject positions, without moving towards some form of reversal in which female fantasy, because it is an active psychic process, becomes a morally liberating activity for women. Fantasy, as Modleski suggests, has utopian elements in it; indeed without fantasy we could not imagine utopias. But fantasizing *as such* is, rather, a crucial part of psychic life, a process required for human sexuality and subjectivity to be set in place and articulated than a process that is either good or bad, or of which we can have too much or too little. How fantasy, with its aggrandizing narrative appetite appropriates and incorporates social meaning, structuring through its public narrative forms the historically specific stories and subjectivities available — that aspect of fantasy is open to political analysis and negotiation. But the ways in which the subject/reader engages with textual fantasy that combines original or primal fantasy — in which desubjectivization is characteristic — with reverie and daydream in which 'first person' identification is more common, is clearly more complex than most accounts of reading romance have allowed.

The least satisfactory element in Freud's exploration of fantasy is his phylogenetic solution to the question of the 'origins' of the basic fantasy scenarios, the witnessing of sexual intercourse between parents, seduction and castration. The search for a pre-history for these fantasies which themselves pose the question of origins is, as Laplanche and Pontalis note, only one aspect of Freud's many-sided discussion of fantasy. Phylogenetic explanation places the 'acts' and 'scenes' of primal fantasy as 'real occurences in the primaeval times of the human family ... children in their phantasies are simply filling in the gaps in individual truth with prehistoric truth.'[18] In fact phylogenetic explanation itself fills in, to some extent, the gap left when Freud abandons the seduction theory, and with it the notion that the analyst can uncover a verifiable real event behind

---

17. Ibid., p. 2.
18. Laplanche and Pontalis, 'Primal Phantasies', *The Language of Psychoanalysis*, p. 331.

the adult history. Phylogenetic explanation both works in tandem with and competes with Freud's concept of 'psychical reality', which gives psychic life an autonomous identity. Its presence indicates how much it mattered to Freud that a 'bedrock of the event' be located somewhere outside the recounted fantasies of the adult patient, in primal fantasy first, and then, if necessary, in 'the history of the species.' The search for the true story in the history of an individual subject can be found in Freud's work many years after he rejected the seduction theory, and speaks to his desire to found the theory on a reality principle of some kind, even if its register is mythic rather than historic, metaphysical rather than material.

Modern psychoanalytic theory is, understandably, unhappy with mythical pre-histories, and its tendency is to ignore or displace the search for the origin of primal fantasy, or, simply to confess with Laplanche and Pontalis that it is a project for 'philosophers.' Nevertheless Freud's own need for such a theory, and its literal embodiment in notions of the 'primitive' and 'archaic', as a set of social practices suggests the ways in which primal fantasy remains morally and ethically ambiguous. Not only are its scenes dramas of prohibition, but they remain tainted with the taboo they enact. The foundation of sociality and identity, they are also, always, scripts that define otherness and exclusion. Imagining a mythic prehistory for the classic primal scenarios, in which fathers *actually* castrated children, evokes contemporary ideas of 'primitive' practice, invites us to think synchronically, across cultures, as well as diachronically back through history. In short phylogenetic explanation calls on other systems of difference, the difference between cultures, between subjectivities to account for the foundation of sexual difference. It intrudes into the discussion of fantasy the colonial discourse of 'otherness' in which degraded subjects act out the prohibited scenarios of European cultures.

The subliminal moralizing of the different levels of fantasy via the invocation of racial hierarchy is expressed very directly at one point in Freud's discussion of the 'hybrid' nature of fantasy as conscious and unconscious forms, in day-dream and dream facade. In 'The Unconscious' (1915) Freud uses the example of 'individuals of mixed race' to illustrate the way in which primal fantasy both hides and reveals its origins when it is embedded in apparently coherent, sophisticated fantasy narrative. The educated fantasies that present themselves as 'highly organized, free from self-contradiction' seem, at first glance part of the rationally integrated system of consciousness. But, Freud noted, interpretation unmasks them: 'Their origin is what decides their fate. We may compare them with individuals of mixed race who, taken all round, resemble white men, but who betray their coloured descent by some striking feature or other, and on that account are excluded from society and enjoy none of the privileges of white people.'[19]

In his comparison Freud uses a biological basis of racial difference. His assumption that the social recognition of difference will automatically lead to exclusion maps the politics of racism over the rules that govern the hierarchy of psychic discourses. Less metaphor than metonym, this disturbing image invokes both biological and social notions of degraded subjectivity and social forms of exclusion as a way of indicating the incomplete integration of fantasy discourses. The imbrication of sexuality and race in Freud's example is complete when we learn that it is through the tell-tale shape of 'nose' and kink of 'hair' that the outlaw primitive will be identified. More than anything else this passage reveals the insistent connection between fantasy, social law, and the related forms of degraded and excluded subjectivity, a connection that remains politically opaque and therefore ambiguous in Freud's own writing.

Text: *The Thorn Birds*

In 'Returning to Manderley' Alison Light reclaims du Maurier's *Rebecca* as a text that provides 'a classic model of romance fiction while at the same time exposing many of its terms.'[20] I would like to adopt a similar critical strategy towards Colleen McCullough's *The Thorn Birds*, a family saga whose events start in 1915 in rural New Zealand and end in 1965 in a London town house. Written by an Australian emigrée living in America in the mid-seventies, the novel subtly appropriates elements of feminist discourse, integrating the language of romance fictions with new languages

---

19. S. Freud, 'The Unconscious' (1915), in *On Metapsychology: The Theory of Psychoanalysis*, Harmandsworth, 1984. The Pelican Freud Library, vol. 11, p. 195.
20. Light, p. 7.

of sexuality and sexual difference. Fantasy is quite unashamedly mobilized in *The Thorn Birds* both at the level of content — the narrative scenario — and at the level of rhetoric — the various styles that mark out its different registers within the story. Through these means the novel weaves a seeming social realism together with a series of original fantasies so that the text resembles the heterogeneous or hybrid form of fantasy described by psychoanalysis. As in a retold dream, the text rationalizes fantasy scenes into a coherent narrative sequence, but in fact the plot is full of unlikely incident and coincidence that characters and authorial voice are constantly trying to justify. The implausible elements of the plot and their elaborate rationalization signal the presence of original fantasy in the text. Like many family sagas, *The Thorn Birds* inscribes all of the generic original fantasies, often mapping them over each other, and repeating them with variations in the experience of different generations. Laplanche and Pontalis describe these fantasy categories as: 'Fantasies of origins: the primal scene pictures the origin of the individual; fantasies of seduction, the origin and upsurge of sexuality; fantasies of castration, the origin of the difference between the sexes.'[21]

Ambiguities about paternity run through the text. Intimations of incest affect almost all the familial and extra-familial relations, affecting father-daughter, mother-son and brother-sister ties. These fantasy scenes are structured and elaborated from the woman's position, which sometimes means only that they offer a mildly eccentric elaboration of the classic fantasy scripts. For example castration fantasy in the narrative emphasizes both lack and power in women and mothers on the one hand and retribution by that eternally absent father, God, on the other. The third person narration, typical of family saga romance allows a very free movement between masculine and feminine positions, and different discursive genres and registers. It also permits the narrative as a whole to be contained within a set of determinate political ideologies for which the characters themselves bear little responsibility. Like *Gone With the Wind*, but with significant differences, *The Thorn Birds* pursues an interesting occasionally radical interrogation of sexual difference inside a reactionary set of myths about history.

---

21. 'Fantasy and the Origins of Sexuality', p. 11.

At the heart of *The Thorn Birds* lies a scandalous passion, between a Catholic priest, Ralph de Bricassart and Meggie Cleary whose family are the focus of the novel. Ralph meets Meggie when she is nine years old, the only and somewhat neglected girl child in a large brood of boys. Ralph himself is a strikingly hand- some and ambitious Irish born priest in his late twenties sent into temporary exile in this remote bit of rural New South Wales because he has quarreled with his bishop. Ralph loves the child for her beauty, and for her 'perfect female character, passive yet enormously strong. No rebel, Meggie: on the contrary. All her life she would obey, move within the boundaries of her female fate.' The whole first half of the novel follows the Cleary's fortunes on Drogheda, the vast Australian sheep station, which belongs first to the widowed millionaire matriarch Mary Carson, and after her death to the Church, with Ralph as its agent. Its narrative moves in a tantalizingly leisurely fashion towards the seduction of the proud, virginal Ralph by Meggie, whose female fate seems to include some fairly fundamental disobedience to church and state. Ralph 'makes' Meggie, as he tells his Vatican superior and confessor later in the text, shaping her education and sensibility from childhood. She, like a dutiful daughter in *someone's* fantasy returns his seemingly non-sexual love with a fully libidinized intensity. The text plays with great skill on the two narratives of prohibition, familial and ecclesiastic, that are bound together in Meggie and Ralph's romance. 'Don't call me Father,' he keeps insisting, while disentangling himself reluct- antly from the arms of the teenage girl who assaults him at every opportunity. Ralph is represented as mother, father and lover in relation to Meggie. Somehow it is Ralph, in the confessional, who has to tell the fifteen year old Meggie about menstruation, because mother Fee is too busy with the boys. Somehow it is Ralph, not Meggie's negligent macho husband, who arrives in a distant bit of the outback to hold her hand in her first painful experience of childbirth.

The ideal feminine man (he has a way, he tells us, with babies), Ralph is bound to the Church by pride and ambition, sure that it will give him a transcendent identity — 'Not a man, never a man; something far greater, something beyond the fate of a mere man.'[22] Losing his virginity at forty odd Ralph discovers *in media res* that he is a 'mere man' after all, while Meggie finds out that only symbolic incest and transgression can make a woman of her. Their brief week's consummation takes place on a remote south sea island. After an Edenic interlude Ralph leaves for Rome and his rising career in the Church. Meggie gestating his son returns to the Cleary family base at Drogheda with her daughter Justine, by her husband Luke. Here under her mother's benign matriarchy (her biological father, significantly dies before her marriage and adultery) she will raise her children and even enjoy a short second honeymoon when Ralph comes to Drogheda to visit years later.

The novel, 591 pages long, deals with major events in the life of three generations of Clearys as well as Ralph's trajectory from country priest to cardinal via his broken vows. Like *Gone With the Wind* and other family saga romances part of its pleasure is in the local, historical detail. Most of the energy of the text however is reserved for the emotional encounters; its power to hold the female reader, in the first half anyway is linked to the inexorable unfolding of Meggie and Ralph's story, a seduction scenario played through the narrative of another durable fantasy, the family romance in which a real-life parent is discarded as an impostor and a more exalted figure substituted.

The incest motif is everywhere in the novel, saturating all the literal familial relations as well as the metaphorical ones. Within the Cleary household, all the boys remain unmarried; they are, as Meggie tells Ralph during their island idyll 'terribly shy ... frightened of the power a woman might have over them ... quite wrapped up in Mum.'[23] Most wrapped up in Fee Cleary is her eldest son Frank, the illegitimate child of a New Zealand politician, half Maori. Through her affair with him Fee has lost her social position; her upper class Anglican family marry her off to their shy dairy hand, Irish Catholic immigrant Paddy Cleary and then disown her. Frank acts out an oedipal drama with Paddy whom he believes is his real father until he goads Paddy into revealing his illegitimate status. They quarrel. Frank calls his father 'a stinking old he-goat ... a ram in rut' for making his mother Fee pregnant yet again, and the father stung, calls the boy 'no better than the shitty old dog who fathered you, whoever he was!' This quarrel takes place in front of the child

---

23. Ibid., p. 358.

Meggie, and Father Ralph. After it Frank leaves home, eventually commits murder and is given a life sentence. His fate is seen in the text quite specifically as Fee's punishment for her sexual transgression. In the second half of the novel, Meggie too will lose her much loved son by Ralph, first to the Church and then by death. These symmetrical events are reinforced by the deep but sexually innocent attachment of brother-sister pairs in each generation: Frank and his half sister Meggie; Justine and her half-brother Dane. Within the male Cleary brood there are homosocial attachments too, the twin boys Patsy and Jims represented as a symbiotic couple. And *The Thorn Birds* extends and elaborates the homosocial, homoerotic themes, though never in a very positive way, through Meggie's husband Luke's preference for his workmate Arne, and, within the church, through Ralph's friendship with his Italian mentor. Male bonding is seen as something of a problem in the book, a problem certainly for Meggie who, as she says, seems drawn to men who don't have much need of women and fear too much closeness with them.[24]

Meggie (and Ralph) witness two primal scenes — in discursive form to be sure — in watching and hearing the revelations in the argument between Paddy and Frank. They hear a graphic, animalized account of the act between Paddy and Fee, and between Fee and some unknown lover, who we later discover to be the half-caste politician. (Children often interpret parental coitus as a fight.) Ralph fears that Meggie will be psychologically damaged by witnessing the argument. The text doesn't follow this up with any reflexive comment. At a narrative level, in relation to the sequence of fantasy scenes involving Meggie that now begin to move inevitably towards the seduction scenario, the fight, as a stage in the destruction of her innocence, and perhaps an erosion of her father's authority is certainly important. Having sorted out one part of the question of the origin of babies, the next fantasy sequence is the one in which Ralph tells the super-innocent fourteen year old that she is menstruating, not dying of cancer. Meggie is presented as peculiarly ignorant of the facts of life for a girl who lives on a working farm. The author has to insert a long justifying didactic passage which claims, incredibly, that the sexual division of labour on the station, together with the patriarchal puritanism of Paddy Cleary has

---

24. Ibid., p. 119.

kept her wholly innocent.[25] Even this touching moment of instruction stops short of full knowledge. When Ralph asks Meggie whether she knows how women get pregnant her answer is wholly within the register of fantasy:

> 'You wish them.'
> 'Who told you that.'
> 'No one. I worked it out for myself.' she said.[26]

The next scene in the seduction sequence is the first unintended kiss between Ralph and the sixteen-year-old Meggie, which she half initiates. Ralph then leaves Drogheda for some time. In his absence Meggie has a conversation with her father in which it is clear that she believes that Ralph will, when she tells him to, leave the church and marry her. Paddy tries, without much luck to disabuse her of this illusion 'Father de Bricassart is a *priest* Meggie ... Once a man is a priest there can be no turning away ... a man who takes those vows knows beyond any doubt that once taken they can't be broken, ever. Father de Bricassart took them, and he'll never break them ... Now you know, Meggie, don't you? From this moment you have no excuse to daydream about Father de Bricassart.'[27] But Paddy is unconvincing as bearer of the reality principle, either to the reader or to Meggie.

After one more unsuccessful attempt to seduce Ralph in the hours after her father's death, Meggie is temporarily persuaded to give him up. She marries Luke, one of the seasonal sheep shearers, because he reminds her of Ralph physically. The substitution is an abominable failure, although it gives McCullough a rich opportunity to expand on the incompetent sexual style and homosocial tendencies of working-class Aussie males. Luke is like Ralph in that he can do without women, preferring the world of work and men, but he is unlike Ralph in that he has no nurturant qualities whatever. The text records in ironic, graphic detail that combines the style of a sixties sex manual with a feminist debunking of heterosexuality, Meggie's painful, incompetent deflowering. Luke sets her to work as a servant for

25. Ibid., p. 144.
26. Ibid., p. 151.
27. Ibid., p. 209.

a crippled farmer's wife and goes off with the boys to cut cane. The section of the book that records Luke and Meggie's brief marriage is convincingly realistic and down to earth in its local incident, but the extremity of Luke's punitive treatment of Meggie actually extends the fantasy register of the narrative. Ralph's accidental arrival during Meggie's difficult labour is the penultimate scene in the seduction sequence. He takes her through the menarche and childbirth, and will, on Matlock Island answer her wish at last and take her sexually.

Throughout the novel sexuality is discussed in at least two different languages; sex which is pleasurable for women is narrated in the generic style of historical romance, steamy suggestive and vague — 'It had been a body poem, a thing of arms and hands and skin and utter pleasure'[28] — while bad sex is exposed in the new pragmatic realism of post-war prose — 'with a great indrawn breath to keep her courage up she forced the penis in, teeth clenched.'[29] Ralph fucks Meggie in Barbara Cartland's best mode. In the process of losing his virginity he also forgoes his exalted notion of himself as above sexual difference. In sexual pleasure Meggie's femininity is confirmed. Meggie and Ralph conceive a male child, though Ralph's punishment is to be ignorant of this fact until after his son's death. Since this is a fantasy from the women's position, keeping men in ignorance of their paternity can be seen as one of their prerogatives. The question of origins is thus reopened for the next generation in the final seduction, but the question of identity, sexuality and difference is temporarily resolved for Ralph, Meggie and reader.

Narrative rationalization binds the fantasy scenarios together. No amount of tricky discursive justification really explains why Meggie should witness Frank and Paddy's quarrel, need to be told by a priest about menstruation, time her labour for Ralph's visit — and so on. Yet all these events are necessary to construct a complex fantasy, a series of scenarios in which the reader's position vis à vis Ralph and Meggie is constantly shifting. Until the sequence reaches its penultimate moment it is fair to say that the reader oscillates from the woman's position to the man's position — represented as poles of subjectivity rather than fixed, determinate identities. For it is wholly unclear that these subject

---

28. Ibid., p. 356.
29. Ibid., p. 317.

positions can be actually identified with the gendered characters Ralph and Meggie.

What, in text and context creates this reading effect, which is responsible in great part for the pleasure of the novel? *The Thorn Birds* is directed at a female audience, one that, by the late seventies had certainly been affected by debates around feminism if only in their most populist and watered-down form. Even through media representations of feminist discourse there had developed among women a more inquiring attitude towards traditional masculinity and femininity. The acceptable social content of daytime fantasies had shifted enough to allow the woman to be the sexual initiator, especially if, like Meggie she is also the model of femininity who only wants marriage and babies, content to stay out of modern, urban public space, down on the farm. Within the terms of the fantasy Meggie is allowed to be both active **and** feminine. With certain fundamental reservations about her social role *The Thorn Birds* offers the female reader a liberated derepressed version of the seduction fantasy, a written out, up front story of 'A daughter seduces a father.' in place of that old standard 'A father seduces a daughter.'

Most mass-market romance, as Modleski and others point out has stuck with the conservative androcentric version, counting on the third person narrative that looks down on the woman in the text to inscribe the active female as the knowing reader in the narrative 'a man seduces a woman.' Shifts in the public discourses about sexuality, specifically feminist discourse, permit the seduction fantasy to be reinscribed in a more radical way in popular fiction, allowing the narrative itself to express the terms of original fantasy from the place of the woman, while reassuring us through Meggie's character that such a fantasy, however transgressive in social terms is perfectly feminine. If the text stopped there it would still be disruptive, for if we put the relationship between femininity and transgression another way the fantasy sequence suggests also that in order to be perfectly feminine, a woman's desire must be wholly transgressive. But the role reversal of the seduction fantasy is only the first and simplest stage in the transformation of the seduction story.

More unexpected and eccentric is the way in which Ralph as the feminine man and virgin priest is mobilized within the fantasy. Critiques of traditional macho masculinity abound in the popular fictions of the seventies, especially perhaps in Holly-

wood film. Decentred masculinity can be represented through a
figure like Ralph whose maternal characteristics are balanced by
his public power. However Ralph's feminine side is also signified
by his great personal beauty, which he himself calls attention to
in the early scenes, and his prized virginity. As a beautiful and
pure object of desire he stands in the text in place of the woman,
often obscuring Meggie. As decentered man, Ralph displaces
Meggie as the object to be seduced. This blurring of masculine
and feminine positions is worked through all but the last seduction scene.

Meggie's passion is usually straightforwardly expressive;
Ralph's is held back by taboo so that his desire is accompanied
by shame, disgust and horror at his own wayward libido on
whose control he so prides himself. 'I can get it up. It's just that I
don't choose to.'[30] 'Spider's poison', 'snakes', 'ghastly drive' are
the phrases used to describe Ralph's illicit desire for Meggie. Yet
Ralph is at last moved by his love of her, and his suppressed
desire, to consummate the relationship; in the final scenario it is
Ralph who pursues and takes action restoring the initiatives of
sexual difference to their right order. The moment of absolute
transgression, when Ralph breaks his vows to the Church is later .
described by him as another kind of 'sacrament'. It is also the
moment when the even more transgressive definitions of sexual
difference that have been offered the reader are withdrawn:
incest makes real men and women of us all.

It is not simply plot and character that structure the text's
unstable inscriptions of sexual difference. The narrative strategy
and the language of the novel contribute centrally to this effect.
Third person narrative helps a lot. Although the novel starts out
with Meggie's early childhood traumas, setting her up as a figure
who endures loss and punishment at an early stage, her psyche
is always held at one remove; the authorial voice is adult and
knowing about her, its tone sympathetic and realistic but never
really intimate. Ralph's consciousness on the other hand,
especially where it touches on his feeling for Meggie is presented
consistently in lyric and philosophical terms. Long paragraphs
speculate on Meggie's attraction for the priest. 'Perhaps, had he
looked more deeply into himself, he might have seen that what
he felt for her was the curious result of time, and place and

---

30. Ibid., p. 166.

person ... she filled an empty space in his life which God could not ...'[31] Ralph 'redecorates' a room for Meggie at the presbytery in which she is installed as surrogate daughter. The text 'decorates' Ralph's feelings for her, offering us a running inner narrative on them, while Meggies's growing feeling for Ralph is rarely given such discursive space. The text gives us a 'natural' identification with Meggie because of her initial priority in the story and because she is the woman in the novel, but it offers us a seductive alternative identification with Ralph, as a more complex and expressive subjectivity. The oscillation between the realistic and lyric modes, the disruption of the terms of sexual difference is both titillating and vertiginous, making obvious what perhaps is always true in romance reading for women, that the reader identifies with both terms in the seduction scenario, but most of all with the process of seduction. In *The Thorn Birds* seduction sequence the term in which subjectivity is most profoundly inscribed is the verb: *seduces*. It is both disappointing and a relief when the scenario reverts to a more conventional set of positions:

> Go, *run*! Run, Meggie, get out of here with the scrap of pride he's left you! ...

> Before she could reach the veranda he caught her, the impetus of her flight spinning her round against him ...[32]

It is as if the act itself, so long deferred, textually speaking, so long the subject of daydream within the narrative, stabilizes the scandalous encounter in terms of socially-normative gendered activity and passivity.

There is a whole further generation of things to say about the rewriting of sexual difference in *The Thorn Birds*, but for the purposes of this argument it is perhaps enough to note that Meggie's 'liberated', 'bitchy', actress daughter makes, in the end a typically feminine match with a macho German financier into whose hands Ralph delivers the stewardship of the Cleary family estates. The novel ends in the moment of European modernity

---

31. Ibid., p. 105.
32. Ibid., p. 354.

with the union of Rainer and Justine. Twin 'stars' in public life, they also represent socially acceptable and highly polarized versions of late twentieth century masculinity and femininity in which tough public men are privately tender and ambitious, successful women are little girls at heart. There are fantasy elements in the 'European' part of the novel, but they are relatively superficial ones. And the seduction scenario between Rainer and Justine is definitely the right way round: 'A man seduces a woman.' Modernity turns out to be pretty old-fashioned after all.

The most daring interrogation of gendered subjectivity is located in the story of Meggie and Ralph and articulated through original fantasy. The English speaking sub-continent, New Zealand and Australia, before World War II, and especially its idealized rural locations, Drogheda and Matlock Island, stand in as the 'archaic' and 'primitive' setting for the origins of modern sexuality and difference. They work in this way *historically* for the Australian reader, just as the pre-Civil War American South does for the American reader, or early nineteenth century Yorkshire for the British reader. But for the 'foreign' reader — and *The Thorn Birds* is written with an international reading market in mind, the setting is doubly displaced and mytholigized through distance and history. It is as if, to paraphrase John Locke's famous colonial metaphor about America: 'In the beginning, all the world was down under.'

Myths of origin need actors as well as settings. *The Thorn Birds* does not revise biblical wisdom in this respect; transgression and sexuality are set in motion by Fee's adulterous, cross racial affair with the half-Maori Pakeha. And I must admit, dear reader, that I have been an unreliable narrator and have held back a crucial piece of information from the text so that it can round out my argument. When Fee and Meggie confess their transgressions to each other Fee lets slip an important piece of information. 'I have a trace of Maori blood in me, but Frank's father was half Maori. It showed in Frank because he got it from both of us. Oh, but I loved that man! Perhaps it was the call of our blood ... He was everything Paddy wasn't — cultured, sophisticated, very charming. I loved him to the point of madness ...'[33]

How does this 'trace' of 'Maori blood' — McCullough, like

---

33. Ibid., p. 421-422.

Freud chooses a racist definition of race — work to explain an heredity of transgression in the text? In the first place the inscription of sexual difference at any historical moment not only requires an 'original' myth of a primal scene, it frequently takes on a third term of social difference and prohibition, which acts as defense perhaps against the scandal of the child watching the scene of its own origins, or, in castration and seduction fantasy the scandal of sexual difference itself. In any case it is interesting that this social difference frequently takes in modern western myth both a racial and specular form, projecting and displacing sexual taboo and illicit desire into cultural taboo and hierarchy.

Racial and religious taboo serve, in *The Thorn Birds* to express the transgressive and asocial character of original fantasy, just as class, race and symbolic incest do in *Wuthering Heights*. Although the men in these texts may threaten social coherence by their 'hybrid' nature and their deceptive veneer of civilization, it often turns out that it is the women who love them whose 'savage' nature and original taint is most profoundly disruptive. It is Cathy, not Heathcliff who stands most absolutely outside the social, knocking at the window in vain. In these texts written by and for women, women nevertheless end up responsible for the scandalous origins of sexuality and difference. *The Thorn Birds* makes this point quite explicitly, adding Fee's own drop of 'primitivism' as a gratuitous racialist confirmation. These two anarchic women are contained in the narrative by their chosen role as mothers and matriarchs. Kept on the plantation, they are not allowed to affect the modern resolution of sexual difference and invade the public sphere. '... "where *do* we go wrong?"' Meggie asks Mum. '"In being born,"' Fee replies.[34]

The last half of the novel disappoints in terms of its normalization of sexual difference, rather like the last section of *Wuthering Heights*. But the really worrying elements of the European portions of the narrative reside in its overt politics. I have said very little about the novel's lengthy and interesting treatment of the Catholic church and priesthood, a treatment which was in dialogue, no doubt, with elements of the reformist debates within Catholicism in the seventies. But while the author takes a liberal Catholic line on the chastity of priests the rest of her views on the Church are anything but progressive. While acknowledg-

34. Ibid., p. 422.

ing its economic opportunism and political infighting the novel is largely uncritical of the Church's international influence. Indeed it openly defends the Vatican's record in relation to fascism. Certainly it is seen as correctly and steadfastly in opposition to revolution. When Meggie and Ralph's son Dane becomes the perfect priest he goes on holiday to Greece where his visit is shadowed by a threatening crowd who are 'milling' and 'chanting' in support of 'Pap-an-dreo'.

Although the story contains a rags to riches element, the origins and morality of wealth are never questioned. Rainer's rise to fortune and power endow him, in the novel, with wholly admirable and desirable qualities. With Ralph and Dane dead, he becomes the secular inheritor of the power that the Church held earlier in the narrative. Fantasies of wealth and power find a lot of scope in family saga, where they intersect with and support the original fantasies represented there. Like *Lace*, *Dallas* or *Dynasty*, *The Thorn Birds* masks the origin of wealth, naturalizing and valorizing it even as it exposes, and up to a certain point reflects upon, the nature of social myth and psychic fantasy about the origins of sexuality and sexual difference. It is this appropriation of fantasy, not fantasy itself that is implicitly dangerous.

Reading *The Thorn Birds* should warn us away from those half-baked notions embedded in certain concepts of 'postmodern' culture and 'post-feminism' that see the disruption of subjectivity and sexual difference as an act with a radical autonomy of its own, and a power to disrupt hierarchies beyond it.

The Thorn Birds is a powerful and ultimately reactionary read. In its unashamed right-wing bias the text assumes that its millions of women readers have become progressively reflective about sexuality, but remain conservative, uninterested and unreflective in their thinking about other political and social concerns. Indeed, going back to my initial analysis of the pleasure of reading *Gone With the Wind*, the reactionary political and social setting, secures, in some fashion, a privileged space where the most disruptive female fantasy can be 'safely' indulged.

If we ask why women read and watch so much popular romance, the answers seem on the one hand very mundane and banal. Still excluded in major ways from power if not labour in the public sphere where male fantasy takes on myriad discursive forms, romance narrative can constitute one of women's few entries to the public articulation and social exploration of psychic life. It seems wrong to suggest, as many studies of romance reading implicitly do, that fantasizing is a female speciality. On the contrary fantasy is, as Freud's work suggests, a crucial part of our constitution as human subjects. It is not either the contents of original fantasy, nor even necessarily the position from which we imagine them that can, or ought, to be stigmatized. Rather it is consciousness of the insistent nature of those fantasies for men and women and the historically specific forms of their elaboration that need to be opened up. Our priority ought to be an analysis of the progressive or reactionary politics to which fantasy can become bound in popular expression. Those narratives, which include of course issues of sexual difference, as well as race, class and the politics of power generally, can be rewritten.

> The Thorn Birds, *first published in hardcover in America in May 1977, has sold more copies than any other novel of the past ten years, and rights have been sold all over the world for more money than publishers have ever paid for a book before.*[35]

---

35. Inside cover blurb, *The Thorn Birds*.

7.

Pandora's Box: Subjectivity, Class and Sexuality in Socialist Feminist Criticism

Feminist criticism, as its name implies, is criticism with a Cause, engaged criticism. But the critical model presented to us so far is merely engaged to be married. It is about to contract what can only be a *mésalliance* with bourgeois modes of thought and the critical categories they inform. To be effective, feminist criticism cannot become simply bourgeois criticism in drag. It must be ideological and moral criticism; it must be revolutionary.

Lillian Robinson, 'Dwelling in Decencies' (1978)[1]

The 'Marriage' of marxism and feminism has been like the marriage of husband and wife depicted in English common law: marxism and feminism are one, and that is marxism ... we need a healthier marriage or we need a divorce.

Heidi Hartmann, 'The Unhappy Marriage of Marxism and Feminism (1981)[2]

1

In spite of the attraction of matrimonial metaphor, reports of feminist nuptials with either mild-mannered bourgeois criticism or macho mustachioed Marxism have been greatly exaggerated. Neither liberal feminist criticism decorously draped in traditional humanism, nor her red-ragged rebellious sister, socialist feminist criticism, has yet found a place within androcentric literary criticism, which wishes to embrace feminism through a legitimate

---

1. Lillian S. Robinson, 'Dwelling in Decencies: Radical Criticism and the Feminist Perspective', in *Sex, Class and Culture*, Bloomington, Indiana 1978, pp. 3-21.
2. Heidi Hartmann, 'The Unhappy Marriage of Marxism and Feminism: Towards a more Progressive Union', in *The Unhappy Marriage of Marxism and Feminism: A Debate on Class and Patriarchy*, London 1981, pp. 1-42.

public alliance. Nor can feminist criticism today be plausibly evoked as a young deb looking for protection or, even more problematically, as a male 'mole' in transvestite masquerade. Feminist criticism now marks out a broad area of literary studies, eclectic, original and provocative. Independent still, through a combination of choice and default, it has come of age without giving up its name. Yet Lillian Robinson's astute pessimistic prediction is worth remembering. With maturity, the most visible, well-defined and extensive tendency within feminist criticism has undoubtedly bought into the white, middle-class, heterosexist values of traditional literary criticism, and threatens to settle down on her own in its cultural suburbs. For, as I see it, the present danger is not that feminist criticism will enter an unequal dependent alliance with any of the varieties of male-centred criticism. It does not need to, for it has produced an all too persuasive autonomous analysis which is in many ways radical in its discussion of gender, but implicitly conservative in its assumptions about social hierarchy and female subjectivity, the Pandora's box for all feminist theory.

This reactionary effect must be interrogated and resisted from within feminism and in relation to the wider socialist feminist project. For, without the class and race perspectives that socialist feminist critics bring to the analysis both of literary texts and of their conditions of production, liberal feminist criticism, with its emphasis on the unified female subject, will unintentionally reproduce the ideological values of mass-market romance. In that fictional landscape the other structuring relations of society fade and disappear, leaving us with the naked drama of sexual difference as the only scenario that matters. Mass-market romance tends to represent sexual difference as natural and fixed — a constant, transhistorical femininity in libidinized struggle with an equally 'given' universal masculinity. Even where class difference divides lovers, it is there as narrative backdrop or minor stumbling-block to the inevitable heterosexual resolution. Without overstraining the comparison, a feminist literary critic-ism that privileges gender in isolation from other forms of social determination offers us a similarly partial reading of the role played by sexual difference in literary discourse, a reading bled dry of its most troubling and contradictory meanings.

The appropriation of modern critical theory — semiotic with an emphasis on the psychoanalytic — can be of great use in

arguing against concepts of natural, essential and unified identity: against a static femininity and masculinity. But these theories
about the production of meaning in culture must engage fully
with the effects of other systems of difference than the sexual, or
they too will produce no more than an anti-humanist avant-
garde version of romance. Masculinity and femininity do not
appear in cultural discourse, any more than they do in mental
life, as pure binary forms at play. They are always, already,
ordered and broken up through other social and cultural terms,
other categories of difference. Our fantasies of sexual transgression as much as our obedience to sexual regulation are expressed
through these structuring hierarchies. Class and race ideologies
are, conversely, steeped in and spoken through the language of
sexual differentiation. Class and race meanings are not metaphors for the sexual, or vice versa. It is better, though not exact,
to see them as reciprocally constituting each other through a
kind of narrative invocation, a set of associative terms in a chain
of meaning. To understand how gender and class — to take two
categories only — are articulated together transforms our analysis of each of them.

The literary text too often figures in feminist criticism as a
gripping spectacle in which sexual difference appears somewhat
abstracted from the muddy social world in which it is elsewhere
embedded. Yet novels, poetry and drama are, on the contrary,
peculiarly rich discourses in which the fused languages of class,
race and gender are both produced and re-presented through
the incorporation of other discourses. The focus of feminist analysis ought to be on that heterogeneity within the literary, on the
intimate relation there expressed between all the categories that
order social and psychic meaning. This does not imply an attention to content only, but also entails a consideration of the
linguistic processes of the text as they construct and position
subjectivity within these terms.

For without doubt literary texts do centre the individual as
object and subject of their discourse. Literature has been a traditional space for the exploration of gender relations and sexual
difference, and one in which women themselves have been
formidably present. The problem for socialist feminists is not the
focus on the individual that is special to the literary, but rather
the romantic theory of the subject so firmly entrenched within
the discourse. Humanist feminist criticism does not object to the

idea of an immanent, transcendent subject but only to the exclusion of women from those definitions which it takes as an accurate account of subjectivity rather than as an historically constructed ideology. The repair and reconstitution of female subjectivity through a rereading of literature becomes, therefore, a major part, often unacknowledged, of its critical project. Psychoanalytic and semiotically oriented feminist criticism has argued well against this aspect of feminist humanism, emphasizing the important structural relation between writing and sexuality in the construction of the subject. But both tendencies have been correctly criticized from a socialist feminist position for the neglect of class and race as factors in their analysis. If feminist criticism is to make a central contribution to the understanding of sexual difference, instead of serving as a conservative refuge from its more disturbing social and psychic implications, the inclusion of class and race must transform its terms and objectives.

II

The critique of feminist humanism needs more historical explication than it has so far received. Its sources are complex, and are rooted in that moment almost 200 years ago when modern feminism and Romantic cultural theory emerged as separate but linked responses to the transforming events of the French Revolution. In the heat and light of the revolutionary decade 1790-1800, social, political and aesthetic ideas already maturing underwent a kind of forced ripening. As the progressive British intelligentsia contemplated the immediate possibility of social change, their thoughts turned urgently to the present capacity of subjects to exercise republican freedoms — to rule themselves as well as each other if the corrupt structures of aristocratic privilege were to be suddenly razed. Both feminism as set out in its most influential text, Mary Wollstonecraft's *A Vindication of the Rights of Woman* (1792), and Romanticism as argued most forcefully in Wordsworth's introduction to *Lyrical Ballads* (1800) stood in intimate, dynamic and contradictory relationship to democratic politics. In all three discourses the social and psychic character of the individual was centred and elaborated. The public and private implications of sexual difference as well as of the imagination and its products were both strongly linked to the optimistic, speculative construction of a virtuous citizen subject for a brave new egalitarian world. Theories of reading and writing — Wollstonecraft's and Jane Austen's as well as those of male Romantic authors — were explicitly related to contemporary politics as expressed in debate by such figures as Tom Paine, Edmund Burke and William Godwin.

The new categories of independent subjectivity, however, were marked from the beginning by exclusions of gender, race and class. Jean-Jacques Rousseau, writing in the 1750s, specifically exempted women from his definition; Thomas Jefferson, some twenty years later, excluded Blacks. Far from being invisible ideological aspects of the new subject, these exclusions occasioned debate and polemic on both sides of the Atlantic. The autonomy of inner life, the dynamic psyche whose moral triumph was to be the foundation of republican government, was considered absolutely essential as an element of progressive political thought.

However, as the concept of the inner self and the moral psyche from the eighteenth century onwards was used to denigrate whole classes, races and genders, late nineteenth-century socialism began to de-emphasize the political importance of the psychic self, and redefine political morality and the adequate citizen subject in primarily social terms. Because of this shift in emphasis, a collective moralism has developed in socialist thought which, instead of criticizing the reactionary interpretation of psychic life, stigmatizes sensibility itself, interpreting excess of feeling as regressive, bourgeois and non-political.

Needless to say, this strand of socialist thought poses a problem for feminism, which has favoured three main strategies to deal with it. In the first, women's psychic life is seen as being essentially identical to men's, but distorted through vicious and systematic patriarchal inscription. In this view, which is effectively Wollenstonecraft's, social reform would prevent women from becoming regressively obsessed with sexuality and feeling. The second strategy wholly vindicates women's psyche, but sees it as quite separate from men's, often in direct opposition. This is frequently the terrain on which radical feminism defends female sexuality as independent and virtuous between women, but degrading in a heterosexual context. It is certainly a radical reworking of essentialist sexual ideology, shifting the ground from glib assertions of gender complementarity to the logic of separatism. The third strategy has been to refuse the issue's relevance altogether — to see any focus on psychic difference as itself an ideological one.

Instead of choosing any one of these options, socialist feminist criticism must come to grips with the relationship between female subjectivity and class identity. This project, even in its present early stages, poses major problems. While socialist feminists have been deeply concerned with the social construction of femininity and sexual difference, they have been uneasy about integrating social and political determinations with an analysis of the psychic ordering of gender. Within socialist feminism, a fierce and unresolved debate continues about the value of using psychoanalytic theory, because of the supposedly ahistorical character of its paradigms. For those who are hostile to psychoanalysis, the meaning of mental life, fantasy and desire — those obsessive themes of the novel and poetry for the last two centuries — seems particularly intractable to interpretation. They are reluctant to grant much autonomy to the psychic level, and often most attentive to feeling expressed in the work of non-bourgeois writers, which can more easily be read as political statement. Socialist feminism still finds unlocated, unsocialized psychic expression in women's writing hard to discuss in non-moralizing terms.

On the other hand, for liberal humanism, feminist versions included, the possibility of a unified self and an integrated consciousness that can transcend material circumstance is represented as the fulfilment of desire, the happy closure at the end of the story. The psychic fragmentation expressed through female characters in women's writing is seen as the most important sign of their sexual subordination, more interesting and ultimately more meaningful that their social oppression. As a result, the struggle for an integrated female subjectivity in nineteenth-century texts is never interrogated as ideology or fantasy, but seen as a demand that can actually be met, if not in 1848, then later.

In contrast, socialist feminist criticism tends to foreground the social and economic elements of the narrative and socialize what it can of its psychic portions. Women's anger and anguish, it is assumed, should be amenable to repair through social change. A positive emphasis on the psychic level is viewed as a valorization of the anarchic and regressive, a way of returning women to their subordinate ideological place within the dominant culture, as unreasoning social beings. Psychoanalytic theory, which is by and large morally neutral about the desires expressed by the psyche, is criticized as a confirmation and justification of them.

Thus semiotic or psychoanalytic perspectives have yet to be integrated with social, economic and political analysis. Critics tend to privilege one element or the other, even when they acknowledge the importance of both and the need to relate them. A comparison of two admirable recent essays on Charlotte Brontë's *Villette*, one by Mary Jacobus and the other by Judith Lowder Newton, both informed by socialist feminist concerns, can illustrate this difficulty.

Jacobus uses the psychoanalytic and linguistic theory of Jacques Lacan to explore the split representations of subjectivity that haunt *Villette*, and calls attention to its anti-realist gothic elements. She relates Brontë's feminized defence of the imagination, and the novel's unreliable narrator-heroine, to the tension between femininity and feminism that reaches back to the eighteenth-century debates of Rousseau and Wollstonecraft. Reading the ruptures and gaps of the text as a psychic narrative, she also places it historically in relationship to nineteenth-century social and political ideas. Yet the social meanings of *Villette* fade and all but disappear before 'the powerful presence of fantasy', which 'energizes *Villette* and satisfies that part of the reader which also desires constantly to reject reality for the sake of an obedient, controllable, narcissistically pleasurable image of self and its relation to the world'.[3] In Jacobus's interpretation, the psyche, desire and fantasy stand for repressed, largely positive elements of a forgotten feminism, while the social stands for a daytime world of Victorian social regulation. These social meanings are referred to rather than explored in the essay, a strategy that renders them both static and unproblematically unified. It is as if, in order to examine how *Villette* represents psychic reality, the dynamism of social discourses of gender and identity must be repressed, forming the text's new 'unconscious'.

Judith Lowder Newton's chapter on *Villette* in her impressive

---

3. Mary Jacobus, 'The Buried Letter: Feminism and Romanticism in *Villette*' in *Women Writing and Writing about Women*, Mary Jacobus ed., London 1979, p.51.

study of nineteenth-century British fiction, *Women, Power, and Subversion* (1981), is also concerned with conflicts between the novel's feminism and its evocation of female desire. [4] Her interpretation privileges the social meanings of the novel, its search for a possible *détente* between the dominant ideologies of bourgeois femininity and progressive definitions of female autonomy. For Newton, 'the internalized ideology of women's sphere' includes sexual and romantic longings — which for Jacobus are potentially radical and disruptive of mid-Victorian gender ideologies. The psychic level as Newton describes it is mainly the repository for the worst and most regressive elements of female subjectivity: longing for love, dependency, the material and emotional comfort of fixed class identity. These desires which have 'got inside' are predictably in conflict with the rebellious, autonomy-seeking feminist impulses, whose source is a rational understanding of class and gender subordination. Her reading centres on the realist text, locating meaning in its critique of class society and the constraints of bourgeois femininity.

The quotations and narrative elements cited and explored by Jacobus and Newton are so different that even a reader familiar with *Villette* may find it hard to believe that each critic is reading the same text. The psychic level exists in Newton's interpretation, to be sure, but as a negative discourse, the dead weight of ideology on the mind. For her, the words 'hidden', 'private' and 'longing' are stigmatized, just as they are celebrated by Jacobus. For both critics, female subjectivity is the site where the opposing forces of femininity and feminism clash by night, but they locate these elements in different parts of the text's divided selves. Neither Newton nor Jacobus argues for the utopian possibility of a unified subjectivity. But the *longing* to close the splits that characterize femininity — splits between reason and desire, autonomy and dependent security, psychic and social identity — is evident in the way each critic denies the opposing element.

---

4. Judith Lowder Newton, *Women, Power, and Subversion: Social Strategies in British Fiction 1778-1860*, Athens, Georgia 1981.

III

My comments on the difficulties of reading *Villette* from a materialist feminist stance are meant to suggest that there is more at issue in the polarization of social and psychic explanation than the problem of articulating two different forms of explanation. Moral and political questions specific to feminism are at stake as well. In order to understand why female subjectivity is so fraught with *Angst* and difficulty for feminism, we must go back to the first full discussion of the psychological expression of femininity, in Mary Wollstonecraft's *A Vindication of the Rights of Woman*. The briefest look will show that an interest in the psychic life of women as a crucial element in their subordination and liberation is not a modern, post-Freudian preoccupation. On the contrary, its long and fascinating history in 'left' feminist writing starts with Wollstonecraft, who set the terms for a debate that is still in progress. Her writing is central for socialist feminism today, because she based her interest in the emancipation of women as individuals in revolutionary politics.

Like so many eighteenth-century revolutionaries, she saw her own class, the rising bourgeoise, as the vanguard of the revolution, and it was to the women of her own class that she directed her arguments. Her explicit focus on the middle class, and her concentration on the nature of female subjectivity, speaks directly to the source of anxiety within socialist feminism today. For it is at the point when women are released from profound social and economic oppression into greater autonomy and potential political choice that their social and psychic expression becomes an issue, and their literary texts become sites of ambivalence In their pages, for the last 200 years and more, women characters seemingly more confined by social regulation than women readers today speak as desiring subjects. These texts express the politically 'retrograde' desires for comfort, dependence and love as well as more acceptable demands for autonomy and independence.

It is Mary Wollstonecraft who first offered women this fateful choice between the opposed and moralized bastions of reason and feeling, which continues to determine much feminist thinking. [5] The structures through which she developed her ideas,

---

5   Mary Wollstonecraft, *A Vindication of the Rights of Woman*, New York 1975.

however, were set for her by her mentor Jean-Jacques Rousseau, whose writing influenced the political and social perspectives of many eighteenth-century English radicals. His ideas were fundamental to her thinking about gender as well as about revolutionary politics. In 1792, that highly charged moment of romantic political optimism between the fall of the Bastille and the Terror when *A Vindication* was written, it must have seemed crucial that Rousseau's crippling judgement of female nature be refuted. How else could women freely and equally participate in the new world being made across the Channel? Rousseau's ideas about subjectivity were already immanent in Wollstonecraft's earlier book *Mary: A Fiction* (1788). Now she set out to challenge directly his offensive description of sexual difference which would leave women in post-revolutionary society exactly where they were in unreformed Britain, 'immured in their families, groping in the dark'.[6]

Rousseau had set the terms of the debate in his *Emile* (1762),[7] which describes the growth and education of the new man, progressive and bourgeois, who would be capable of exercising the republican freedoms of a reformed society. In Book V, Rousseau invents 'Sophie' as a mate for his eponymous hero, and here he outlines his theory of sexual asymmetry as it occurs in nature. In all human beings passion was natural and necessary, but in women it was not controlled by reason, an attribute of the male sex only. Women, therefore, 'must be subject all their lives to the most constant and severe restraint, which is that of decorum; it is therefore necessary to accustom them early to such confinement that it may not afterwards cost them too dear ... we should teach them above all things to lay a due restraint on themselves.'[8]

To justify this restraint, Rousseau allowed enormous symbolic power to the supposed anarchic, destructive force of untrammelled female desire. As objects of desire Rousseau made women alone responsible for male 'suffering'. If they were free agents of desire, there would be no end to the 'evils' they could cause. Therefore the family, and women's maternal role within it, were, he said, basic to the structure of the new society.

---

6. Ibid., p. 5.
7. Jean-Jacques Rousseau, *Emile*, London 1974.
8. Ibid., p. 332.

Betrayal of the family was thus as subversive as betrayal of the state; adultery in *Emile* is literally equated with treason. Furthermore, in Rousseau's regime of regulation and restraint for bourgeois women, their 'decorum' — the social expression of modesty — would act as an additional safeguard against unbridled, excessive male lust, should its natural guardian, reason, fail. In proscribing the free exercise of female desire, Rousseau disarms a supposed serious threat to the new political as well as social order. To read the fate of a class through the sexual behaviour of its women was not a new political strategy. What is modern in Rousseau's formulation is the harnessing of these sexual ideologies to the fate of a new progressive bourgeoisie, whose individual male members were endowed with radical, autonomous identity.

In many ways, Mary Wollstonecraft, writing thirty years after *Emile*, shared with many others the political vision of her master. Her immediate contemporary Thomas Paine thought Rousseau's work expressed 'a loveliness of sentiment in favour of liberty', and it is in the spirit of Rousseau's celebration of liberty that Wollstonecraft wrote *A Vindication*. Her strategy was to accept Rousseau's description of adult women as suffused with sensuality, but to ascribe this unhappy state of things to culture rather than nature. It was, she thought, the vicious and damaging result of Rousseau's punitive theories of sexual difference and female education when put into practice. Excessive sensuality was for Wollstonecraft, in 1792 at least, as dangerous if not more so than Rousseau had suggested, but she saw the damage and danger first of all to women themselves, whose potential and independence were initially stifled and broken by an apprenticeship to pleasure, which induced psychic and social dependency. Because Wollstonecraft saw pre-pubescent children in their natural state as mentally and emotionally unsexed as well as untainted by corrupting desire, she bitterly refuted Rousseau's description of innate infantile female sexuality. Rather, the debased femininity she describes is constructed through a set of social practices which by constant reinforcement become internalized parts of the self. Her description of this process is acute: 'Every thing they see or hear serves to fix impressions, call forth emotions, and associate ideas, that give a sexual character to the mind ... This cruel association of ideas, which every thing conspires to twist into all their habits of thinking, or, to speak with more precision of feeling, receives new force when they begin to act a little for themselves.'[9]

For Wollstonecraft, female desire was a contagion caught from the projection of male lust, an ensnaring and enslaving infection that made women into dependent and degenerate creatures, who nevertheless had the illusion that they acted independently. An education that changed women from potentially rational autonomous beings into 'insignificant objects of desire' was, moreover, rarely reversible. Once a corrupt subjectivity was constructed, only a most extraordinary individual could transform it, for 'so ductile is the understanding and yet so stubborn, that the association which depends on adventitious circumstances, during the period that the body takes to arrive at maturity, can seldom be disentangled by reason'.[10]

What is disturbingly peculiar to *A Vindication* is the undifferentiated and central place that sexuality as passion plays in the corruption and degradation of the female self. The overlapping Enlightenment and Romantic discourses on psychic economy all posed a major division between the rational and the irrational, between sense and sensibility. But they hold sensibility *in men* to be only in part an antisocial sexual drive. Lust for power and the propensity to physical violence were also, for men, negative components of all that lay on the other side of reason. Thus sensibility in men included a strong positive element too, for the power of the imagination depended on it, and in the 1790s the Romantic aesthetic and the political imagination were closely allied. Sexual passion controlled and mediated by reason, Wordsworth's 'emotion recollected in tranquility', could also be put to productive use in art — by men. The appropriate egalitarian subjects of Wordsworth's art were 'moral sentiments and animal sensations' as they appeared in everyday life.[11] No woman of the time could offer such an artistic manifesto. In women the irrational, the sensible, even the imaginative are all drenched in an overpowering and subordinating sexuality. And in Wollstonecraft's writing, especially in her last, unfinished novel *Maria, or the Wrongs of Woman* (1798), which is considerably

---

9. Wollstonecraft, p. 177.
10. Ibid., p. 116.
11. William Wordsworth and Samuel Taylor Coleridge,*Lyrical Ballads*, R.L. Brett and A.R. Jones eds., London 1971, p. 261.

less punitive about women's sexuality in general than *A Vindica-tion*, only maternal feeling survives as a positively realized element of the passionate side of the psyche. By defending women against Rousseau's denial of their reason, Wollstonecraft unwittingly assents to his negative, eroticized sketch of their emotional lives. At various points in *A Vindication* she interjects a wish that 'after some future revolution in time' women might be able to live out a less narcissistic and harmful sexuality. Until then they must demand an education whose central task is to cultivate their neglected 'understanding'.

It is interesting and somewhat tragic that Wollstonecraft's paradigm of women's psychic economy still profoundly shapes modern feminist consciousness. How often are the maternal, romantic-sexual and intellectual capacity of women presented by feminism as in competition for a fixed psychic space. Men seem to have a roomier and more accomodating psychic home, one which can, as Wordsworth and other Romantics insisted, situate all the varieties of passion and reason in creative tension. This gendered eighteenth-century psychic economy has been out of date for a long time, but its ideological inscription still shadows feminist attitudes towards the mental life of women.

The implications of eighteenth-century theories of subjectivity were important for early feminist ideas about women as readers and writers. In the final pages of *A Vindication*, decrying female sentimentality as one more effect of women's psychic degrada-tion, Wollstonecraft criticizes the sentimental fictions increasingly written by and for women, which were often their only education. 'Novels' encouraged in their mainly young, mainly female audience 'a romantic twist of the mind'. Readers would 'only be taught to look for happiness in love, refine on sensual feelings and adopt metaphysical notions respecting that passion'. At their very worst the 'stale tales' and 'meretricious scenes' would by degrees induce more than passive fantasy. The captive, addicted reader might, while the balance of her mind was disturbed by these erotic evocations, turn fiction into fact and 'plump into actual vice'.[12] A reciprocal relationship between the patriarchal socialization of women and the literature that supports and incites them to become 'rakes at heart' is developed in this passage. While Wollstonecraft adds that she would rather

---

12. Wollstonecraft, p. 183.

women read novels than nothing at all, she sets up a peculiarly gendered and sexualized interaction between women and the narrative imaginative text, one in which women become the ultimately receptive readers easily moved into amoral activity by the fictional representation of sexual intrigue.

The political resonance of these questions about reader response was, at the time, highly charged. An enormous expansion of literacy in general, and of the middle-class reading public in particular, swelled by literate women, made the act of reading in the last quarter of the eighteenth century an important practice through which the common sense and innate virtue of a society of antonomous subject-citizens could be reached and moulded. An uncensored press, cheap and available reading matter and a reading public free to engage with the flood of popular literature, from political broadsheets to sensational fiction, was part of the agenda and strategy of British republicanism. 'It is dangerous,' Tom Paine warned the government in the mid-1790s after his own writing had been politically censored, 'to tell a whole people that they shall not read.' Reading was a civil right that supported and illustrated the radical vision of personal independence. Political and sexual conservatives, Jane Austen and Hannah More, as well as the republican and feminist left, saw reading as an active, not a passive function of the self, a critical link between the psychic play of reason and passion and its social expression. New social categories of readers, women of all classes, skilled and unskilled working-class males, are described in this period by contemporaries. Depending on their political sympathies, observers saw these actively literate groups as an optimistic symptom of social and intellectual progress or a dire warning of imminent social decay and threatened rebellion.

Wollstonecraft saw sentiment and the sensual as reinforcing an already dominant, approved and enslaving sexual norm, which led women to choose a subordinate social and subjective place in culture. The damage done by 'vice' and 'adultery', to which sentimental fiction was an incitement, was a blow to women first and to society second. Slavish legitimate sexuality was almost as bad for women in Wollstonecraft's view as unlicensed behaviour. A more liberal regime for women was both the goal and the cure of sentimental and erotic malaise. In *A Vindication* women's subjection is repeatedly compared to all illegitimate hierarchies of power, but especially to existing aristocratic hegemony. At every possible point in her text, Wollstone-craft links the liberation of women from the sensual into the rational literally and symbolically to the egalitarian transforma-tion of the whole society.

'Passionlessness', as Nancy Cott has suggested, was a strategy adopted both by feminists and by social conservatives.[13] Through the assertion that women were not innately or excess-ively sexual, that on the contrary their 'feelings' were largely filial and maternal, the imputation of a degraded subjectivity could be resisted. This alternative psychic organization was represented as both strength and weakness in nineteenth-century debates about sexual difference. In these debates, which were conducted across a wide range of public discourses, the absence of an independent, self-generating female sexuality is used by some men and women to argue for women's right to participate equally in an undifferentiated public sphere. It is used by others to argue for the power and value of the separate sphere allotted to women. And it is used more nakedly to support cruder justifications of patriarchal right. The idea of passionlessness as either a natural or a cultural effect acquires no simple ascendancy in Victorian sexual ideology, even as applied to the ruling bourgeoisie.

As either conservative or radical sexual ideology, asexual femininity was a fragile, unstable concept. It was constructed through a permanently threatened transgression, which fictional narrative obsessively documented and punished. It is a gross historical error to infer from the regulatory sexual discourses in the novel the actual 'fate' of Victorian adulteresses, for novels operated through a set of highly punitive conventions in relation to female sexuality that almost certainly did not correspond to lived social relations. However, novels do call attention to the difficulty of fixing such a sexual ideology, precisely because they construct a world in which there is no alternative to it.

IV

One of the central weaknesses of humanist criticism is that it

---

13. Nancy F. Cott, 'Passionlessness: An Interpretation of Victorian Sexual Ideology, 1790-1850', *Signs*, vol. 2, no. 2, pp. 219-33.

accepts the idea advanced by classical realism that the function of literature is mimetic or realistic representation. The humanist critic identifies with the author's claim that the text represents reality, and acts as a sympathetic reader who will test the authenticity of the claim through the evidence of the text. The Marxist critic, on the other hand, assumes that author and text speak from a position within ideology — that claims about fictional truth and authenticity are, in themselves, to be understood in relation to a particular historical view of culture and art that evolved in the Romantic period. Semiotic and psychoanalytic theories of representation go even further in rejecting the possibility of authentic mimetic art. They see the literary text as a system of signs that constructs meaning rather than reflecting it, inscribing simultaneously the subjectivity of speaker and reader. Fiction by bourgeois women writers is spoken from the position of a class-specific femininity. It constructs us as readers in relation to that subjectivity through the linguistic strategies and processes of the text. It also takes us on a tour, so to speak, of a waxworks of other subjects-in-process — the characters of the text. These fictional characters are there as figures in a dream, as constituent structures of the narrative of the dreamer, not as correct reflections of the socially real.

It is hard for feminism to accept the implications of this virtual refusal of textual realism, if only because literature was one of the few public discourses in which women were allowed to speak themselves, where they were not the imaginary representations of men. None the less, the subjectivity of women of other classes and races and with different sexual orientations can never be 'objectively' or 'authentically' represented in literary texts by the white, heterosexual, middle-class woman writer, however sympathetically she invents or describes such women in her narrative. The nature of fiction and the eccentric relation of female subjectivity itself both to culture and to psychic identity, as understood from a psychoanalytic perspective, defeats that aim. We can, however, learn a great deal from women's writing about the cultural meanings produced from the splitting of women's subjectivity, especially her sexuality, into class and race categories. But before we say more about this way of reading women's writing we need a more precise working definition of 'class'.

Unlike subjectivity, 'class' has been a central category for socialist feminist criticism, but remains somewhat inert within it, if not within socialist feminist theory as a whole. Socialist critics hesitate to identify their own object of study, the literary text, as a central productive site of class meaning, because it seems too far away from 'real' economic and political determinations. The same worry, conversely, can induce a compensatory claim that *all* the material relations of class can be discovered within the discourse; indeed, that they are most fully represented there, because language is itself material. These positions, which I confess I have parodied a little, remain unresolved in current debate, although efforts at *détente* have been made. They indicate the uneasy relationship between the political and the literary in the Marxist critical project, an unease shared by socialist feminists too.

Among socialist historians in the last few years the understanding of the history of class has undergone vigorous reappraisal in response to debates about the changing composition and politics of the working class in modern capitalist societies. In a recent collection of essays, *The Languages of Class*, the British historian of the nineteenth century, Gareth Stedman Jones, proposes some radical approaches to that history which have an immediate relevance for the analysis of representation. First of all, Stedman Jones asks for a more informed and theoretical attention by historians to the linguistic construction of class. '"Class" is a word embedded in language and should be analysed in terms of its linguistic content,' he states. In the second place, 'class' as a concept needs to be unpacked, and its differential construction in discourse recognized and given a certain autonomy: 'because there are different languages of class, one should not proceed upon the assumption that "class" as an elementary counter of official social description, "class" as an effect of theoretical discourse about distribution or productive relations, "class" as the summary of a cluster of culturally signifying practices or "class" as a species of political or ideological self-definition, share a single reference point in anterior social reality.' [14]

This formulation helps to break down the oppressively unitary character of class as a concept. Through it class can be seen as defined in different terms at different levels of analysis.

---

14. Gareth Stedman Jones, *Languages of Class: Studies in English Working Class History 1832-1982*. Cambridge 1983, pp. 7-8.

However we still need to understand in more detail how class is experienced by class subjects. 'Anterior social reality' hangs slightly loose in Stedman-Jones' model. How does it exist, if it exists at all as a site where these conflicting and competing discourses meet? Class is lived, after all, as if it were a set of coherent social relations. Yet, at the same time there is a gap between what people think they are doing, and what they are actually doing, and it is important to think about what happens in that gap both in the everyday and at moments of crisis in class relations. Take, for example that most visible instance of working class protest, the strike. Most strikes do not set out to challenge capitalism, but rather to gain specific demands from employer and state. Yet strikes do disrupt the smooth running of capitalism at a macrocosmic level, and in consequence shift the terms in which capitalism is perceived for the striking community itself. Indeed the field of meaning of social and economic relations and, not incidentally of the subjectivity of strikers and owners is changed by a strike. Whether the strike is lost or won a partly new paradigm, though not necessarily a more radical one for the striking community, is constructed. This process is not marked by a simple progression from one position or one subjectivity to another. Rather it is characterized by an oscillation between moments of relative incoherence — the breaking-up of old political languages and positions — and moments when new formulations — often tentative and transitory — are being realised. Nor are these processes of transformation always or even mostly, willful, argued through, fully conscious realignments. Class is 'made' and 'lived' in both conscious and unconscious registers through a variety of languages and practices at any given point in history.

How can this pulling apart of the languages of class help socialist feminist critics to put class and gender, the social and the psychic together in a non-reductive way? First of all, these distinctions put a useful space between the economic overview of class — the Marxist or socialist analysis — and the actual rhetoric of class as it appears in a novel. The class language of a nineteenth-century novel is not only or even primarily characterized by reference to the material circumstances of the protagonists, though that may be part of its representation there. The language of class in the novel foregrounds the language of the self, the inner discourse of the subject *as* class language, framing that discourse through the dissonant chorus of class voices that it appropriates and invents. In the novel, class discourse *is* gendered discourse; the positions of 'Emile' and 'Sophie' are given dramatic form. Class is embodied in fiction in a way that it never is either in bourgeois economic discourse or in Marxist economic analysis. In those discourses of class, *gender* is mystified, presented in ideological form. In fiction, though difference may be presented through sexual ideologies, its immanent, crucial presence in the social relations of class, as well as its psychic effects, is strongly asserted. Fiction refuses the notion of a genderless class subjectivity, and resists any simple reduction of class meaning and class identity to productive forces. This refusal and resistance cannot be written off, or reduced to the humanist ideologies of transcendence that those fictions may also enunciate, for the presence of gendered subjectivity in nineteenth-century fiction is always 'in struggle' with the Romantic ideologies of unified identity.

Within socialist feminist cultural analysis it has been easier to describe the visual or linguistic fusion of class and gender meanings in representation than it has been to assess the role such fusion plays in the construction of either category. Let us assume that in these signifying practices class is powerfully defined through sexual difference, and vice versa, and that these representations are constitutive of certain class meanings, not merely a distorted or mendacious reflection of other languages. 'Class' needs to be read through an ensemble of these languages, often contradictory, as well as in terms of an economic overview. The overpowering presence of gender in some languages of class and its virtual absence in others needs to be related not to a single anterior definition of class reality, but to the heterogeneous and contradictory nature of that reality.

Literature is itself a heterogeneous discourse, which appropriates, contextualizes and comments on other 'languages' of class and gender. This process of intertextuality — the dialogic, as the Russian critic Bakhtin called it undermines the aspirations of the text towards a unifying definition.[15] The language of class in the nineteenth-century novel obsessively inscribes a class system whose divisions and boundaries are at once absolute and

---

15. M.M. Bakhtin, *The Dialogic Imagination: Four Essays*, Michael Holquist, ed., Austin, Texas 1981.

impregnable and in constant danger of dissolution. Often in these narratives it is a woman whose class identity is at risk or problematic; the woman and her sexuality are a condensed and displaced representation of the dangerous instabilities of class and gender indentity for both sexes. The loss and recuperation of female identity within the story — a favourite lost-and-found theme from *Mansfield Park* to *Tess* — provides an imaginary though temporary solution to the crisis of both femininity and class. Neither category — class or gender — was ever as stable as the ideologies that support them must continually insist. The many-layered, compacted representations of class and gender found in imaginative literature are not generic metaphors, peculiar to fiction, drama and poetry, though in them they are given great scope. They occur in many other nineteenth-century discourses — metonymic, associative tropes linked by incomparable similarities, through a threat to identity and status that inheres to both sets of hierarchies, both structures of difference.

The class subjectivity of women and their sexual identity thus became welded together in nineteenth-century discourses and took on new and sinister dimensions of meaning. Ruling groups had traditionally used the sexual and domestic virtue of their women as a way of valorizing their moral authority. By focusing on the issue and image of female sexual conduct, questions about the economic and political integrity of dominant groups could be displaced. When the citizen–subject became the crucial integer of political discourse and practice, this type of symbolization, which was always 'about' sexual difference as well as 'about' the political, took on new substantive, material meaning. The moral autonomy of individuals and the moral behaviour of social groups now converged in a political practice and theory — liberal, constitutional and legitimated through an expanding franchise — in which the individual voter was the common denominator of the political. Women, as we have seen, were explicitly excluded from these political practices, but, as we have also seen, attempts to naturalize that exclusion were never wholly successful. Feminism inserted itself into the debate just at the point where theories of innate difference attempted to deny women access to a full political identity. The debate about women's mental life signalled, as I have suggested, a more general anxiety about non-rational, unsocial behaviour. Female subjectivity, or its synecdochic reference, female sexuality, became the displaced and condensed site for the general anxiety about individual behaviour that republican and liberal political philosophy stirred up. It is not too surprising that the morality of the class as a whole was better represented by those who exercised the least power within it, or that the punishment for female sexual transgression was fictionally represented as the *immediate* loss of social status.

The ways in which class is lived by men and women, like the ways in which sexual difference is lived, are only partly open to voluntary, self-conscious political negotiation. The unconscious processes that construct subjective identity are also the structures through which class is lived and understood, through which political subjection and rebellion are organized. Arguing for the usefulness of psychoanalysis in historical analysis, Sally Alexander emphasizes that its theories do not imply a universal human nature. Rather, 'Subjectivity in this account is neither universal nor ahistorical. First structured through relations of absence and loss, pleasure and unpleasure, difference and division, these are simultaneous with the social naming and placing among kin, community, school, class which are always historically specific.'[16]

Literary texts give these simultaneous inscriptions narrative form, pointing towards and opening up the fragmentary nature of social and psychic identity, drawing out the ways in which social meaning is psychically represented. It is this symbolic shaping of class that we should examine in fiction. Literary texts tell us more about the intersection of class and gender than we can learn from duly noting the material circumstances and social constraints of characters and authors.

However mimetic or realistic the aspirations of fiction, it always tells us less about the purely social rituals of a class society organized around the sexual division of labour than about the powerful symbolic force of class and gender in ordering our social and political imagination. The doubled inscription of sexual and social difference is the most common, characteristic trope of nineteenth-century fictions. In these texts, the difference between women is at least as important an element as the difference between the sexes, as a way of representing both class and

16. Sally Alexander, 'Women, Class and Sexual Difference', *History Workshop Journal*, 17, pp. 125-49.

gender. This salient fact often goes unnoticed in the emphasis of bourgeois criticism on male/female division and opposition. In turn, this emphasis on heterosexual antagonisms and resolutions effaces the punitive construction of alternative femininities in women's writing. If texts by women reveal a 'hidden' sympathy between women, as radical feminist critics often assert, they equally express positive femininity through hostile and denigrating representations of women. Imperiled bourgeois femininity takes meaning in relation to other female identities, and to the feminized identities of other social groups that the novel constructs and dialogizes. The unfavourable symbiosis of reason and passion ascribed to women is also used to charcterize both men and women in the labouring classes and in other races and cultures. The line between the primitive and the degraded feminine is a thin one, habitually elided in dominant discourse and practically used to limit the civil and political rights of all three subordinated categories: Blacks, women and the working class.

Through that chain of colonial associations, whole cultures became 'feminized', 'blackened' and 'impoverished' — each denigrating construction implying and invoking the others. 'True womanhood' had to be protected from this threatened linguistic contamination, not only from the debased subjectivity and dangerous sexuality of the lower-class prostitute, but from all other similarly inscribed subordinate subjectivities. The difference between men and women in the ruling class had to be written so that a slippage into categories reserved for lesser humanities could be averted. These fragmented definitions of female subjectivity were not only a mode through which the moral virtue of the ruling class was represented in the sexual character of its women; they also shaped, and were shaped by, the ways in which women of the middle and upper classes understood and represented their own being. It led them towards projecting and displacing on to women of lower social standing and women of colour, as well as on to the 'traditionally' corrupt aristocracy, all that was deemed vicious and regressive in women as a sex.

It is deeply troubling to find these projected and displaced representations in the writing of sexual and social radicals, and in the work of feminists from Wollstonecraft to Woolf, as well as in conservative sexual and social discourses. They are especially marked in those texts and writers who accept in whole or in part the description of mental life and libidinal economy of the Enlightenment and the moral value attached to it. In *A Vindication*, working-class women are quite unselfconsciously constructed as prostitutes and dirty-minded servants corrupting bourgeois innocence. Turn the page over and you will also find them positioned in a more radical sense as the most brutalized victims of aristocratic and patriarchal despotism. Note the bestial descriptions of the female poor in Elizabeth Barrett Browning's *Aurora Leigh*. Remember the unhappy, ambivalent and contradictory relationship to black subjectivity, male and female, of many mid-nineteenth-century American feminists and abolitionists. Most distressing of all, because nearer to us in time, think about the contrast between Woolf's public polemical support of working-class women and the contempt with which the feelings and interests of her female servants are treated in her diaries, where they exist as lesser beings. These representations are neither natural nor inevitable. They are the historic effects of determinate social divisions and ideologies worked through psychic structures, worked into sexual and social identity. If they are understood they can be changed.

In Ann Radcliffe's *Mysteries of Udolpho*, one of the most popular of the Enlightenment gothic novels of the 1790s, the heroine, Emily, flees from the sinister importunities of her titled foreign host. The scene is rural Italy, as far away as possible from genteel British society. Emily's flight from the castle is precipitous, and in her terror and haste she forgets her hat. Within the world of the text, Emily's bare head threatens her identity as pure woman, as surely as do the violent, lascivious attentions of her pursuer. Both the narrative and her flight are interrupted while Emily restores her identity by purchasing 'a little straw hat' from a peasant girl. A woman without a hat was, in specular terms, a whore; the contemporary readership understood the necessary pause in the story. They understood too that the hat, passed from peasant to lady, securing the class and sexual status of the latter, was not only a fragment of domestic realism set against gothic fantasy. Hat and flight are part of a perfectly coherent psychic narrative in which aristocratic seducer, innocent bourgeois victim, peasant girl and straw hat play out the linked meanings of class and sexuality.[17]

---

17. Ann Radcliffe, *The Mysteries of Udolpho*, London 1966.

Stories of seduction and betrayal, of orphaned, impoverished heroines of uncertain class origin, provided a narrative structure through which the instabilities of class and gender categories were both stabilized and undermined. Across the body and mind of 'woman' as sign, through her multiple representations, bourgeois anxiety about identity is traced and retraced. A favourite plot, of which *Jane Eyre* is now the best-known example, sets the genteel heroine at sexual risk as semi-servant in a grand patriarchal household. This narrative theme allowed the crisis of middle-class femininity to be mapped on to the structural sexual vulnerability of all working-class servants in bourgeois employment. Such dramas were full of condensed meanings in excess of the representation of sexuality and sexual difference. A doubled scenario, in which the ideological and material difference between working-class and bourgeois women is blurred through condensation, it was popular as a plot for melodrama with both 'genteel' and 'vulgar' audiences.

We do not know very much so far about how that fictional narrative of threatened femininity was understood by working-class women, although it appeared in the cheap fiction written for servant girls as well as in popular theatre. Nineteenth-century bourgeois novels like *Jane Eyre* tell us almost nothing about the self-defined subjectivity of the poor, male or female. For, although they are rich sources for the construction of dominant definitions *of* the inner lives of the working classes, they cannot tell us anything about how even these ideological inscriptions were lived *by* them. For an analysis of the subjectivity of working-class women we need to turn to non-literary sources, to the discourses in which they themselves spoke. That analysis lies outside the project of this paper but is, of course, related to it.

I want to end this chapter with an example of the kind of interpretative integration that I have been demanding of feminist critics. No text has proved more productive of meaning from the critic's point of view than Charlotte Brontë's *Jane Eyre*. I have referred to the condensation of class meanings through the characterization and narrative of its heroine, but now I want to turn to that disturbing didactic moment in volume 1, chapter 12, which immediately precedes the entry of Rochester into the text. It is a passage marked by Virginia Woolf in *A Room of One's Own*, where it is used to illustrate the negative effect of anger and inequality on the female imagination. Prefaced defensively —

'Anybody may blame me who likes' — it is a passage about need, demand and desire that exceed social possibility and challenge social prejudice. In Jane's soliloquy, inspired by a view reached through raising the 'trap-door of the attic', the Romantic aesthetic is reasserted for women, together with a passionate refusal of the terms of feminine difference. Moved by a 'restlessness' in her 'nature' that 'agitated me to pain sometimes', Jane paces the top floor of Thornfield and allows her 'mind's eye to dwell on whatever bright visions rose before it': 'to let my heart be heaved by the exultant movement which, while it swelled it in trouble, expanded it with life; and, best of all, to open my inward ear to a tale that was never ended — a tale my imagination created, and narrated continuously; quickened with all of incident, life, fire, feeling, that I desired and had not in my actual existence.'[18]

This reverie is only partly quoted by Woolf, who omits the 'visionary' section, moving straight from 'pain . . .' to the paragraph most familiar to us through her citation of it:

> It is in vain to say that human beings ought to be satisfied with tranquillity; they must have action; and they will make it if they cannot find it. Millions are condemned to a stiller doom than mine, and millions are in silent revolt against their lot. Nobody knows how many rebellions besides political rebellions ferment in the masses of life which people earth. Women are supposed to be very calm generally: but women feel just as men feel; they need exercise for their faculties, and a field for their efforts as much as their brothers do; they suffer from too rigid a restraint, too absolute a stagnation, precisely as men would suffer; and it is narrow-minded in their more privileged fellow-creatures to say that they ought to confine themselves to making puddings and knitting stockings, to playing on piano and embroidering bags. It is thoughtless to condemn them, or laugh at them, if they seek to do more or learn more than custom has pronounced necessary for their sex.
>   When thus alone I not unfrequently heard Grace Poole's laugh . . .[19]

This shift from feminist polemic to the laugh of Grace Poole is the 'jerk', the 'awkward break' of 'continuity' that Woolf

---

18. Charlotte Brontë, *Jane Eyre*, Margaret Smith ed., London 1976, p. 110.
19. Ibid., p. 110-11.

criticizes. 'The writer of such a flawed passage will never get her genius expressed whole and entire. Her books will be deformed and twisted. She will write in a rage where she should write calmly. She will write foolishly where she should write wisely. She will write of herself when she should write of her characters. She is at war with her lot. How could she help but die young, cramped and thwarted?'[20]

It is a devastating, controlled, yet somehow uncontrolled indictment. What elements in this digression, hardly a formal innovation in nineteenth-century fiction, can have prompted Woolf to such excess? Elaine Showalter analyses this passage and others as part of Woolf's 'flight into androgyny', that aesthetic chamber where masculine and feminine minds meet and marry. Showalter's analysis focuses on Woolf's aesthetic as an effect of her inability to come to terms with her sexuality, with sexual difference itself. Showalter's analysis is persuasive in individual terms, but it does not deal with all of the questions thrown up by Brontë's challenge and Woolf's violent response to it. In the sentences that Woolf omits in her own citation, Brontë insists that even the confined and restless state could produce 'many and glowing' visions. Art, the passage maintains, can be produced through the endless narration of the self, through the mixed incoherence of subjectivity spoken from subordinate and rebellious positions within culture. It was this aesthetic that Woolf as critic explicitly rejected.

However, the passage deals with more than sexual difference. In the references to 'human beings' and to unspecified 'millions', Brontë deliberately and defiantly associates political and sexual rebellion even as she distinguishes between them. In the passage the generic status of 'men' is made truly trans-class and trans-cultural when linked to 'masses', 'millions' and 'human beings', those larger inclusive terms. In 1847, on the eve of the second great wave of modern revolution, it was a dangerous rhetoric to use.

Its meaningful associations were quickly recognized by contemporary reviewers, who deplored the contiguous relationship between revolution and feminism. Lady Eastlake's comments in the *Quarterly Review* of 1849 are those most often quoted: 'We do not hesitate to say, that the tone of mind and

---

20. Virginia Woolf, *A Room of One's Own*, Harmondsworth 1973, p. 70.

thought which has overthrown authority and violated every code human and divine abroad, and fostered chartism and rebellion at home is the same which has also written *Jane Eyre.*'

Yet Charlotte Brontë was no political radical. How is it then that she is pulled towards the positive linking of class rebellion and women's revolt in this passage, as she will be again in *Shirley*? Perhaps my earlier example of the process through which class meaning is transformed for class subjects during a strike is helpful here. For this passage does not mark out a moment of conscious reformulation of Bronte's class politics. Rather it is a significant moment of incoherence, where the congruence between the subordination of women and the radical view of class oppression becomes, for a few sentences, irresistible. It is a tentative, partial movement in spite of its defiant rhetoric, a movement which threatens to break up the more general, self-conscious class politics of the text. And it brings with it, inexorably, its own narrative reaction which attempts, with some success, to warn us quite literally that the association of feminism and class struggle leads to madness. For Jane's vision is checked, instantly, by the mad mocking female laughter, and turned from its course a few pages later by the introduction of Rochester into the narrative.

For Woolf, Jane's soliloquy spoils the continuity of the narrative with its 'anger and rebellion'. Woolf turns away, refuses to comprehend the logical sequence of the narration at the symbolic level of the novel.

Jane's revolutionary manifesto of the subject, which has its own slightly manic register, invokes that sliding negative signification of women that we have described. At this point in the story the 'low, slow ha' ha!' and the 'eccentric murmurs' that 'thrilled' Jane are ascribed to Grace Poole, the hard-featured servant. But Grace is only the laugh's minder, and the laugh later becomes correctly ascribed to Rochester's insane wife, Bertha Mason. The uncertain source of the laughter, the narrator's inability to predict its recurrence — 'There were days when she was quite silent; but there were others when I could not account for the sounds she made' — both mark out the 'sounds' as the dark side of Romantic female subjectivity.[21]

Retroactively, in the narratives the laughter becomes a threat

---

21. Bronte, p. 111.

to all that Jane had desired and demanded in her roof-top reverie. Mad servant, mad mistress, foreigner, nymphomaniac, syphilitic, half-breed, aristocrat, Bertha turns violently on keeper, brother, husband and, finally, rival. She and her noises become the condensed and displaced site of unreason and anarchy as it is metonymically figured through dangerous femininity in all its class, race and cultural projections. Bertha must be killed off, narratively speaking, so that a moral, Protestant femininity, licensed sexuality and a qualified, socialized feminism may survive. Yet the text cannot close off or recuperate that moment of radical association between political rebellion and gender rebellion, cannot shut down the possibility of a positive alliance between reason, passion and feminism. Nor can it disperse the terror that speaking those connections immediately stirs up — for Woolf in any case.

Woolf was at her most vehement and most contradictory about these issues, which brought together for her, as for many other feminists before and after, a number of deeply connected anxieties about subjectivity, class, sexuality and culture, Over and over again in her critical writing, Woolf tries to find ways of placing the questions inside an aesthetic that disallows anger, unreason and passion as productive emotions. Like Wollstonecraft before her, she cannot quite shake off the moral and libidinal economies of the Enlightenment. In 'Women and Fiction' (1929) she frames the question another way:

'In *Middlemarch* and in *Jane Eyre* we are conscious not merely of the writer's character, as we are conscious of the character of Charles Dickens, but we are conscious of a woman's presence — of someone resenting the treatment of her sex and pleading for its rights. This brings into women's writing an element which is entirely absent from a man's, unless, indeed, he happens to be a working man, a Negro, or one who for some other reason is conscious of disability. It introduces a distortion and is frequently the cause of weakness. The desire to plead some personal cause or to make a character the mouthpiece of personal discontent or grievance always has a distressing effect, as if the spot at which the reader's attention is directed were suddenly two-fold instead of single.[22]

---

22. Virginia Woolf, 'Women and Fiction', in *Women and Writing*, Michèle Barrett, ed., London 1979, p. 47.

Note how the plea for a sex, a class, a race becomes reduced to individual, personal grievance, how subordinate position in a group becomes immediately pathologized as private disability, weakness. Note too how 'man' in this passage loses its universal connotation, so that it only refers normatively to men of the ruling class. In this passage, as in *Jane Eyre*, degraded subjectivities are metonymically evolved — 'disability', 'distortion' — and degradation is expressed as an effect of subordination, not its rationale nor its cause. But the result is still a negative one. For the power to resist through fictional language, the language of sociality and self; the power to move and enlighten, rather than blur and distress through the double focus, is denied. Instead, Woolf announces the death of the feminist text, by proclaiming, somewhat prematurely, the triumph of feminism. 'The women writer is no longer bitter. She is no longer angry. She is no longer pleading and protesting as she writes. ... She will be able to concentrate upon her vision without distraction from outside.'[23] This too is a cry from the roof-tops of a desire still unmet by social and psychic experience.

Although the meanings attached to race, class and sexuality have undergone fundamental shifts from Wollstonecraft's (and Woolf's) time to our own, we do not live in a post-class society any more than a post-feminist one. Our identities are still constructed through social hierarchy and cultural differentiation, as well as through those processes of division and fragmentation described in psychoanalytic theory. The identities arrived at through these structures will always be precarious and unstable, though *how* they will be so in the future we do not know. For the moment, women still have a problematic place in both social and psychic representation. The problem for women of woman-assign has made the self-definition of women a resonant issue within feminism. It has also determined the restless inability of feminism to settle for humanist definitions of the subject, or for materialism's relegation of the problem to determinations of class only. I have emphasized in this chapter some of the more negative ways in which the Enlightenment and Romantic paradigms of subjectivity gave hostages to the making of subordinate identities, of which femininity is the structuring instance. Although psychoanalytic theories of the construction of

---

23. Ibid., p. 48.

gendered subjectivity stress difficulty, antagonism and contradiction as necessary parts of the production of identity, the concept of the unconscious and the pyschoanalytic view of sexuality dissolve in great part the binary divide between reason and passion that dominates earlier concepts of subjectivity. They break down as well the moralism attached to those libidinal and psychic economies. Seen from this perspective, 'individualism' has a different and more contentious history within feminism than it does in androcentric debates.

That is the history we must uncover and consider, in both its positive and its negative effects, so that we can argue convincingly for a feminist rehabilitation of the female psyche in non-moralized terms. Perhaps we can come to see it as neither sexual outlaw, social bigot nor dark hiding-place for treasonable regressive femininity waiting to stab progressive feminism in the back. We must redefine the psyche as a structure, not as a content. To do so is not to move away from a feminist politics that takes race and class into account, but to move towards a fuller understanding of how social divisions and the inscription of gender are mutually secured and given meaning. Through that analysis we can work towards change.

8.

Keeping the Color in
The Color Purple

Teaching literature from a Marxist and a feminist perspective means fighting a continual rearguard action against those dominant forms of cultural interpretation that find and prefer universal, transhistorical and essentialist meanings in the literary text, rendering them all, in the end, expressive of a single 'human condition'. No texts are more vulnerable to that kind of reading than foreign texts, perhaps especially those foreign texts deceptively written in our 'own' language. Unless we are actually specialists in the area from which these foreign anglophone literatures come, and teaching them in that context, our more than usually fragmented and partial knowledge of the history, politics and culture in which they were produced and originally read, frequently leads us into teaching and thinking about these texts through an unintentionally imperialist lense, conflating their progressive politics with our own agendas, interpreting their versions of humanism through the historical evolution of our own.

Moreover texts that address racial difference express an alterity that cannot be subsumed in the 'otherness' of the national culture from which they also speak. These texts evoke and interrogate an historical continuum of attitudes towards racial difference within the West upon which normative concepts of white, male bourgeois subjectivity is constructed. They produce in the middle-class reader today a level of anxiety about the disruption of those unconsciously held positions that can,

177

ironically, move the unreflective reader even further towards a universal reading that suppresses these disturbing effects. More often than not, texts by Black American authors will be read by white Britons with a minimal attention to their cultural specificity and an active suppression of the challenge they pose to a liberal understanding of racial difference. We need to integrate these texts into current debates on race and culture but our appropriative reading must be a political one, connecting rather than blurring distinctions between cultures. In order for it to be more than another ideological bleaching of the text into an all-purpose human garment, it must come out of a specific understanding of the other cultural moment and histories in which it was written, published and read. As an American expatriate who has taught American literature and history in a British university for fifteen of my twenty years of voluntary exile, I have felt with particular acuteness the problems of 'translating' American texts for English readers. My own education in English literature in the United States has been an object lesson in the dangers of assuming that one can understand the literature of another society through the peculiarly selective images that represent it abroad. We were taught, in my posh women's college during the heyday of the New Criticism, the romantics without revolution and the entire nineteenth century fictional canon without class. Teaching American literature to British students highlights the distortion and absences in the everyday transmission of American history and culture here. Some omissions are worse than others. English students come to the course with a reasonable working sketch of the history of American imperialism abroad and an almost complete ignorance of the history of race in America. Teaching these issues through nineteenth and twentieth century fiction and poetry by both white and Black authors has involved a formidable amount of historical filling-in, so that even the simplest references can be glossed. Moreover such an endeavour must have fairly modest ambitions, for one is not only dealing with gaps in knowledge about another continent but with a skewed understanding and fundamental ignorance of British history. British students still live in the choking legacies of the class society of the nineteenth century and are therefore quite quick at interpreting its historical meanings once they are given some analytic help and some collateral reading. But the historical complicity of Imperial Britain with racial subordination is played down in their education, and in spite of the media attention to the 'problem' of racism in Britain in recent years they themselves (unless they are Black) do not think of racism as a complex issue. Insofar as they mostly share and have shared a progressive outlook on the world they come to these nineteenth and twentieth century fictions, from James Fenimore Cooper's *The Last of the Mohicans* through Alice Walker's *The Color Purple* with that liberal moral complacency that begins from the individual belief that they themselves are not racist, and that in any case eradicating racism is a matter of changing individual prejudice. Changing this perspective means getting them to reassess racism as a structural and historical effect, one which occurs at economic, political and ideological levels, and, most important of all, has been resisted through the struggle of Blacks themselves at every one of those levels over a very long period of time. This task itself has changed over time in relation to shifts in Black politics and consciousness in the United States and political events in the U.K.

When I taught these issues and texts in the late sixties and early seventies students had a ready empathy with young Black revolutionaries or with popular leaders like Martin Luther King as symbolic comrades in what then seemed to them like an international movement against a uniform oppression. However debates *within* the Black social and political movements in the fifties and sixties were hard to 'get across'; no equivalence with class or even with anti-colonial struggles really conveys the specificity of those differences, or the traumatic nature of even the most peaceful and 'reformist' assault on segregation in the South and institutional racism in the north. The year in the United States that most British students of American Studies spend within the racism of that society, engaging with its institutions, seeing how it is presented in the American media, talking with Black and white Americans about it does more for their conceptual understanding of the issues, and their ability to read fictions about them than any academic course. For in spite of the intransigence of racism in the United States, and the generally liberal political language in which progressive debates about it are often couched, the legacy of twenty years of activism, struggle and change, of consistent intervention and argument by and between Americans of colour has meant that awareness of the complexity of racism and of the problems endemic in the

fight against it is infinitely richer and more nuanced in the
United States. However, much of that debate and history is available in this country, even if, for different reasons both the right
and the left are likely to be condescending towards it. The white
left's ignorance of the history and debate over race in America is
particularly dismaying and must necessarily dishearten Black
Britons who engage in dialogue with it, or who try to work from
within its British political structures. The discussion within the
Labour Party about Black sections is a case in point. Whatever
the appropriateness of Black sections as a strategy, and there
may be many good reasons why the U.S. example might not
apply, the efficacy of Black caucusses and other forms of autonomous Black organisation inside and outside the party structures in getting more Black citizens involved in the political
process and elected to office needs to be considered in depth,
before they are rejected in the simple-minded ahistorical fashion
that the quoted position of Kinnock implies. Similarly the
sudden flood of Black women's writing that is appearing on the
market through the various feminist presses has been, unsur-
prisingly, heralded as a cultural phenomenon that owes its
source and energy to American feminism. The post-war Black
cultural renaissance in the United States, triggered by the civil
rights movement and Black Power activism has been forgotten —
if it ever was fully known there — though it in itself provided
the model and pioneered the strategies of cultural politics
appropriated to such advantage by the women's movement in
America.

In particular it is forgotten that Black writing in the United
States developed a community of writers, and a tradition of
Black poetry, fiction, drama and political polemic over several
generations. This writing in turn constructed and addressed an
audience in which there was an implicit hierarchy of preferred
readers. If these writers spoke to both Black and white Americans their 'ideal' reader was always Black.

Anyone who has read the literature of the Harlem Renaissance in the twenties and thirties and the plays, poetry, fiction
and polemic of Black men writing in the fifties cannot fail to see
the women writers who have come to prominence in the seventies and eighties as engaged in fierce intimate dialogue with that
writing and its androcentric politics. Moreover the tradition of
older Black women writers, from the nineteenth century

onwards — Frances Ellen Watkins Harper, through Zora Neale Hurston, Ann Petry and Gwendolyn Brooks has been, as Alice Walker among others has insisted, a powerful influence on a younger generation of Black women writers. Some older Black women poets and novelists have been writing throughout what we might crudely designate the ascendent male and ascendent female moments in Black American cultural expression since the war. (Although shifts in the public prominence of one gender of writer over another must be seen in part as marketing devices to do with the political economy of publishing.)

Much of the poetry of Gwendolyn Brooks, the early fiction of Paule Marshall, recently republished, was written prior to the emergence of the women's movement in the late sixties and early seventies. It nevertheless is deeply conscious of the 'triple oppression' of Black women — the axis of race, class and gender, through which their subordination and struggle is lived. The difference between that writing and the work of black women writers in the seventies and eighties is that these later texts are self consciously part of an ongoing and painful debate between black and white feminists about the ways in which American feminism, past and present, has been deeply complicit with racism. It is no small task, taking on your brothers and your would–be sisters as well as the dominant culture in its most reactionary embodiment. The writing of Toni Morrison, Ntsozake Shange, Sonia Sanchez, Carolyn Rodgers, Toni Cade Bambara, Audre Lorde, Paule Marshall, Nikki Giovanni, Lucille Clifton and Alice Walker (among many others) speaks into and out of contemporary debates with complex and contradictory histories. Moreover many, even most, of these novelists have not chosen updated versions of classical realist forms for their writing, so that even if one was lazy enough to rely on the fictional text to provide its own historical context, these new fictions refuse that project.[1] These novels dialogize the

---

1. For a provocative discussion of the realtion of genre and form in Black writing see the seminal essay by Richard Wright, 'The Literature of the Negro in the United States', *White Man Listen*, Garden City 1964, pp. 69-106. Wright, in 1957 saw the postwar Black writing as characterized by a sharp loss of lyricism, a drastic reduction of the racial content, a rise in preoccupation with urban themes and subject matter both in the novel and the poem.' The merging of 'Negro expression' with 'American expression' would, he thought, occur if racial tension lessened, and an increase of 'racial themes'

languages, Black and white, in which race, class and gender have been discussed in America, but they demand to be read inter-textually with other discourses, other fictions as part of a wider debate. Political and polemic, even didactic, their use of and transformations of popular fictional forms as well as their appropriation of modernist and post-modernist strategies is specifically rooted in ongoing debates about Black cultural politics and its appropriate discursive forms — as much if not more than in contemporary feminist discussions of similar issues.

How can we then, in Britain, 'read' *The Color Purple* so that its cultural and political conditions of production are not deraci-nated, so that its narrative retains its rich, polychromatic texture, its provocative politics? How can we keep it from being bleached into a pallid progressive homily, an uncontentious, sentimental, harmless piece of international libertarianism? It has been suggested that there are worrying elements in the novel that collude with such a reading, and that the marketing of the book in the United States has made the most of this anodyne popular appeal. Is there a political price for the book's appeal to the tradition of the sentimental novel, à là *Uncle Tom's Cabin,* the reconstituted rural family (*The Waltons*) or a vaguely defined and potentially reactionary 'spirituality'? The fact that 'history' as a series of dated events is not employed in the novel, but appears obliquely collapsed in its narrative chronology, makes it hard to use internal evidence to give the book back its wider history. Set in a somewhat mythical version of the South (Walker's own Georgia, but ranging over a period deliberately longer than Celie's own personal life history can sustain) it invites compar-ison with other treatments of Black family life and identity in the South as they have appeared in both white and Black writing.[2]

Alice Walker herself has discussed her debt to the work of

---

would be a sign of sharpened conflict. Toni Morrison takes up the issue of form and genre in relation to the bourgeois history of the novel and Black writing in 'Rootedness: The Ancestor as Foundation' in *Black Women Writers: Arguments and Interviews,* Mari Evans, ed., London 1985, pp. 339-45.

2. It must be remembered that for all American readers — Black and white — the South has long been not only a significant geographical and historical site, but also an imaginative landscape on which black/white relations are played out.

another Black southern woman writer, Zora Neale Hurston whose novel *Their Eyes Are Watching God* also takes place in a rural southern, mostly all-Black setting. There is a useful comparison to be made between the development and fate of Hurston's heroine and Celie's in *The Color Purple*, especially in their relation to sexuality, community and family. But that comparison provides only one fragment of Alice Walker's own intellectual history, and a relatively late discovery too because she herself had not been 'allowed to know' about other Black, southern women writers. An earlier 'influence' was Flannery O'Conner whom Walker read 'endlessly' as 'a college student in the sixties' ... 'scarcely conscious of the difference between her racial and economic background' and her own. After a period where she rejected O'Conner and pursued the work of forgotten Black women writers, Walker concluded that 'though the rest of America might not mind, having endured it so long, I would never be satisfied with a segregated literature. I would have to read Zora Hurston *and* Flannery O'Connor, Nella Larsen *and* Carson McCullers, Jean Toomer *and* William Faulkner, before I could begin to feel *well* read at all.'[3] For us to teach Walker *well* we too need to read white and Black southern fiction in the twentieth century, for it is in part through and in response to those writings that her critique and reconstruction of 'family', 'community' and 'femininity' has been made.

It is especially useful perhaps to be aware of how the southern Black women's experience in the work of Richard Wright, James Baldwin, and Ralph Ellison has been handled, if we want to assess Walker's radical intervention into the field of Black writing. I feel strongly that these intertextual relationships — the ones that Walker explores as a writer explicitly in resistance to existing fictions and politics must be understood and developed for students before suggesting the ways in which Walker's novel might be 'recuperated' into dominant American ideologies of family, community and self. For in selecting Stowe or *The Waltons* as traditional conservative fictions with which a radical text must not collude or intersect we are, inevitably, reflecting the selective transmission of literary texts and television drama

---

3. Alice Walker, *In Search of Our Mother's Gardens: Womanist Prose*, London 1984. p. 43.

from America to England, and representing a normative readership as one that would encounter those narratives and not
others. And if one sticks to 'literary relations' alone one is
reinforcing too, the notion that fictional narrative itself, on the
page or the TV and cinema screens is exclusively in dialogue with
other fictional narratives rather than forming a part of much
wider debates about race, community, sexuality and family.

However it *is* important to specify texts, politics, movements
with which *The Color Purple* might be in dialogue. One set of
texts must be the 'southern' writings of older Black male writers.
How are Black women represented in these works? What do
these novels and autobiographies have to say about the relationship between racial oppression, the aspiration of their Black male
protagonists and the social and sexual dynamics of the Black
family? These questions are crucial, for it is centrally the handling of these questions in these canonical Black male texts that a
whole generation of Black women writers have through their
own fictions successfully challenged and revised.

Wright's autobiography, *Black Boy* (1945), for instance, is a
deeply misogynistic text in which the women in his southern
childhood and young manhood are either presented as bigoted,
punitive and repressive or part of an amoral, lumpen proletariat.
Ellison's *Invisible Man* (1952) reinvents the migration from South
to North not as a progessive *bildungsroman* but as bleak
picaresque, his hero a black Candide, ripped off and betrayed by
both whites and Blacks. In Ellison's imaginary South, Black
women are represented by an incestuous daughter who enjoys
her father's embrace and an outraged but fundamentally
resigned wife. This comic cameo of incest told by the Black father
is used to illustrate the ways in which whites displace sexual
anxiety and transgressive desire on to the Black community and
family. In no way however does this incident pose the question
of the exploitation of Black women; in its telling their subjectivity
is profoundly negated.[4]

James Baldwin's fictional treatment of sexuality, the family
and women is consistently more subtle and more sympathetic to
women than that of most male novelists of the macho and

4. Toni Morrison in *The Bluest Eye*, 1970 rewrites the 'incest story' from a female
    perspective, as indeed does Maya Angelou in the first volume of her auto-
    biography *I Know Why the Caged Bird Sings*, 1970.

misogynist fifties and early sixties. *Go Tell it On the Mountain* (1953) also traces the Black migration from South to North. His southern scenes describing the transformation of Gabriel from hell-raiser to preacher and patriarch include an episode in which a Black girl is raped by white men, rendering her sexually frigid. Although Baldwin is one of the first and major analysts of the intimate relationship between dominant notions of masculinity and oppression within the Black family, his view of women as somehow inevitably confined to heterosexual relations is one of the historical limitations of his writing. I offer this extremely episodic and partial account of these major texts by Black male writers, simply to suggest some of the intertextual resonances in *The Color Purple* that British readers will not hear. Black male writing although published here never had the vogue that it enjoyed, if only briefly and partially, in the United States, and does not any longer form part of the reading that might be thought essential to a non-professional literacy in twentieth century American writing. The narrative choices and the construction of emblematic female figures — Celie, Shug, Sophia — in *The Color Purple* need to be read in relation to these prior constructions of southern Black social relations that represent women as either powerless or repressive, and which focus (with Baldwin as an honorable exception) on the imperilled masculinity of Black men. Alice Walker's first novel, *The Third Life of Grange Copeland* (1970) is an exploration in a tragic mode of the ways in which Black masculinity has been lived in the terms constructed by the post-Civil War South. *The Color Purple* is its more optimistic 'sequel' offering a paradigm of change through the agency of Black women and a fictional celebration of their capacity to assess and affect the social relations in which they find themselves, an ability to survive the brutal exploitation of their bodies and their labour, by both the dominant culture and their own world of social relations. The 'utopianism' of *The Color Purple* and its seemingly apolitical model of change as a familial dialectic looks rather less simple when read as a polemic against the deeply negative imaginative interpretations of southern Black life in much male Black fiction and autobiography. *The Color Purple* offers a dynamic version of Black female subjectivity that, in effect, rewrites its representations as they appear in both white and Black, male and female southern fictions.

I have offered here, in the briefest and most schematic way, one frame for the literary contextualization of *The Color Purple*.[5] However as I suggested earlier the political and cultural discourses through which the novel might be read in the United States are much more heterogeneous than this, and 'literary' reference is possibly the most 'elite' and 'specialized' order of intertextual understanding that the book would receive. At a different and more immediately political level, *The Color Purple* intervenes in a long standing historical and political debate about the signification and the 'real' history of Black familial relations since the eighteenth century. The deeply racist and sexist nature of this struggle over the representation of the Black family was fully exposed in the mid-sixties when the infamous report by the sociologist Daniel Moynihan blamed the 'matriarchal' structure of the Black family — the female-headed household — for the poverty, unemployment and general immiseration of urban black life.[6] Moynihan traced this so-called 'matriarchal' pattern back to slavery, absolving twentieth-century institutional racism and capitalism from responsibility for twentieth-century depriva- tion. While the pathologizing of the Black family was by no means a new strategy for displacing the causes of Black poverty, the timing of Moynihan's intervention proved particularly provocative. Not only did the report meet with widespread liberal and left antagonism, it moved historians of slavery, both white and Black, to research and analyse the historical reality of the Black family in and after slavery. Not all of the writing that emerged from this exploration was adequately informed by feminist concerns (most of it was done initially by men) but it formed the base for a feminist exploration of those historical questions. Within popular representations (television and film) of Black life the way that Black familial and sexual relations were described became a highly sensitive issue. The most obvious dominant 'solution', partly adhered to in the scripting of *Roots* was to offer a much less melodramatic and normative account of Black family life, with fathers more present and women less

---

5. I have not dealt with the question of spirituality in the novel, an element that needs to be traced through the history of spirituality in Black expression and its use as a mode of entry to the political sphere. See Wright and Morrison, cited above, for brief discussion of this wide topic.

6. L. Rainwater, W.L. Yancey and D.P. Moynihan *The Moynihan Report and the Politics of Controversy*, Cambridge, Mass. 1967.

obviously the 'emasculating' strong Black mother projected by Moynihan.[7] The terrain and terms of this debate, involving as it does crucial social policy affecting the Black community and especially the single parent family on social security, is an on-going one, and takes on new dimensions and permutations with the development of 'new right' anti-feminist, pro-family initiatives. It is of course deeply connected to a more general misogyny that sees autonomous female sexuality and power as threatening and pathological, but its historical displacement on to Black women in the United States must be strongly emphasized. Given that political context and the dominant liberal response to it, the reconstruction of 'family life' in Walker's novel which includes resistance to both heterosexuality and the nuclear family must be seen as a feminist response to a specifically racial set of discourses about the family and femininity. It is one that criticizes the utopian agendas of white feminism, that do not see the representation of a denigrated Black femininity in white culture as a problem. That aspect of *The Color Purple* is I think understood here through current British conflicts between Black and white feminism, but its somewhat different history in the United States still needs to be understood and discussed. Resistance to racial and sexual subordination, and the forms of oppression themselves do not have a 'universal', 'trans-historical' expression. If *The Color Purple* is in great part a parable of the history of Black female subjectivity — a psychic history that relates to other fictional and historical accounts of such subjectivity — let us read it and teach it, insofar as we can, in a three dimensional, diachronic and dialectical manner. Any other way will reproduce those forms of cultural imperialism that the novel is attempting to refuse and resist. Unless we have some sense of the complex histories through which Walker's modes of resistance have been shaped we cannot begin to argue with her alternatives.

---

7. Margaret Walker's *Jubilee*, 1966, a novel that also takes an historical, panoramic look at the Black southern experience is thought by its author and others to be an unacknowledged source of *Roots*.

III

Autobiography, Gender and History

9.

Wicked Fathers: A Family Romance

'Whether one has killed one's father or has abstained from doing so is not really the decisive thing. One is bound to feel guilty in either case . . . So long as the community assumes no other form than that of the family, the conflict is bound to express itself in the Oedipus complex, to establish the conscience and to create the first sense of guilt.'

Sigmund Freud, *Civilisation and its Discontents*[1]

'But what you do not see, what you cannot see, is the deep tender affection behind and below all those patriarchal ideas of governing grown-up children . . . The evil is in the system — and he simply takes it to be his duty to rule . . . like the Kings of Christendom, by divine right.'

Elizabeth Barrett to Robert Browning, August 1845[2]

This essay was begun as a brief feminist reprise of a parent-child encounter that has achieved modern mythic status. I started out by thinking I could integrate my own experience as a daughter with that of Elizabeth Barrett Browning, for I have always prided myself on my ability to let my own life stand as one example of the road women take to feminism. But after writing a page or two about myself and my father I realised how deeply — and irrationally — I felt such a public exposure of our embattled but loving history to be an attack, a betrayal. It is with some chagrin that I acknowledge that there are quite ordinary areas of my personal history which I can not yet transform into public prose. This revelation has led me back to enquire how this problem was met by the subject of my piece. I had thought, at first, that I would concentrate on discovering how such a 'wicked father' came into being in cultural and psychological terms. Instead I

---

1. Sigmund Freud, *Civilization and Its Discontents*, James Strachey, ed., London 1975, p. 69.
2. Robert Browning and Elizabeth Barrett Browning, *The Letters of Robert Browning and Elizabeth Barrett Browning, 1845-1846*, New York 1898, vol. 1, pp. 174-75.

have centred more fully on the daughter, exploring the oblique and fragmented ways in which she constructed the meaning of paternal authority in her autobiographical and imaginative writings, placing the 'private' personal texts of her youth against the great feminist achievement of her maturity, the novel-poem *Aurora Leigh*, in which she draws us the portrait of the poet as a young woman. In following her struggle to understand and come to terms with the complex meanings that fathers hold for daughters as they can and cannot be represented in writing, I have made some sense of my own inhibition, my own father-daughter history. I hope this exploration will be as enlightening for others as it has been for me.

Literary Legend

Elizabeth Barrett Browning's name is remembered today less as the major nineteenth-century poet she was than as the defiant daughter, semi-invalid, turned forty, who, in September 1846, fled her father's oppressive household with a younger, penniless and unknown poet, Robert Browning. Given our culture's consuming reductive interest in the life stories of women writers in preference, often, to their work, it is not surprising that Elizabeth is best known for this romantic biographical fragment, sentimentally framed by her love poems to Browning, *Sonnets from the Portuguese*. In fact we might never have known under what circumstances Browning acquired a wife had she not been one of the most well-known poets of her day. It is that, in the end, which makes her courtship and elopement visible and immortalized her tyrannical parent Edward Barrett Moulton-Barrett. There he stands on our mantelpiece, propped up next to his fictional contemporary, Dicken's Paul Dombey, senior, one of the two most wicked fathers in Victorian culture.

Selective popular memory has been helped along by Rudolph Besier's 1930 play. *The Barretts of Wimpole Street*, adapted in turn for screen and television. Besier gave the story a post-Freudian twist, and a new tang for the twentieth century, by exposing Edward Barrett's paternal cruelty as barely disguised incestuous desire. 'My father is not like other men,' Elizabeth is made to cry in terror and disgust as she grabs her spaniel Flush and exits from Wimpole Street for ever, closely followed by her loyal

servant Wilson staggering under the weight of Victorian impedi-
menta. The unveiling of an incest motif (which to be fair to
Besier lies embedded though slumbering in the contemporary
letters and accounts) serves to weaken the feminist implications
of Elizabeth Barrett's actions. By emphasizing the normal and
feminine in the daughter and the pathological and villainous in
the father Besier suppressed the ways in which Edward was
precisely 'like other men' and his poet daughter something more
than a nice girl protecting her person from a nasty, over-age
seducer.

Besier's melodrama toys with the potentially subversive
notion that resistance to tyranny begins at home, and with the
women of the family, only to draw back from such a dangerous
interpretation. Instead the play roots Edward's perverted invest-
ment in the illness and celibacy of his talented child back in his
own sexually unsatisfying marriage to a terrified but compliant
woman. Like a Hitchcock film or Ross MacDonald thriller the
play constructs a crude family psychohistory, an outrageous
trauma in the closet, as the reason for skewed and oppressive
family relations in the present. In order for Elizabeth to be the
heroine of Besier's story she must be carefully absolved of any
collusion with her lecherous jailer, beyond of course the formal
obedience supposedly natural to a resigned Christian daughter of
the period. By spicing the story up, Besier masks its more interesting textures and flavours. His version covers up the passionate and tormented affection Elizabeth bore her unforgiving father
for the rest of her life; it denies the complex interaction between
them that led to their final impasse. If wicked fathers and their
surrogates were not, often, also loved and living figures; if their
female children bore them only the just measure of hatred due to
abstract tyranny then they would not pose the kinds of problems
that they do for feminism.

What evidence has come down to us, in an adolescent autobiography and a recently discovered diary kept for a crucial year
in her mid-twenties, points towards a more contradictory and
interesting narrative than Besier's highly coloured popularization
allows. If we read these personal accounts together with
Elizabeth's poetic transformation of them we can begin to see the
boundaries within which a mid-nineteenth-century middle-class
woman could enact and imagine her liberation from patriarchal
structures.

It is sometimes forgotten that Edward Moulton-Barrett's eccentric ban on marriage extended to all of his surviving children of whom seven were male. Only Elizabeth, the eldest, had an independent income; she alone could afford to defy her father's prohibition, which was so rooted and fixed that Browning was persuaded by his fiancée that to ask for her hand would mean his instant banishment from the house. Yet, in spite of the extreme peculiarity of Barrett's stance, to marry without parental consent was almost, as Elizabeth noted wryly in the months following her elopement, to cohabit without the benefit of clergy. To marry *so*, in middle age, and then to marry poorer and younger was, if one was female, to add insult to injury. It offered other restless daughters of the bourgeoisie a dangerous and dangerously attractive precedent of filial ingratitude, romantic excess and economic recklessness. As she had foreseen, Elizabeth's social circle took sides after the event with the most unqualified support coming from those older men who stood in quasi-paternal relationship to her — her cousin John Kenyon and the blind Greek scholar Hugh Stuart Boyd. Her sisters and her younger women friends were quickly reconciled, but her brothers and many other friends were only reluctantly persuaded. Although the Brownings visited England several times in the years following their flight, these visits were always somewhat clouded for her. While Elizabeth lived, the couple made their permanent home abroad.

As the scandal first entered the public domain in 1846 it intersected and merged with a wide range of contemporary representations about the meaning of family, childhood and marriage, as well as a very particular debate about gender that ran under the heading of 'the woman question'. Fiction and poetry were seen as perfectly appropriate mediums for such debates and both Tennyson's *The Princess*, a pantomime in verse about an all-woman's university, written while Robert and Elizabeth were courting, as well as the darker vision of Dicken's *Dombey and Sons*, serialized in the months after the Brownings' emigration, were read as serious contributions to these public discussions. Indeed Florence Dombey's flight from *her* father's house in chapter forty-seven reads spookily like an inner narration of Elizabeth's last months in Wimpole Street: 'She looked at him, and a cry of desolation issued from her heart. For as she looked, she saw him murdering that fond idea to which she had held in spite of him. She saw his cruelty, neglect and hatred dominant above it, and stamping it down. She saw she had no father upon earth, and ran out orphaned, from his house.'

To these popular images of father-daughter relations, Elizabeth would, in 1856, add her own comment through her widely acclaimed novel-poem *Aurora Leigh*. Here she would rewrite in more bearable terms the emotional and artistic genesis of a woman poet, reaching back into the 1840s to rethink the debates on marriage, feminism, class warfare, art and love. A year after its publication Edward Moulton-Barrett died without acknowledging his daughter's marriage, marking a bleak end to their long estrangement. 'So it is all over now,' Browning wrote helplessly to a family friend, 'all hope of better things or a kind answer to entreaties such as I have seen Ba write in the bitterness of her heart. There must have been something in the organization, or education, at least that would account for and extenuate all this ...'[3] Elizabeth grieving wrote to the same friend of her bitterness, 'and some recoil against myself ... Strange, that what I called "unkindness" for so many years, in departing should have left me such a sudden desolation. And yet, it is not strange perhaps.'[4]

Family History

The father. The daughter. The family. How far, and at what width of angle does one rewind from that moment of departure, well enough imitated on stage and screen? Elizabeth left behind not only the father she still 'tenderly loved' but nine other intimate companions, forty years of her life torn through by an act of disobedience. 'Remember that I shall be killed — it will be so infinitely worse than you can have an idea,' she wrote to Browning a day or two after their secret wedding while she still lived at home.[5] Her last hours at Wimpole Street were filled with 'agitation and deepest anguish. It is dreadful ... dreadful ... to have

3. Robert Browning to Mrs Martin Florence, May 3, 1857. Elizabeth Barrett Browning, *Letters of Elizabeth Barrett Browning*, Frederic G. Kenyon, ed., London 1897, vol. 2, pp. 263-4.
4. Elizabeth Barrett Browning to Mrs Martin, July 1, 1857. Ibid., pp. 264-5.
5. RBB and EBB, *The Letters*, vol. 2, p. 545.

to give pain here by a voluntary act — for the first time in my life.'[6] A murder. A sacrifice. In Elizabeth's last letters to Browning in the week before the elopement it is hard to tell who is being killed, who doing the killing.

'Something in the organization, or education ...' — Browning's question is ours, but like him we are not quite sure whose organization or education we need most to understand. About Edward Moulton-Barrett's we know very little, except that it was ostensibly for his education that in 1794 his mother and grandparents brought him and his younger brother to England from their West Indian properties which they would one day inherit. The boys' father had run off when they were infants. There is no evidence that this 'difficult, insensitive, self-willed and isolated young man' did much more than have his name registered at Harrow and Trinity College, Cambridge. Eager to end his childhood he was married before his twentieth birthday to Mary Graham-Clarke, an heiress six years his elder. Edward was just twenty-one when the first of his twelve children, Elizabeth, was born. More insistently perhaps than most men of his time, fatherless Edward made a career of fatherhood.[7]

His inheritance secured, he went looking for a country estate of his own, and found it at Hope End, Herefordshire. 'The more I see of the property the more I like it and the more I think I shall have it in my power to make yourself, Brother and Sister and dear Mama happy,' he wrote to his infant daughter.[8] The power of money; the power of paternity. It seems unlikely that 'dear Mama' recovering from the birth of a third child in three years was consulted about the decision.

In later life, Elizabeth would see her overextended childhood at Hope End as too secluded, too tranquil. Yet they seem on the whole to have been happy years for the young father and his

---

6. Ibid., vol. 2, p. 562.
7. Elizabeth Barrett Browning, *The Barretts at Hope End: The Early Diary of Elizabeth Barrett Browning*, Elizabeth Berridge, ed., London 1974 pp. 1-2. Biographical information on Edward Barrett Moulton-Barrett comes from Berridge's introduction to the Hope End diaries. She notes that 'Edward's mother had come to England as a protest against the three different native households her husband maintained.'
8. Quoted in the Introduction to *Diary by E.B.B.: The Unpublished Diary of Elizabeth Barrett Browning, 1831-1832*, Phillip Kelley and Ronald Hudson eds., Athens, Ohio 1969.

children. It was a strictly religious household but not a sombre one; if Edward was often autocratic, moody and stern, he was also by all accounts witty, playful and merry in the bosom of his family. He was the children's intimate and master, a typical, loving, patriarchal figure. The children, girls included, were allowed space and leisure to develop individual interests. 'Books and dreams were what I lived in — and domestic life only seemed to buzz gently around, like bees about the grass,' Elizabeth remembered. For its time it sounds a child-centred, relaxed regime.

What tensions there were in these early years surface especially in Elizabeth's clouded descriptions of her mother — 'very tender ... of a nature harrowed up into some furrows by the pressure of circumstances ... A sweet, gentle, nature, which the thunder a little turned from its sweetness ...' ... 'one of those women who can never resist, but in submitting and bowing themselves, make a mark, a plait, within — a sign of suffering'. The thunder, the forces not resisted but submitted to and suffered, these are never exactly named. Mary Barrett died in 1828 when Elizabeth was twenty-two, worn out one might guess, though no one says so, with bearing twelve children in eighteen years.

Elizabeth's adult portrait of her mother is of a woman so distinct from herself that she might be another species. This disavowal of her mother's way of being began young. It is certainly explicit in the manuscript autobiography *Glimpses into My Own Life and Literary Character* written when she was fourteen. In this manifesto of personal and artistic identity, she traces her passionate, active temperament back to early childhood:

> I was always of a determined and if thwarted violent disposition. My actions and temper were infinitely more inflexible at three years than now at fourteen. At an early age I can remember reigning in the Nursery and being renowned amongst the servants for self-love and excessive passion.[10]

The author is transparently pleased and barely apologetic about

9. Robert Browning and Elizabeth Barrett Browning, *The Letters*, vol. 2, p. 482.
10. Elizabeth Barrett Browning, 'Glimpses Into My Own Life and Literary Character', *Hitherto Unpublished Poems and Stories With an Inedited Autobiography*, H. Buxton Forman ed., Boston 1914, p. 6. Forman also paraphrases a

this shocking self-portrait, and returns a few pages later to the irresistible subject of her unchanged, unregenerate character which was 'still as proud, as wilful, as impatient of control, as impetuous', although now 'thanks be to God it is restrained.' The 'habitual' command of herself is represented as a social cover, not a moral necessity, a surface 'revolution' of disposition that might fool her friends, 'But to myself it is well known that the same violent inclinations are in my inmost heart . . .'[11]

Violence, energy and impetuosity of character were assets and their impenitent owner looked 'upon that tranquillity which I cannot enjoy with a feeling rather like contempt as precluding in great measure the intellectual faculties of the human mind!'[12] Poor Mary Barrett! While Elizabeth defiantly embraced a romantic definition of creative intellect infused with passion she was careful to distinguish it from the kind of feminine excess criticized by both Mary Wollstonecraft and Jane Austen — 'nothing is so odious in my eyes as a damsel famed in story for a superabundance of sensibility'.[13] In spite of her assurance that she has mastered techniques of self-control, it is her 'good heart' and its right to acute feeling that the essay defends against the invisible accuser, surely not just her gentle mother, who might think her 'vain, deceitful or vindictive',[14] 'envious or obstinate'.

Near the end of the essay, conscious that she has throughout boldly presented a self almost wholly at odds with contemporary ideologies of the feminine, an 'I' modelled on a full-blooded male romanticism, Elizabeth confronts the issue directly.

---

story found in some autobiographical notes of E.B.B.'s which may have been prompted by an autobiographical letter written to Richard Henigst Horne at his request in 1843, which illustrates her absence of deference and hatred of conventional behaviour. Indications in the text are that she was about ten when the incident occured. . . . she describes a meeting with her father on the stairs in the morning. She 'smiled at him, for she loved him,' 'Not a word,' said he. 'No' she said — 'I have nothing to say.' 'Will you not ask me if I am well?' 'No — if you had been ill you would have told me.' Her father was angry and led her by the hand into the breakfast room. 'Here is a little girl who thinks it too much trouble to ask her father how he is.' She says she blushed and was sorry, though she knew in her heart that she did not 'think it too much trouble, but too much falsehood.' *HUP*, p. xxxiii, xxxiv.

11. Ibid., p. 16.
12. Ibid., p. 17.
13. Ibid., pp. 21-2.
14. Ibid., p. 18.

My mind is naturally independant and spurns that subserviency of opinion which is generally considered necessary to feminine soft-ness. ... I feel within me an almost proud consciousness of independance which prompts me to defend my opinions and to yield them only to conviction!!!!!!!'[15]

The seven exclamation points mark out this passage as the climax of the piece, and its moment of greatest anxiety.

'Glimpses' is addressed to her younger brother by a year Edward, 'Bro' whose lessons and play she had always shared, and who remained her favorite sibling until his tragic death by drowning in 1840. 'Glimpses' was written soon after Bro was sent to Charterhouse school, and this inevitable separation, through which Elizabeth lost both her loved companion and the male tutor who could assist her progress in classical studies, brought home to her with shattering clarity the social meaning of sexual difference. Bro was an ordinary boy of no special intellec-tual gifts; yet the classical and literary education for which the precocious Elizabeth yearned was his by right. The expressive rage of 'Glimpses' suggests that it was triggered by some parti-cular domestic conflict which we cannot identify, but we can guess that it involved her father. In this detailed review of her intellectual progress from infancy to adolescence 'Papa' appears only once, as the donor of a ten-shilling prize addressed to the 'Poet Laureat of Hope End' for a six-year-old effort on the subject of virtue. The pages of the autobiography burn with an angry silent denial of his influence and aid. Whether Edward Moulton-Barrett read his daughter's broadside is not known. Had he done so, and noted her warning that she could never love those she could not 'admire, respect and venerate', her ultimate defection might not have come as a surprise.[16]

Yet the father, whose minimal presence in 'Glimpses' already

---

15. Ibid., p. 24. This distaste for the feminine is reiterated in the paraphrased notes cited above: 'She regarded it as her great misfortune that she was born a woman. She says that in those days of childhood she despised all the women in the world except Madame de Stael — she could not abide their littlenesses called delicacies, their pretty headaches, and soft mincing voices, their nerves and affectations. ... One word she hated in her soul — and the word was 'feminine'. She thanked her gods that she was not and never would be feminine,' *HUP*, p.xxvii.

16. *HUP*, p. 18.

marks out an area of resistance and rebellion in the daughter, was, in quite straightforward ways, responsible for his daughter's intellectual progress and literary ambitions. Her precocity was consistently approved and rewarded throughout her childhood. She had almost the free run of his library which was extensive for a man of little formal education and no special intellectual interests. At four she was reading fairy tales; at eleven she had given up novels for philosophy. In spite of his devout belief, Edward Moulton-Barrett's library was stocked with radical texts. Elizabeth read Tom Paine's *Age of Reason*, Voltaire's *Philosophical Dictionary*, Hume's essays — as well as Goethe, Rousseau and Wollstonecraft, all this before she was fifteen. Only a few books — Gibbon and *Tom Jones* are the ones she mentions — were considered too blasphemous or obscene for her scrutiny. From the age of twelve she was allowed to sit in on her brother's lessons with his tutor Mr McSwinney; these helped with classical and modern languages although she was mostly self-taught. More than this casual permission most nineteenth-century daughters could not expect to receive. In the year of 'Glimpses' her father had her juvenile 'epic' in four books, *The Battle of Marathon*, written when she was twelve, privately printed. It is suitably dedicated 'to the father, whose never-failing kindness, whose unwearied affection I never can repay' but the poem's intellectual parent, Byron, is also recognized. One of her first adult poems accepted by the *London Globe and Traveller* in 1824, *Stanzas on the Death of Lord Byron*, pleased both parents and *An Essay on Mind, with Other Poems* (1826) was highly commended by her proud father. Edward Barrett's support for his daughter's aspiration was constrained but not wholly bound by contemporary prejudice. His kindness, affection and encouragement, his expressive pleasure in her efforts stood behind the arrogant energetic and independent mind of 'Glimpses'. Until Bro's elevation to Charterhouse showed Elizabeth where her gender marked the limit of parental indulgence, it might be said that Edward Barrett was rather the pattern for a feminist father than the model of paternal tyranny.

Her mind 'a turmoil of conflicting passions, not so much influenced by exterior forces as by internal reflection and impetuosity', Elizabeth spent her childhood at Hope End in study and dreams. 'Glimpses' records, with some humour, a twenty-four-hour religious crisis when she was twelve, but there is nothing but the evidence of the autobiography itself to predict the severe and mysterious illness that struck her at fifteen, and which kept her bedridden for almost eighteen months. It was preceded by a riding injury to her spine which would later prove more serious, but its character is clearly that of an hysterical illness, of the kind that would, at the end of the century, give Freud his first clues to the working of the unconscious. The nerve specialist, Dr Coker, kept a detailed account of the symptoms, which started with weeks of headache, then shifted to attacks of severe pain in 'various parts of the body'.

> The suffering is agony — and the paroxysms continue from a quarter of an hour to an hour and upwards — accompanied by convulsive twitches of the muscles, in which the diaphragm is particularly concerned — The attack seems gradually to approach its acme and then suddenly ceases — During its progress the mind is for the most part conscious of surrounding objects but towards its close, there is generally some, and occasionally very considerable confusion produced by it — There are generally three attacks in the day and none during the night ... Opium at one time relieved the spasms but it has ceased to have that effect ...[17]

Hysteria, Freud wrote, frequently affects 'people of the clearest intellect, strongest will, greatest character and highest critical power'; things that cannot be put into words — fantasies and feelings psychically and socially unacceptable — are spoken instead through the physical symptom.[18] Elizabeth herself seems to predict her illness in 'Glimpses' warning that 'were I once to loose the rigid rein I might again be hurled with Phaeton far from every thing human ... everything reasonable!'[19] The illness should be read as another expressive text whose 'subject' was, probably, the powerful set of emotional conflicts set out in her autobiography. She was paying a high price for her restraint and control. Perhaps too, the 'independance' she desired was harder to enact, femininity a more pressing psychic

---

17. *Diary by E.B.B.*, pp. xviii — xix.
18. Josef Breuer and Sigmund Freud, 'On the Psychical Mechanism of Hysterical Phenomena: Preliminary Communication (1893)', *Studies on Hysteria*, James and Alix Strachey eds., Harmondsworth 1974, p. 64.
19. *HUP*, p. 23.

obligation than she was willing to admit. How closely after the onset of menstruation her illness followed is not recorded, but she would herself in *Aurora Leigh* call daring attention to the importance of the menarche in emotional development, especially the traumatic changes it could trigger in father-daughter relations.

Aurora Leigh traces the growth of a woman poet from infancy to maturity, an adult epic version of 'Glimpses'. In this re-imagined life, the girl poet is raised by her widower father, an 'austere Englishman' transformed from a 'common man' by his passionate love for his Florentine wife. In his grief he retreats with his daughter to a remote mountain hideaway where he gives her a liberal education in the fallibility of patriarchal knowledge — 'out of books/He taught me all the ignorance of men ...' After nine years this isolated childhood and idyllic relationship is shattered. 'I was just thirteen,/Still growing like the plants from unseen roots/ In tongue-tied Springs, — and suddenly awoke/To full life and life's needs and agonies/ With an intense, strong, struggling heart beside/A stone-dead father. Life struck sharp on death,/ Makes awful lightening.' Menstru-ation and the death of the father. For Elizabeth, physical puberty was closely tied to the emergence of the 'intense, strong, strugg-ling heart' so vividly evoked in the autobiography. In *Aurora Leigh* the fictional father enjoins his daughter to 'love' and then, providentially, removes himself as potent and potentially taboo love object — 'Ere I answered he was gone,/And none was left to love in all the world.'[20]Aurora's nurturant born-again father, whose new creed was love, was created in the fruitful middle years of the Brownings' marriage against the background of Edward Moulton-Barrett's 'unkind' silence. But the poem reaches back perhaps to the unclouded pre-pubescent years at Hope End. Female adolescence and the death of the loving father are made coincident, their conjunction a bolt from heaven. The symbolic parallel to Elizabeth's history continues as the grieving Aurora's suffering mirrors, in part, the period of her illness.

> There, ended childhood. What succeeded next
> I recollect as, after fevers, men

---

20. Elizabeth Barrett Browning, *Aurora Leigh and Other Poems*, Cora Kaplan, ed., London 1978. First Book, p. 44.

Thread back the passage of delirium,
Missing the turn still, baffled by the door;
Smooth endless days, notched here and there with knives,
A weary, wormy darkness, spurred i' the flank
With flame that it should eat and end itself
Like some tormented scorpion.[21]

Elizabeth's illness weakened her permanently. Although she would walk and ride again, after it she tired quickly, cried easily, was subject to fainting fits and bouts of nerves — all external marks of the feminine sensibility she despised. Illness of various kinds became both a burden and a form of defence against a fully social public existence, a response to crises and conflicts she could not always confront or resolve through action. By 1824 this initial serious illness had played itself out, and she was on her feet and writing again. The first major crisis had been negotiated.

Thoughts of the Heart

One more episode from Elizabeth's youth, opened up to us through her single successful attempt to keep a diary, suggests how difficult it is to isolate the father-daughter relationship from the wider resistance to patriarchal culture in Elizabeth's demand for recognition as an independent, creative woman.

The period 1827-32 were harsh years for the Barrett ménage. Mary Barrett died in 1828 after a year's illness. By 1831 Edward Barrett's financial affairs were in such disarray that it became necessary to sell Hope End. Absorbed in his business troubles, Edward was frequently absent. Fortunately for Elizabeth the publication in 1826 of *An Essay on Mind* brought her to the attention of a new neighbour, the forty-five-year-old blind Greek scholar, Hugh Stuart Boyd. His 'quenched' sight, his age, and the fact that he was respectably flanked by a wife and daughter made him an ideal candidate for platonic intellectual friendship. Even so, Barrett warned his daughter that it would be improper for her as a 'young female' to make the first call. Once begun, the acquaintance thrived on their mutual need for intellectual companionship, respect and admiration. Boyd, in fact, had a

---

21. Ibid.

stable of young female protégées who served as readers and amanuenses, among whom Elizabeth had a somewhat perilous position as favourite. We can see Boyd as Elizabeth herself would do in maturity, as a cranky and rather narrow pedant. In the years of their confidential friendship — 'no confidence, no friendship', Boyd decreed — Elizabeth used him to explore her capacity for strong feeling outside the family. Impeded by their different temperaments, the jealous interference of both families and Elizabeth's fragile health their connection had some of the character of a love affair, and gave Elizabeth a taste of her father's growing exclusiveness towards his children.

In March 1831, when Elizabeth began the diary, her relationship with Boyd was at fever pitch and suspense about the fate of Hope End was also rising. The diary shows the whole family hanging on to Edward's letters and moods for clues to their future. Barrett had instructed brother Sam to 'say nothing on the subject of removal to the girls'. His proud silence about the impending loss of his kingdom emphasised his unqualified power within the family.

Like 'Glimpses', the diary was a place to record 'the thoughts of my heart as well as my head', and the long episodic opening entry was written in the wake of a real and inner thunderstorm that provoked 'hot & cold' anxiety for 'myself & everybody near me & many bodies not near me; viz for Papa and Bro who were out — for Mr Boyd who is at Malvern where the storm was travelling. Arabel dreamt last night that *he* was dead, & that I was laughing! Foolish dream —' The *he* of Arabel's becomes through Elizabeth's associations all the men she loved — and hated. Then the entry descends into a gloomy review of her friendship with Boyd — 'I suspect that his regard for me is dependent on his literary estimation of me & is not great enough for me to lose any part of it.' This negative assessment of her worth in the eyes of men is implicit in the last fragment of the entry, a seemingly cheery report at Edward Barrett's pleasure at Bro's reported success as an after-dinner speaker — 'Dear Papa! dear Bro!'[22] The discontinuous 'bits' make up a revealing associative narrative of anxiety, anger, longing and threatened loss, with her sexual and her creative selves as uncertain protangonists. No wonder she was worried that her 'very exacting & exclu-

22. E.B.B., *The Barretts at Hope End*, p. 61-63.

sive & eager & headlong & *strong'* mind would produce thoughts that she could not 'bear to look on ... after they were written'. The sexualized element of these thoughts was part of their terror and attraction: 'Adam made fig leaves for the mind, as well as for the body.'

Near the end of the diary Elizabeth records a dream that maps out and summarizes her year of distress. 'Dreamt about Adolphe & Endymion, & a lady who was by turns Emily and Amalthea & of her murdering Endymion whose soul was infused into Aldophe. Papa reproached her. But she held up her beautiful face, & said, "I am yet very fair." "Clay Walls" said Papa!'[23] The condensed mythic-romantic figures marry the classical world Elizabeth and Boyd shared with her 'modern' imaginative life. Endymion-Adolphe — Greek youth merged with Constant's Byronic hero — is assassinated by two notable daughters, Amalthea, child of the King of Crete and Zeus' nurse, and Emily, heroine of Anne Radcliffe's *Mysteries of Udolpho,* which Elizabeth had read the summer before. Radcliffe's novel spoke to Elizabeth's fears, for the orphaned Emily sees her safe country home broken up and becomes the prey of lecherous Gothic villains. In the dream this composite daughter murders desire in the shape of its popularly conceived object, a handsome young man. Perhaps the murder also represents the seduction it was designed to avert; perhaps too, it is a killing off of the romantic hero in the dreamer. Certainly all the passive/active identities belong to the dreamer-transgressor, whose seductive self-justification is met with paternal rejection — the blind indifference of a clay death mask to the daughter with clay feet. One of many possible interpretations, this reading of the dream emphasizes the frustration of these critical months when Elizabeth's future as artist, woman and daughter seemed to depend completely on the words and looks of two withholding, possessive men, both sexually barred to her.

In *Aurora Leigh* women's tendency to emotional and artistic dependence on the commendation 'of some one friend' is bitterly detailed and finally rejected in a brilliant passage that ends 'Must I work in vain,/ Without the approbation of a man?/It cannot be; it shall not.'[24] But the diary, another trying out of the meanings

23. Ibid., p. 236.
24. *Aurora Leigh,* Fifth Book, p. 197.

of independence, proved too painfully revealing of this gendered, unrewarding dependence. After a year it was broken off in 'self-disgust'.

Family Romance

The opening lines of 'Family Romances', one of Sigmund Freud's most tantalizing short essays, reminds us how general was the task our romantic heroine faced. Freud believed that the 'liberation of an individual, as he grows up, from the authority of his parents is one of the most necessary though one of the most painful results brought about by the course of his development ... the whole progress of society rests upon the opposition between successive generations'.[25] Persons who failed in that task, generally men in Freud's therapeutic experience, were likely to entertain a typical neurotic fantasy, in which the real-life father is found to be an imposter, and is replaced by a more socially exalted and loving parent. A flexible fantasy, capable of endless elaboration, its narrative can turn siblings into lovers by removing the blood tie — the plot and characters in the subject's family history can be rewritten to fulfil a variety of impossible wishes. Born of the child's sense of being inadequately loved and recognized, and of the guilt engendered by its overtly hostile feelings, family romance stems as much from the overvaluation of the despised parent as from hostility to him. In the fantasy replacement, qualities of the original parent can always be discerned.

The 'family romance' of a woman will always be deeply marked by femininity, the inner and outer construction of sexual difference. Femininity insists that women remain somewhat enchilded throughout adult life, deferential to the authority of all males of their own social class and higher. Women do not always choose to confront paternal authority directly, for they are not of the sex that must compete with or indeed replace it. The demands of adult life allow them, often, to continue in dependent roles; liberation from their fathers often means no more than

25. Sigmund Freud, 'Family Romances', *On Sexuality: Three Essays on the Theory of Sexuality and Other Works*, Angela Richards, ed., Harmondsworth 1977, pp. 221-225.

the passage from paternal to marital household. But femininity is neither an essential attribute of gender nor a very stable psychosocial structure. The adult identity that Elizabeth desired was in some but not all respects at odds with psychic and social femininity, and her experience illustrates just how violent the acquisition of 'normal' femininity can be, and how culturally asymmetrical its terms.

It may be that Edward Moulton-Barrett did more than he could have known to set up the conditions of Elizabeth's ultimate resistance. By treating her in infancy in a way more culturally appropriate to an elder son — his confiding letter to her about his ambitions for Hope End suggests something of this — he reinforced the infant self-will that reigned in nursery and below stairs, Elizabeth never let go of her right to that heady sovereignty, which she pinpoints in 'Glimpses' at around three, an age before the full psychic and social implications of sexual difference are clear to a child. The fourteen-year-old girl clung obstinately to that pre-Oedipal moment of autonomy, agency and passion, for she understood with peculiar prescience that it was the constituent moment of her self-formation, as romantic artist. By encouraging her precocious intelligence and rewarding her poetic efforts, by identifying, as parents sometimes do, with her gifts, Edward inadvertently allowed her to develop unimpeded her vision of herself as 'Poet Laureat' (in 'Glimpses' she leaves out the final feminising 'e'). For the father it was a gentle joke; for the daughter, even before she understood the title, it was deadly serious.

As she moved in her reading from fairy tales to novels, from novels to classical literature, philosophy and modern poetry the image of herself as romantic poet gathered definition. As an eldest child, living in relative social isolation she was freer than most female children to image a world that would let her be that poet — and a woman. The model of the romantic poet was male; it insisted on authority, autonomy and the expression of strong feeling. Emotion expressed by women, as the fourteen-year-old Elizabeth knew from reading and experience, symbolized to others their weakness, inferiority and dependence. The contradictory uses of the word 'control' in 'Glimpses' — control of self, control of meaning — signal the impasse; what made her vulnerable to other people was internally, for her creative self, a necessary strength. When Bro was sent to school, leaving Elizabeth lonely and tutorless, the hard realities of being a daughter and not a son were brought home to her. 'Glimpses' is a *cri de coeur* against the terminal condition of femininity, her illness a year later an equally expressive text of the violent conflicts she could not reconcile. The Hope End diary was another attempt to make sense through writing of this senseless social and spiritual contradiction.

By the time Elizabeth was in her twenties the pathological contours of her father's character were becoming clearly visible. The loss of Hope End was a drastic blow to his image of himself as father; even ten years later the name could not be mentioned in his presence. No other part of his paternal power would be eroded if he could help it; he could use his will and his considerable remaining resources to govern absolutely the lives in his little monarchy. His daughter could win whatever laurels she liked in the cultural community as long as she remained physically dependent upon him.

Elizabeth accepted these unspoken terms for many years, although her recurrent, debilitating illnesses say something about their cost. Two coincident events helped her to break free. In 1845 Browning introduced himself to her through an impassioned, admiring letter which began, 'I love your verses with all my heart, dear Miss Barrett,' and went on to praise 'the fresh strange music, the fluent language, the exquisite pathos and true new brave thought ... my feeling rises altogether. I do, as I say, love these books with all my heart — and I love you too.' [26] Meetings only deepened his infatuation and stirred her affection. How could she resist this late confirmation of her art and her femininity? At the same time her doctors advised her that she must escape south during the cruel English winters if she wished to live much longer. It was her father's unwillingness to bless her reasonable plans to winter abroad with suitable companions that finally moved her to action. With Browning to support and encourage her she found the strength to resist. Edward Barrett's love was not, after all, the kind she was prepared to die for. After years of living out the most disabling aspects of femininity while preserving an inner strength of will, she was offered a position where she might redefine the former, keep the latter. Browning's age, status, poverty and gentle nature

---

26. EBB and RB, *The Letters*, vol. 1, pp. 1-2.

were all in his favour. In personal terms the price of overvaluing
male authority figures had been excessive. Thereafter it was only
political patriarchs that she was prepared to venerate; her fas-
cination with strong men still needed an outlet. And venerate
them she did, from Cavour to the awful Louis Napoleon, Browning's dismay notwithstanding. They became part of her political
romance with Italy.

But in *Aurora Leigh* she memorialized her own troubled
history and the men who figured in it, in a pattern which very
closely follows that of family romance. The loving, liberal,
English father of Book 1 is certainly the father of her early childhood at Hope End who set his daughter free in his library, traced
on top of Emily's idealistic, indulgent daddy from *Mysteries of
Udolpho*. In Aurora's cousin and future husband, Romney Leigh,
the trinity of important male relationships of her youth, Papa,
Bro, Boyd, are all remembered, grafted on to later models. True
to the narrative structure of family romance, Romney shares her
surname, marking him out as the relative to whom she can at
last have sexual access. Like father, brother and Boyd, the young
Romney admires the young Aurora's gifts; lending her books
without really acknowledging her right to an independent
creative identity. And in the sadder-but-wiser older Romney,
'mulcted' of his sight but not of his desire for his cousin, the
erotic element in the relationship with Boyd is tenderly acknowledged. There are much less benign fragments too in this collage
cousin-lover; Romney's tragic flirtation with 'abstract' radical
politics articulates a distaste for radical theory learned at the
knee of her father who was a liberal in politics and an unreconstructed despot at home.

The plot and characters of *Aurora Leigh* nowhere explicitly
recalls the unforgiving old man, still alive during its composition,
but the still embittered author denies any role and influence to
the father in the life of the adult poet, by writing him out of the
narrative. Chaste, hardworking and independent, young Aurora
lives on her own in London through her twenties, the most self-
contained and successful female orphan in Victorian fiction. Yet
further facets of Barrett senior and his domestic history, as they
were transformed by Elizabeth's fantasies, are clearly recognizable. During Romney's picaresque career as a socialist he
plans a loveless political marriage with a pure, devoted, dependent working-class girl, Marian Earle, whose character and Chris-

tian name recall gentle, passive Mary Barrett whose real social
position is signalled by her fictional surname. Through this
doomed cross-class mésalliance, Elizabeth sketches out a critique
of her parents' unequal emotional union, substituting, perhaps,
Romney's politically instrumental courtship for Edward's
supposed economic one. In Elizabeth's family romance only true
and equal love binds; in winning Romney from Marian, Aurora
achieves that perfect union, and her creator, the once usurping
daughter, wins her loved despotic parent from her only serious
rival. Yet Marian is a saint-like portrait, and the passage near the
end of the poem when she, her bastard son and Aurora live
happily together in Italy render in idyllic transformation the
years when Mary and Elizabeth presided over the half-grown,
mostly male Barrett brood. In the harmonious household of her
imagination, where all loves are permitted, the poet-daughter
reigned supreme.

The family romance woven through *Aurora Leigh* is only one
strand of this rich poem, the first and greatest imaginative celebration in English of woman's creative potential. Women's
fictions, especially their utopian writing, are central texts for
feminism; for they remap the terrain political feminism hopes to
alter. In *Aurora Leigh* Elizabeth Barrett Browning tries to rei-
magine the making of a woman poet without the arbitrary parent
who ruled her first forty years, the years of her own making as
an artist. Up to a point she succeeds, but as I have suggested
Papa is clearly visible through the disguises of the fictional father
and cousin-lover, his bad and good qualities dispersed through
the narrative, his love and desire captured in the last pages. Nor
do I read this return of the father in *Aurora Leigh* as an element
that weakens its feminist intent or message. On the contrary, it
poses the problem of fathers, not just wicked ones, in its sever-
est, most demanding form.

Women's utopias are often characterized by the absence or
dispersal of paternal authority — a banishment in itself an
important imaginative reshaping of the landscape of our lives.
Yet the shadow father still lingers within us, as well as in
Elizabeth's poem, constituent of the terms through which both
our femininity and our feminism is constructed and lived. Do we
want to depose him altogether? Elizabeth's life and work as read
through her public and private writing suggest how imperfect is
the fit between the social and the psychic father, between the

offical despot who ruled by 'divine right' and the father whose 'deep tender affection' both fuelled and foiled his daughter's desires. Can we depose the first without sacrificing the second, the loved, loving, imperfect parent from whom we must, as both children and women, struggle free?

When I tried to write about my father and myself I could only catch at the ebb and flow of our struggles. I could not, significantly, recall the text or pretext of a single one of our painful skirmishes, so closely strung from my fifth to my twenty-first year, when I left home. Twenty-one years past that break those desperate battles to establish autonomy seem no more — but no less — important than my father's extraordinary influence, example, support and affection, which have shaped my life in positive ways. Strong-minded daughters of dominating men will inevitably find them a site of 'all those patriarchal ideas' with which our culture is saturated, will often cut their political teeth in opposing their sanctions however mild, will, almost certainly, imagine a gentler, more loving father. I cannot remember my father literally denying me any access to the world I asked for, but his very existence symbolized the way I was to be denied. Elizabeth's story, which I too first encountered in Besier's play, had an instant resonance for me, as it has I am sure for many women, for it places the burden of guilt and illegitimate desire with which father-daughter relations are mutually drenched firmly on the shoulder of the male, where some feminists will say it belongs. My exploration of Elizabeth's life, and my reflections on my own history, suggest a more complex scenario in which love, anger, guilt, and desire are orchestrated as a duet, not a baritone solo, in which daughters cannot be constructed wholly as social and psychic victims of their fathers or their fathers as wholly unregenerate villains. Because they include both social and psychological reality, binding together the worlds of material and imaginative possibility, literary texts express this contradictory relation more fully and accurately than most other discourses. Nowhere is it more poignantly and densely worked through than in the life and writing of Elizabeth Barrett Browning.

10.

Red Christmases

In my post-war New England childhood a red star shone defiantly at the top of my family's Christmas tree, signifying our distance from both the Christian and capitalist meanings of the holiday. For us to celebrate Christmas at all was a complex heterodoxy. Jews, atheists, communists, we nevertheless refused to turn our backs on our national winter carnival; instead we tried to make it ours by emphasizing its pagan pleasures, harnessing the Christian millennium to contemporary radical hopes.

These were Cold War years in which collective radical culture was fragmented and demoralized. I am not sure that we achieved more than a kind of loony cultural pluralism, but at least we tried. On Christmas Eve we sang traditional carols out of a little blue pamphlet distributed free by the Bethlehem Steel Corporation, adding favourite IWW ballads, so that *Silent Night* might be followed by *Joe Hill* and *Good King Wenceslas* by a satisfyingly vicious anti-clerical song beginning 'Long-haired preachers come out every night / just to tell us what's wrong and what's right ...' For the rest our Christmas was straight-up secular Anglo-American — stockings, presents, relatives and an enormous meal cooked by my mother.

The most important holiday on the national calendars of the English speaking world, Christmastime is a notoriously hard moment to radicalize. It has its own radical history; as a day and season it has been used to demonstrate and resist, most especially and recently against militarism, but our dominant culture uses it with sinister success to emphasize traditional definitions of public and private, to impose through its secular and Christian themes the notion of happy families shored up by a benign capitalism. Christmas honours family life as a model of subordinate social relations, privatized units of consumption and pleasure, with work — however appalling its conditions and meagre its rewards — as a necessary evil to sustain it. Christmas unreformed celebrates the family as the only appropriate recept- acle for personal feeling, implying that there is nothing to struggle for beyond its boundaries, no legitimate struggle to be had within it.

It is just such 'national' 'familial' representations that the left has had such difficulty in transforming. Never mind that only some five per cent of British domestic units include a male 'provider', a non-working full-time 'housewife and mother' and young children. This minority household form is represented as the only ideal celebrant of the holiday — the old, single or sick become the symbolic objects of charity of this magical nuclear family. The increasingly undeserving poor — strikers and the long term unemployed —are posed as marginal to it, not only economically unable to be full participants but outside the legi- timate polity. Mary's nuclear family was a curious one, and Jesus, I guess, a bastard, but modern Mariolatry doesn't there- fore honour the single parent or her offspring.

Against the tyrannical ideal most of us are found wanting, and we feel the want unwillingly but dreadfully at Christmas. Many of my socialist and feminist friends hate Christmas for the deeply atavistic and regressive feelings it calls up, for its seductive appeal to repeat, relive and repair the past in the name of child- hood. Its bells toll us home to our conventional places as mothers, fathers and children — or leave us homeless if we are none of these.

Most especially, most awfully, the siren song of a national familial Christmas speaks to mothers. God alone knows why, since the only idle, rested mother at Christmas — except of course for the rich who still keep servants — is Mary, serene in plaster, wood and plastic. Mothers pay dearly for being the symbol and source of the holiday, for it is they who transform the raw products of material culture into an emotionally edible form. Whether there is a little or a lot, mothers buy, decorate, wrap, and cook most of it. They and their mothers, daughters and any other women drawn into a household do most of the manual labour at Christmas, and the lion's share of the caring, emotional labour too.

Very many of these women work outside the home in jobs that are especially hard at Christmastime so that these extra tasks are added on to the ordinary inequities of the sexual division of labour. In my parents' household, for example, socialism only mildly affected the unequal distribution of tasks. My father did a great deal of domestic back-up labour, more than most men, but my mother (who worked outside the home too) bought and wrapped all of the presents and cooked the main meal. I always felt that Christmas was her event, her responsibility.

Thirteen of my eighteen years in Britain have been spent as both a single parent and a working mother. Most of the year I positively enjoy being a single parent in spite of its obvious difficulties. At Christmas nostalgia and confusion reign; I am beset with anxiety that I cannot provide a good-enough Christmas, or, what is the same thing, be a good-enough mother on my own. Every year I try to subvert and remake its symbols and rituals; as an individual exercise in transformation it has severe limitations.

Some years I seem to do all right; others have been spectacular but instructive failures. In 1974 my mother-in-law and a Jewish American friend came to stay. 'What are you *doing?*' asked my mother-in-law, a working actress recently emancipated by divorce and living a nomadic, busy life in cheap hotels. 'What in the *hell* are you doing? asked my friend, childless and single with no dangerous nostalgia for Christmas past for her guilt to feed on. Horrified they watched me spend money I did not have, cook huge, unwanted quantities of food, lavish my son with expensive presents. It was a ludicrous and compulsive private pantomime in which I played mummy *and* daddy, successful producer and affluent consumer. I went through these multiple roles tranced and stubborn, like one of Freud's hysterics, expressing with each gesture the impossibility of being all or any of these symbolic figures.

The somewhat shameful memory of that Christmas must be balanced against the memory of small victories and pleasures: of a delighted child climbing into bed with me to unpack his stocking, of handmade red stars, women's symbols, birds of peace, of good friends with whom to assess the year's gains and losses and think ahead. Nevertheless, my son, now sixteen, has gently but firmly taken the whole business out of my hands. Last year and this he has chosen to go on a skiing holiday organized by his comprehensive school — saving up for the privilege of foregoing family Christmas. I am both grateful to him and, at the same time, bereft, for suddenly there is no place in the secular nativity for me to claim.

Over the last few weeks I have talked about the theme of this article with friends. 'Christmas isn't about mothers', one said. 'Christmas is all about men, about male largesse and the power of money.' I thought about that, about the New Born King, Father Christmas and Dad with his wallet out, coalesced and fused into an icon of male power. But I could take this compounded image only so far in my imagination. There was a Christmas song in my childhood that used to blare through every main street loud-speaker:

> You better not shout, you better not cry
> You better watch out, I'm telling you why,
> Santa Claus is coming to town.
> He sees you when you're sleeping, he knows when you're awake,
> He knows when you are bad or good, so be good for goodness sake.

I lived then in a Massachusetts town famous as the home of one of the great eighteenth century Calvinist preachers, Jonathan Edwards. Here was his God, absolute and punitive, decked out in red: a magical agent of surveillance more powerful than McCarthy and the FBI tracking communists. ('He's making a list, you knew that he would. Of who has been bad, and who has been good . . .') I hated that song and it frightened me, but I did not associate it with the paternal power against which I did daily and intimate battle but rather with the power of the State, as it was levelled in those years against my parents and others for standing brave witness against its unjust decrees.

This distinction — and connection — between the public and private forms of power seems especially relevant this hard Christmas of 1984. This year it will be difficult even for Tories and Social Democrats to argue for the mythical harmony of interests that sustain dominant versions of the holiday. For one effect of the miners' strike is to make sharply visible today what is true every year, that large sections of the population cannot share, if they would, in the annual pig-out, because they are in dire want and without prospects.

There are however much more positive political trans-formations that have emerged from the strike — ones that have undermined the conservative hegemony of Christmas as a unified emblem of national nostalgia smugly celebrating an idealized familial past and future. Although MacGregor's Christ-mas bribe and the Miners' Christmas Appeal both invoke traditional symbols of family and childhood, mobilization inside and outside the striking communities have in important ways broken down the public/private divisions that hold them in place. To keep going the striking communities have undergone dynamic change, socializing the invisible labour of women, shift-ing the burden of child care. Women have taken up central public, political and polemic roles in the struggle.

This Christmas, in these communities, conventional images of them as plaster madonnas or perfect housewives are neither relevant nor credible. Equally the iconic meaning of charity has been challenged. Across the nation those who give and who organize the giving in the Christmas appeal do not do so to pacify a potentially rebellious working class, but to support their rebellion and resistance, to valorize the defence of the mining communities and their collective futures.

Every year we are subjected on the box to an adaptation of Dickens's *A Christmas Carol*, and strong Tory men and women weep at the death of Tiny Tim while Bob Cratchit and his wife wait passively for Scrooge's 'change of heart'. This year, even with MacGregor a shoo-in for Scrooge, we have some reason to rewrite the story differently with both Mr and Mrs Cratchit as active agents of change. The events of the last few weeks in the strike and the mobilization around it have demonstrated just *how* important are the connections between public cultural meaning, private feeling and militant political struggle. We need to hang on to that understanding. We need to take Red Christmas and the social and psychic critiques that shape it out of doors, beyond the individual household into a collective public space, where it will crowd out and displace the wooden nativities, those familial idols of the ruling class, which have stood there for so long.

11.

Speaking/Writing/Feminism

My mother describes me at eleven months, a particularly small baby, bundled, propped and harnessed in my pram outside our New York apartment house, addressing startled passers-by with the adult precision of newly learnt speech: 'Hellow, pretty lady!' Speaking came early, came easy, eliciting surprise, approval and even tangible reward. This first gratifying experience of public speaking (I cannot remember it) seemed to set a pattern which allowed me the courage forever after to break through the patriarchal convention that enjoined women to deferential silence. I have always enjoyed the sound of my own voice, even when it has irritated and offended others. As a young political woman my lack of inhibition about public speaking frequently got me into trouble with the male-dominated left. It also, occasionally, got me where I not so secretly wanted to be — on a soapbox, addressing a crowd. In school, at university, but most of all as an academic, this 'unnatural' articulacy has helped to mark me out as a rebel. In professional gatherings where women are in a very small minority, it is normal for them to accept their marginality by staying relatively quiet. My frequent interventions ensure that my social behaviour as well as my opinions are displeasing to my colleagues. In the last fourteen years a very large part of my political and intellectual life has taken place inside the Women's Movement. Of all the changes that feminism has made in my private and public behaviour none has been so hard to learn or to keep to as shutting up so that others may speak.

All forms of public performance seemed to come from a desire that I could neither rationalize or suppress and that overrode self-consciousness. By the time I was nine I had found a relatively acceptable outlet in acting. From then until my early twenties I had no other ambition, and while acting in no way contained my appetite for oral expression, it helped to explain it in terms of an artistic aspiration which could only spring from an eccentric expressive temperament. Nevertheless speaking up, at home, at school, on the stage, always seemed to involve a sense of danger and challenge which I fed on. Writing, on the other hand, was to begin with an act of conformity with family and school. Writing in my Jewish, middle-class intellectual family was the most approved activity. Books and the written word were so highly valued (I was allowed to throw almost anything in a tantrum *except* a book) that my own written efforts were usually accompanied by a kind of terror that they would be derivative, cliché, inauthentic. From my first attempt at fiction, a garbled pastiche of *Lamb's Tales from Shakespeare* called 'The Lovers', to this piece in process, all my narrative or reflexive writing, including letters and diaries, has felt haunted by the language of others. Every fragment of imaginative prose or verse from the age of six onwards has given me that stale ghosted feeling *as I wrote it*, as well as when I read it back afterwards. It took me a long time to find a voice and a genre of writing that gave me the sense that I was cutting across the 'givenness' of social relations.

The difference in my experience of oral and written expression seems worth pursuing for a bit longer, since the causes and effects of the social sanction against women's speech and writing has, for some years now, been the central feminist issue that shapes all my research. Inside my family, as I have said, all the unspoken pressures and desires on and for me, as a precociously clever child, were towards channelling my talents into some sort of writing. To write was to do what my father did and what my mother valued. Talking, or more accurately, talking back, got me into endless trouble. My childhood and adolescence was one long struggle with a paternal authority which had imagined a gentler, more docile daughter. Neither of my parents thought much of my dramatic ambitions or talents though they did nothing to discourage me; on the contrary they made considerable sacrifices of time and money to help me along. Yet I could not fail to understand their disappointment. A sort of political puritanism made the exploitation of one's own voice and body too bound up with egotism and personal desires. In writing, the family morality seemed to say, the suspect personal gratifications of self-expression were reduced to an acceptable, ethical level through the displacement of words from mouth to printed page. This implicit critique of theatrical self-presentation became linked for me with the whole range of frivolous, sensual, self-indulgent activities from dressing up — an elaborate event in the 1950s — to secret masturbation. All these were practices my parents disapproved of, or would have done, I was sure, if they had known about them. Acting, speaking, showing off my adolescent body, worst of all touching it, were, I was convinced, tainted in my parents' eyes with egotism in general and female narcissism in particular. Dressing up and showing off were complicit in their minds with the worst aspects of femininity as the dominant culture decreed it. How much of this was projected guilt is hard to tell. I couldn't have put all these impressions into words in my teens. Still, if anyone had asked me what their model of a good socialist woman was I would have been able to describe her. She was the woman who had ignored her emergent sexuality in adolescence, sublimated desire, dressed and spoke soberly and used the last leisured years of childhood to learn that she might teach. I was a child of the 1950s and Rosa Luxemburg was a remote and scary figure. My heroine, in so far as I had one, was Sarah Bernhardt. As Hamlet.

The 1950s for left-wing Americans were a frightening, demoralizing decade. Our family clung together. I kept secrets that I had never been told. I shared my parents' politics — (how could I not? — I still do in great part) and found it difficult to criticize the social inflections of their views. In some upside-down way writing became saturated with a set of ethical prescriptions that I could neither refuse nor wholly accept. It became what others desired of me, and only sometimes what I wanted for and of myself. It became the other of an illicit, politically incorrect femininity in which I desperately wanted to be inscribed, the other too, of my formidable and undervalued ambitions as an actress. Although I gave voice to the words of the playwright on the local stage it was there, above all, that I felt I uttered myself. For a very long time, longer than I care to think, even *now*, writing is too often the act of a dutiful daughter.

It was at my desk and my typewriter that I felt spoken, not by the culture that disapproved of women writing only a little less than it disliked women speaking in public, but by that powerful alternative culture in which I was raised.

In my personal history, then, the psychic contradiction between woman's speech and her femininity was given an eccentric twist. If the construction of femininity roughly follows the dominant psychic structures of a given society, any particular instance will have its own inflection. While I understand, as an abstraction, that my wilfully raised voice usurps 'the place and tone of a man', for me speaking out is also deeply entwined with femininity, with, for example, a conventional desire to be looked at. That extended angry verbal struggle with my father — what did I have but words to get his attention, to intervene between him and my mother, and what did he give me back but words? For many women sexuality is spoken through their social silence. For me, language did what my meagre child's body (I could pass easily for ten or eleven at seventeen) could never do. In recent years I have been giving more and more public lectures, often to audiences of women only, but invariably on feminist subjects. My talks are never given from a written text; I rarely refer to notes. These occasions bring the ethical and political imperatives through which I was raised together with my irrepressible and unregenerate desire to speak out, to have a direct, unmediated contact with an audience. Very often the subject of these talks mirrors the meaning of the event for me — an historical and theoretical account of the related suppression of women's speech, writing and sexuality.

There still remains the difficult subject of this essay — my own writing. I have deferred it as long as I could, deferred the actual writing of this section for months because I thought that I could not bear to see what I would say. As I get older — I am forty-two as I write this — the possibility of writing has largely replaced the possibility of new emotional and sexual adventures as a subject for fantasy. It is the activity in which I would now prefer to recognize myself. 'Writer' ranks way above 'mother', 'teacher', 'speaker', as a vocational identity. As a young woman, writing seemed to threaten femininity — to leave me stranded on the dry shores of the incest taboo, my father's daughter and no one's lover. Now, when I feel sure that no one will love me in the body who does not first love me for my words, writing promises too much in the way of fantasized libidinal reward instead of too little. There seems often to be too much invested in its success: political effectiveness, professional status, recognition within feminism, the self-respect that comes with completing a self-imposed task, and sometimes pleasure in the process itself. How did this puritanical work, so often in my teens and twenties an escape from the insistent desire of and for a man, become, in my thirties, the process and polemic of desire? What follows is a narrative that has been only partly worked through. I do not see it as typical or representative. I offer it with some diffidence as a history that might contribute something to the understanding of the relationship of women to writing.

In 1973 I was separated from my husband with a five-year-old child to support, a university job that I needed to hold on to and an ugly battle to acquire academic tenure ahead. I was thirty-three years old and had been working on an unfinished DPhil thesis for some seven years. The subject — Tom Paine and the radical press in the late eighteenth century — was partly inherited from my father who as a young man had adopted Paine as one of his radical heroes. I too was drawn to Paine for his marvellous popular rhetoric, his democratic politics, his personal eccentricities and his vision of self-determination based on a dream of universal literacy. Paine was a figure easily appropriated by the new left politics in which I had been involved in America. Perhaps he was a bit too like the young male left who wanted the women in the movement as tea-makers, typists, envelope lickers, and, in the memorable words of Stokely Carmichael — 'prone'. Certainly the subject was top-heavy with associations that made me nervous of it as well as fascinated by it. In any case I was working on this thesis at some disadvantage, 3,000 miles away from not one but three supervisors, a benign but internally divided trinity of male historians. By 1973 the subject had gone a bit stale on me and I had outgrown the liberal paradigm in which the original project was couched without having acquired the theoretical tools to reformulate it. I had made myself politically extremely unpopular at my workplace by taking an active and vocal part in a bitter row about free speech and the Vietnam War, which split my department and made my subject chairman into an enemy. Even so, he thought well of the thesis, and it seemed crucial that I complete it in order to be given tenure.

At this point, with everything pressing me towards doing what was asked of me by my institution, I abandoned the dissertation, not formally but quite definitively, and began an entirely different project — the construction of a critical anthology of women's poetry. I found a publisher, negotiated a fee and finished the book in about eighteen months. It, and not my uncompleted work on Paine, was assessed finally as the research that secured my job. I have never touched the thesis again, nor have I ever written to my supervisors to explain why. I knew that it was impossible for me to write anything more for the judgement of those fair-minded, affectionate men, nor could I find a language adequate to explain my defection as something other than disability.

Perhaps I should have sent them a copy of the anthology, for in the introductory essay I described women's embattled relationship to poetry, the most highly valued discourse in western culture. There, too, I spoke of the ways in which writing poetry involved women in complex moments that were simultaneously resistant and submissive to the dominant patriarchal culture. There were analogies to my own history, but I did not try to think about them. I never sent my supervisors either the book or a letter of explanation; my boorish silence must have satisfied some need in me for a violent and irrevocable break with a project too intimately tied up with my family. For when I abandoned the dissertation I also seem to have stopped writing simply through and for my father's desire. My thesis especially, but much of the writing I had done as undergraduate and postgraduate were, I now think, intended above all to win my father's approval. Metaphorically these pieces had use value only; I made them for domestic consumption. In so far as they served to further my career as an academic that career too became bound to my father's will, in ways that made me, in the first years as a teacher, dislike this 'second choice' profession as if it were a forced marriage.

At that particular moment in my life, the marketplace offered and supported a kind of freedom, capitalist in its terms, that I could not find in the academy. Because of my personal history, writing for the university system became writing for patriarchy par excellence. It was extraordinarily important to me that my anthology was paid for, circulated and sold, for at that time feminism had almost no purchase or currency within English universities, and especially not within literary studies. In evading some of the conditions of production imposed by the institution and in redefining my subject I had, at last, found a place from which I could write, as I could speak, to a wider audience than one man.

The 'self' that occupies the place-from-which-I-can-write exists as a necessary fiction for writing, a sometimes fantasy of autonomy and authority that persists, if I am exceptionally lucky, until the end of the writing project. There is a temptation, which has found its way into much recent feminist criticism, to celebrate this writing identity both as a temporary escape from femininity, and as a model for a post-feminist female identity that will endure through the history of an individual. It is perhaps a common-sense indulgence to see woman in this supposed moment of defiance and rupture as woman as she must become outside and beyond patriarchal inscription. While I think that defiance is a component of the act of writing for women, I would now prefer to emphasize the fluctuant nature of subjectivity that the contrast between the writing and non-writing identity highlights.

In the early stages of thinking about women and writing I had, in common with other feminists, talked mostly about the ways in which women were denied access to something I have called 'full' subjectivity. While any term so abstract evokes more meaning than it can possibly contain in a given context, what I was working towards was a description of a position within culture where women could, without impediment, exist as speaking subjects. I now think that this way of posing the question of writing/speaking and subjectivity is misleading. It assumes, for instance, that *men* write from a realized and realizable autonomy in which they are, in fact, not fantasy, the conscious, constant and triumphant sources of the meanings they produce. This assumption is part of an unreconstructed romantic definition of the poet as it was most eloquently expressed in Wordsworth's 1800 introduction to *Lyrical Ballads*. Here the poet has a universalized access to experience of all kinds, feels things more deeply, and expresses those feelings 'recollected in tranquillity' for all men. It did not take much thought to point out how difficult it was for women to appropriate this romantic definition of genius and transcendence, given the contemporary restraints on their experience and the contempt in which their gender-specific feelings were held. A more interesting question was about the status of the definition itself, which even today has enormous currency within traditional literary criticism. How far was it an ideological fiction? In what sense could any writing or writer or indeed any *actor* in history *be* that romantic subject? For if one were to accept a modern re-working of the romantic definition of the creative process, then as a feminist 'full subjectivity' would become a political goal for feminism, as well as a precondition for all acts of struggle and intervention, writing included.

In the last few years I have come round to a very different perspective on the problem, drawn from Marxist and feminist appropriations of psychoanalytic and structuralist theories, but confirmed, I think, by my own and other women's fragmented experience of writing and identity. Rather than approach women's difficulty in positioning themselves as writers as a question of barred access to some durable psychic state to which all humans should and can aspire, we might instead see their experience as foregrounding the inherently unstable and split character of all human subjectivity. Within contemporary western culture the act of writing and the romantic ideologies of individual agency and power are tightly bound together, although that which is written frequently resists and exposes this unity of the self as ideology. At both the psychic and social level, always intertwined, women's subordinate place within culture makes them less able to embrace or be held by romantic individualism with all its pleasures and dangers. The instability of 'femininity' as female identity is a specific instability, an eccentric relation to the construction of sexual difference, but it also points to the fractured and fluctuant condition of all consciously held identity, the impossibility of a will-full, unified and cohered subject.

Romantic ideologies of the subject suppress this crucial and potentially hopeful incoherence, or make its absence a sign of weakness and thus an occasion for mourning or reparation. Feminism has been caught up far too often in this elegiac mood, even when on other fronts it has mounted an impressive critique of Western rationalism as a phallocratic discourse of power. One option within feminism to combat the seeming weakness which inheres in women's split subjectivity has been to reassert an economy of control, to deny the constant effect of unconscious

processes in utterance and practice, and to pose an unproblematic rationalism for women themselves, a feminist pysche in
control of femininity. For myself, this avenue is closed, if only
because it makes me feel so demoralized, a not-good-enough
feminist as I was a not-good-enough daughter. I would rather
see subjectivity as always in process and contradiction, even
female subjectivity, structured, divided and denigrated through
the matrices of sexual difference. I see this understanding as part
of a more optimistic political scenario than the ones I have been
part of, one that can and ought to lead to a politics that will no
longer overvalue control, rationality and individual power, and
which, instead, tries to understand human desire, struggle and
agency as they are mobilized through a more complicated, less
finished and less heroic psychic schema.

This perspective makes better sense of my own experience as
writer and speaker, both as a dutiful daughter and now as a
feminist, and gives me some clues as to what enabled the
passage between these two moments. Neither activity or
position has given me a security of identity nor do I any longer
see that as a meaningful objective. However, the stakes and
contradictions involved in writing and speaking as a feminist
have shifted, although not always in easily apparent ways. The
way I write has hardly changed since I was an undergraduate. I
always favoured a rich, fruity prose, leavened and larded with
word play and jokes that fleshed out the didactic skeleton of my
arguments and broke up the high seriousness of academic
discourse. Puns and risqué metaphors are a way of making the
hard puritanical business of writing more fun, more libidinal,
and therefore, more mine. I never need to tell jokes when I am
giving a talk, nor do they seem to be necessary to hold an
audience to a serious theme. Speaking involves a bodily
presence, is itself a pleasure. However, in the teaching situation,
in the solemn, tense occasion of tutorial or seminar, vulgar wise-
cracks spring to my lips unbidden. I understand better now, why
I make these formal rhetorical choices. That knowledge in itself
has changed the condition of utterance.

Tillie Olsen, the American writer and critic, has explored the
multiple ways in which women's silences as writers have been
overdetermined in western culture. Her overview is always both
Marxist and feminist, but she always emphasizes the importance
of the individual situation. In my own family history the

dominant prejudices against female utterance were only ever mobilized against my speaking voice. It is that voice from a position of opposition that has emerged confident, playful and fluent. My pleasure and confidence in writing has been as hard to achieve, as unreliable, though at certain rare moments as thrilling, as sexual pleasure. Familial disavowal and/or support always has complex and mediated effects in relation to dominant ideologies. All my published writing has been within and for feminism. These days, however, the conditions of production have shifted. Now I write into a constituted discipline of recognized intellectual importance. I write for women, rather than as in my early work, constructing a polemic directed against men. And I have noticed a change in the content and direction of my work that is a bit worrying. The critical sections of the poetry anthology were almost always positive appraisals, a revision and revaluation of lost or dismissed writing. These days I have moved away from mildly eulogistic projects, and instead have engaged in a series of fairly heavy debates with other feminists and other feminisms, historical and contemporary. This internal polemic suggests that the habit of writing in opposition is deeply ingrained, in fact the only tolerable mode of writing for me. Even within the women's movement that has given purpose and meaning to my life and my words, I remain something of an ungrateful child.

Index